LA

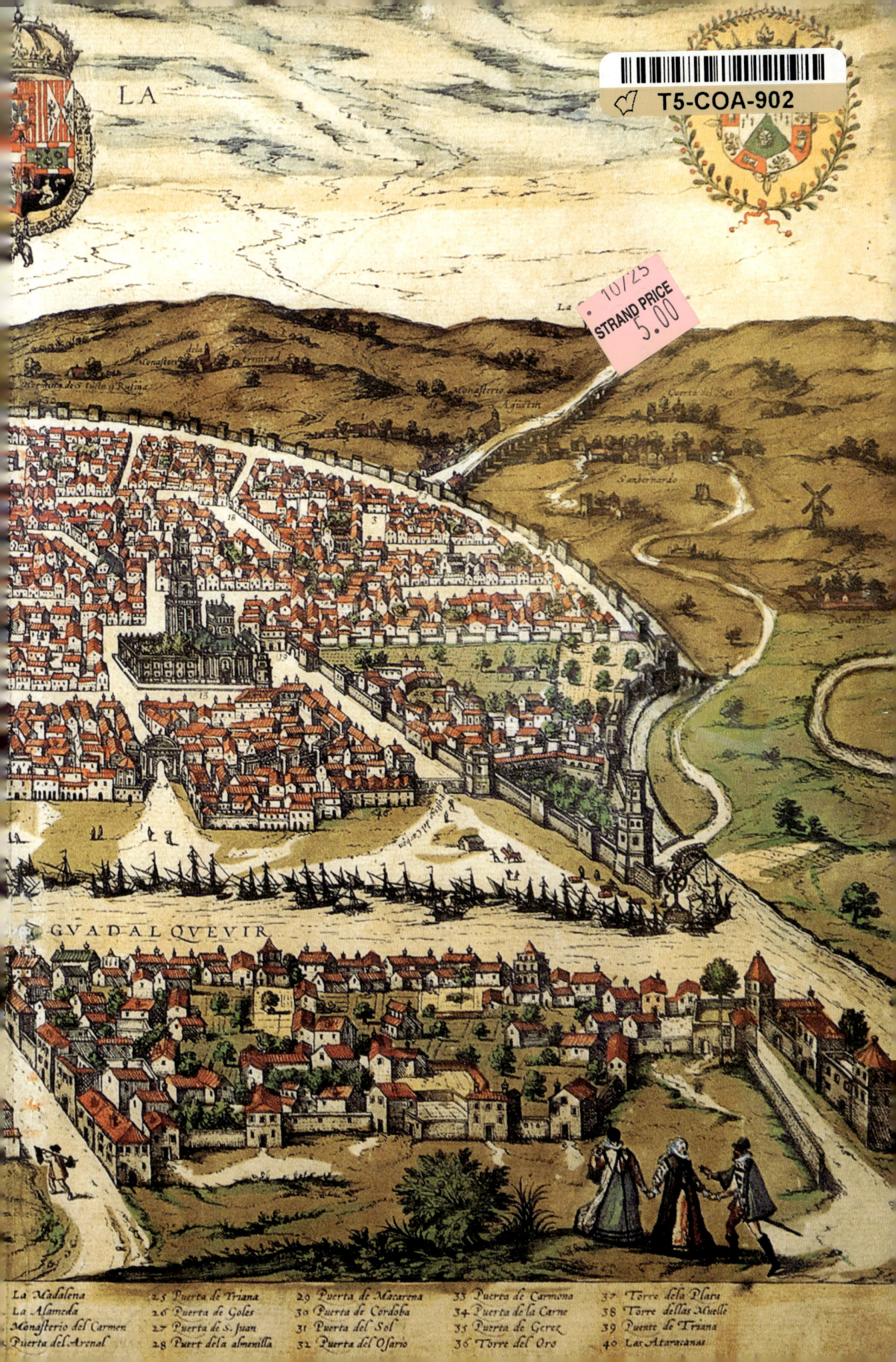

GVADALQVEVIR

La Madalena	25 Puerta de Triana	29 Puerta de Macarena	33 Puerta de Carmona	37 Torre de la Plata
La Alameda	26 Puerta de Goles	30 Puerta de Cordoba	34 Puerta de la Carne	38 Torre dellas Muelle
Monasterio del Carmen	27 Puerta de S. Juan	31 Puerta del Sol	35 Puerta de Gerez	39 Puente de Triana
Puerta del Arenal	28 Puert de la almenilla	32 Puerta del Osario	36 Torre del Oro	40 Las Ataraçanas

IN THE SPIRIT OF
SEVILLE

Text © 2013 Antonio del Junco
© 2013 Assouline Publishing
601 West 26th Street, 18th Floor
New York, NY 10001, USA
Tel: 212-989-6769 Fax: 212-647-0005
www.assouline.com
ISBN: 9781614281481
Endpages: An illustration of Seville in the sixteenth century.
Photograph © Antonio del Junco
Translation by Lawrence Schimel
Printed in China
All rights reserved. No part of this publication may be reproduced, stored in a retrieval system,
or transmitted in any form or by any means, electronic, or otherwise, without prior consent of the publisher.

ANTONIO DEL JUNCO

IN THE SPIRIT OF
SEVILLE

Foreword by the Duchess of Alba

ASSOULINE

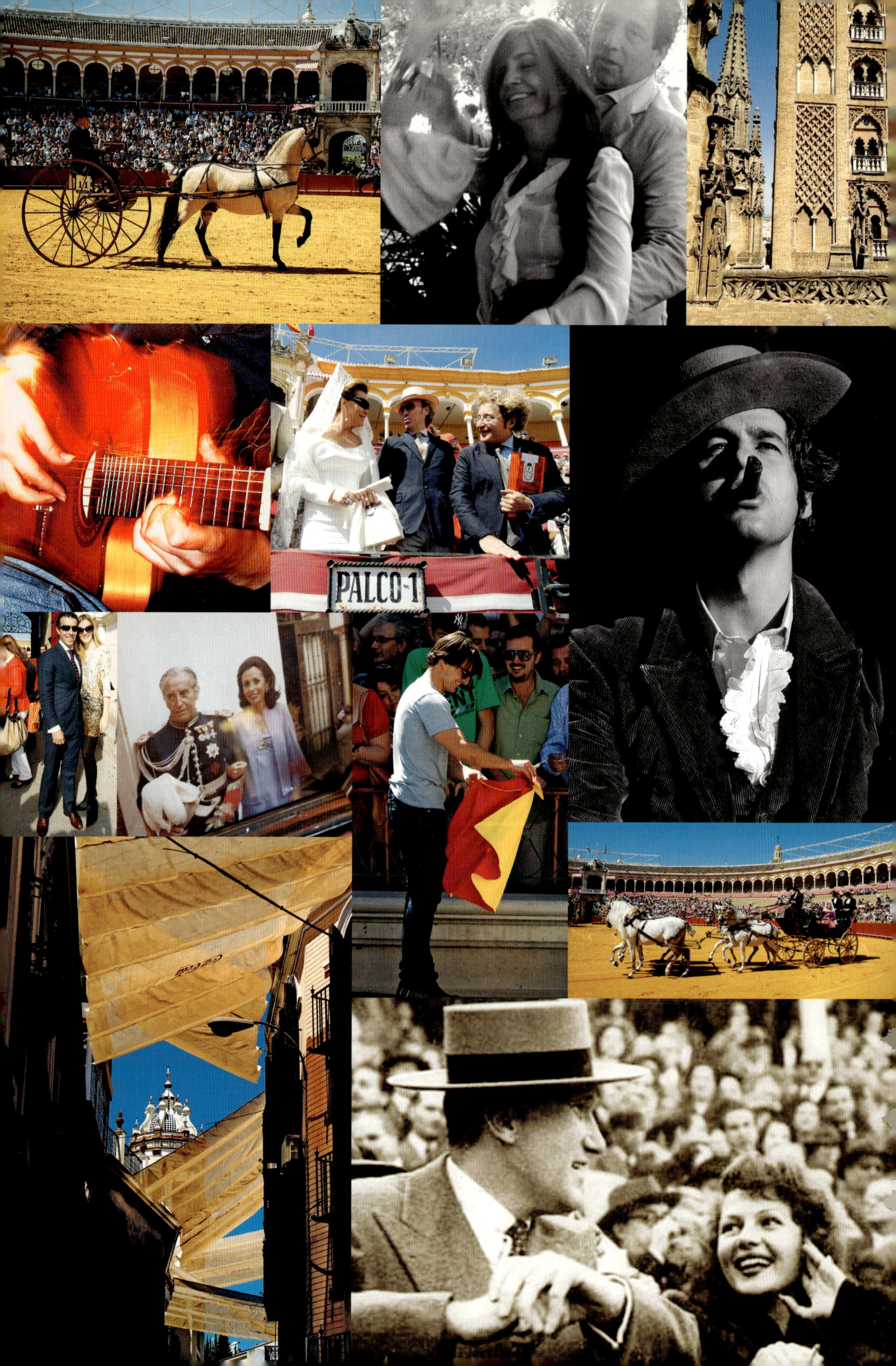
PALCO-1

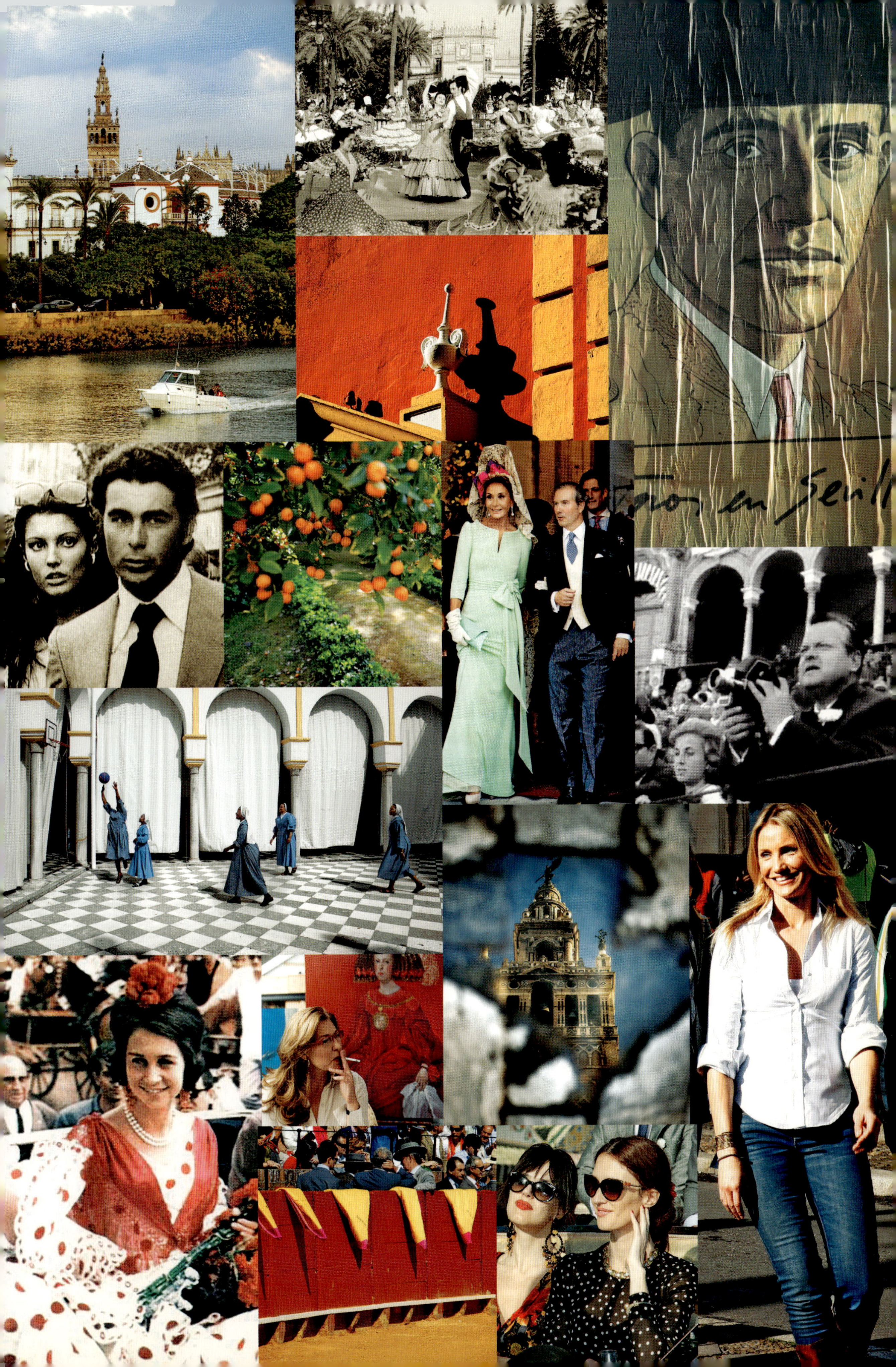

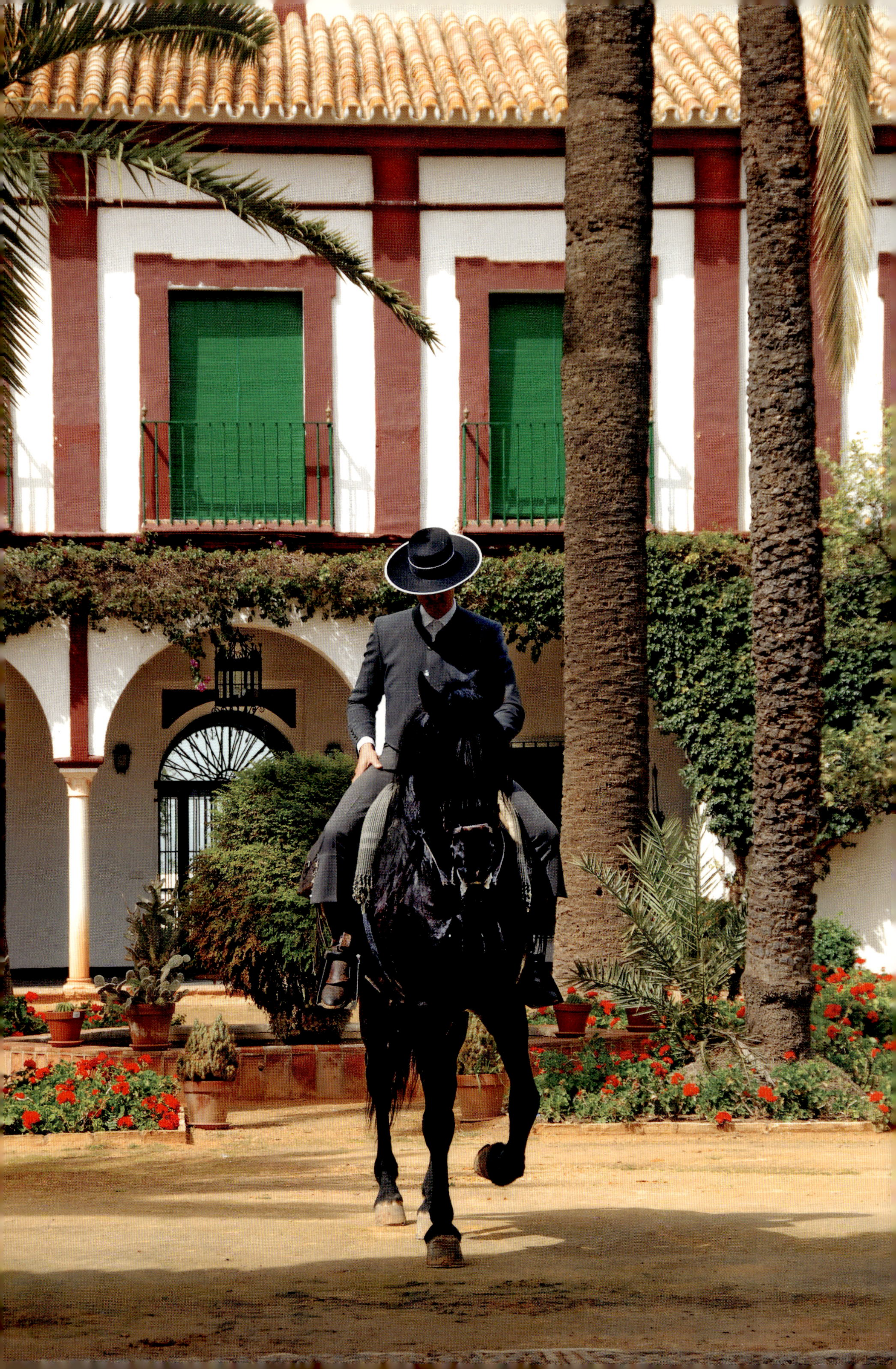

Foreword

by Cayetana Fitz-James Stuart y Silva, Duchess of Alba de Tormes

Seville has always been my home. This city is one of the most special cities in the world. Joy floats through its streets, and it has a very special nature. And not just for its history, which is visible on every corner, nor even just for its colors, nor for its noble buildings, nor just for its skies, so blue—the inspiration for Antonio Machado's final verses, written in Collioure a few hours before he departed for eternity. It is, above all, for the Sevillians.

I have always had a lovely relationship with the inhabitants of Seville. They love me, I know, and I also love them very much, as they know. And it is for that reason that I spend the greater part of the year here in Seville, in the Palacio de las Dueñas, so full of memories, so full of details, and so full of my entire life.

Seville is marvelous in any season. In the fall, the fog at dawn can be seen through transparent and vaporous tulle veils, and the rain adorns the city with tones of gray so sweet that even the puddles serve as mirrors. But the apparel that best suits Seville is, without question, that of springtime.

Spring is when the city begins to show off its lace of orange blossoms, white as pearls, with the scent of nostalgia for those precious memories of our loved ones who are no longer with us.

It is during that luminous springtime when Seville becomes so pretty, when it's obvious that it loves itself, that it shows itself to good advantage. Preparations for Lent have already commenced, continuing with the break of dawn on Palm Sunday. Then Holy Week begins, transforming the city and converting it into a theater setting where the entire city acts, prays, and marvels before such beauty.

I feel much emotion during the Madrugá, when the Brotherhood of the Gypsies passes the door of my house in Dueñas, giving me the opportunity to greet the most holy Christ of Health and Our Lady of Sorrows, of which I am maid of honor.

And after that week, full of emotions and fervor, comes the explosion of joy, with the arrival of the April Fair of Seville, the most beautiful fair in the entire world. During the Seville Fair, I've always liked to dance, ride horseback, and spend time with friends—those who live in the city, and those who come here from around the world. I remember with special fondness

A rider in traditional dress at a farmhouse in Seville.

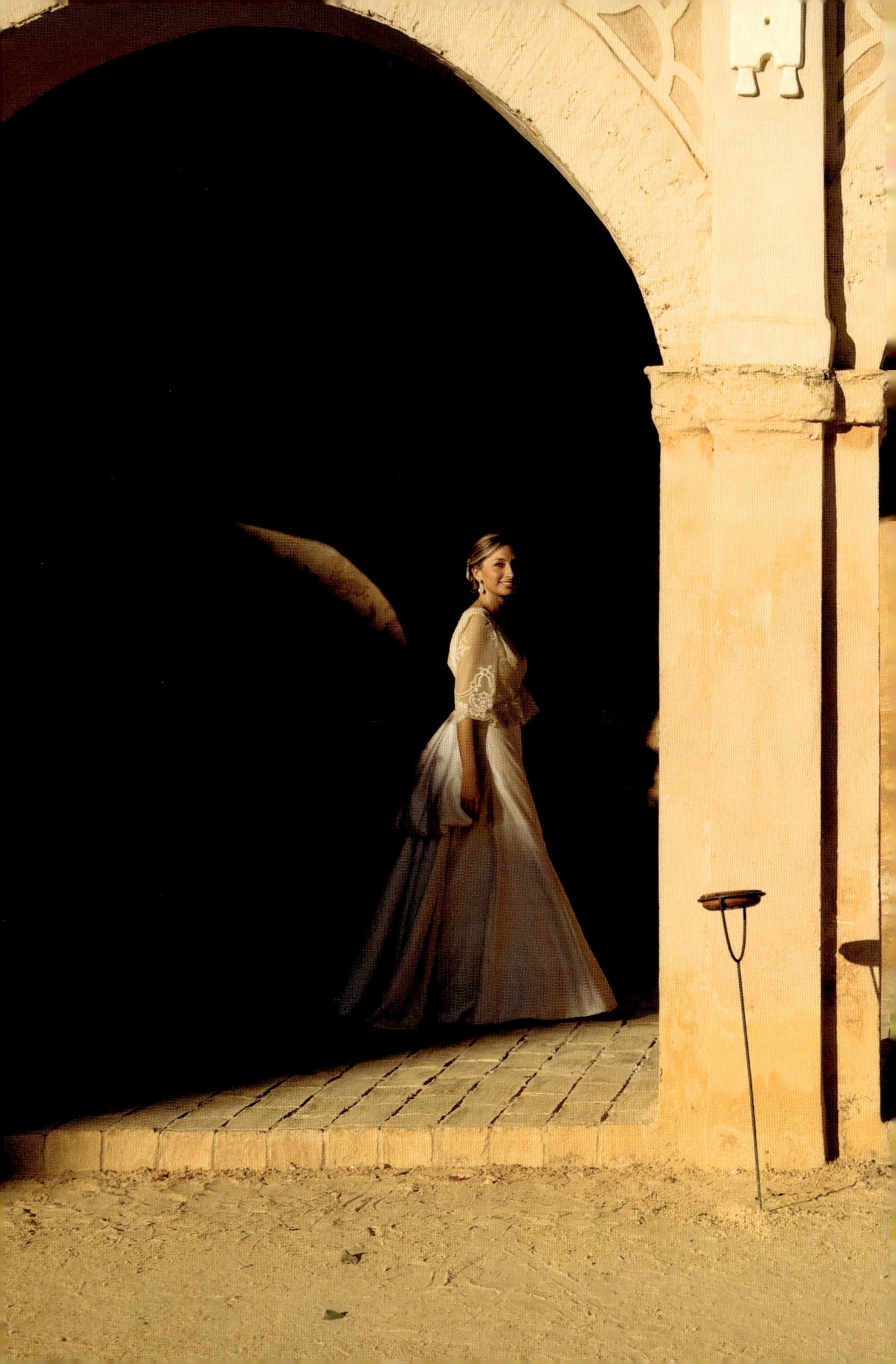

the wife of President Kennedy, Jacqueline, with whom I rode around the Royal Armory on horseback, and Princess Grace of Monaco, among many other personalities. I also like going to the bullfights during the Seville Fair, which are held in the very beautiful plaza of the Royal Cavalry Armory of Seville. I've always had very good friendships with matadors, including Antonio Bienvenida, Antonio Ordóñez, Pepe Luis Vázquez, and the master of masters, the great Curro Romero.

I had the chance to meet the author of this lovely book, Antonio del Junco, when he came to my home, the Palacio de las Dueñas, to take a portrait of me. I think that with his very singular perspective, and with Assouline's proven record of good work and prestigious editors known worldwide, there is no doubt that the spirit of Seville will be perfectly reflected. That's what I desire with all my heart.

Ángela, a friend of the author, at her wedding at a fifteenth-century country estate.

NO 8 DO

Introduction

"The worst thing is not that Sevillians think that they have the most beautiful city in the world… the worst is that they may be right."
—Antonio Gala, author, twentieth century.

Seville doesn't have skyscrapers as New York does. But it has the Giralda, one of the loveliest towers in the world, where the *Giraldillo*, the sculpture that sits atop the structure, acts as a weather vane, watching the sunset every afternoon.

Seville doesn't have the sea as Cádiz does. But it has the Guadalquivir River, which fills the air with the scent of salt and the cries of the seagulls.

Seville doesn't have seven hills as Rome does. But it has the gently sloping Aljarafe, from which the city can be seen, nestled in the lush green space on the banks of the river.

Seville doesn't have the broad, tree-lined avenues of Paris—in fact, the city is essentially a labyrinth. To find the spirit of this three-thousand-year-old city, to understand the allure of Seville, to explain the special fascination that attracts people in search of beauty and joy to this city from all across the world, you must enter the intimate, mystical maze. Once you're in, it's easy to lose yourself inside. It's even easier to decide to stay.

The singular beauty of Seville is the result of three thousand years of history, itself a maze of influences and relationships, a composite of countless layers of culture that have mixed and mingled over time, weaving a richly textured fabric of Sevillian identity that remains unique in the world today. Thus, the city is best understood as the latest in a long line of distinct iterations that preceded this one, each with its own definition of what a "Sevillian" is; taken together, these Sevilles of the past provide a foundational pulse that guides the city's beating heart. The Phoenicians, who knew the city as Ispal when it was nothing more than a settlement of stilt houses along the river—these were Sevillians. The Romans, who founded the legendary city of Hispalis on the banks of the river, the city that bore Trajan and Hadrian—these were Sevillians. And the Moors, who centuries later called it Ixbilia, tracing their curving alleyways atop the rectilinear plans of Roman cities, embellishing the skyline with arches and minarets, including the stunning Alcázar—these were also Sevillians.

A Sevillian coat of arms in the Plaza de San Francisco.
Following pages: A sixteenth-century etching of Seville as seen from the Aljarafe.

HISPALIS

1. die Inquisition
2. St. Laurentz
3. die Trojanische Pforte
4. St. Pauli Kirche
5. St. Magdalene
6. S. Bonaventura
7. Jesuiter Kirche
8. die Kirche der Incarnation
9. S. Francisci Kirche
10. S. Petri

Regni Andalusiæ Metropolis ad flumen Quadalquivir, in qua ex America advectum aurum et argentum in monismata recuditur. Post Madritum est maxima et celeberrima Hispaniæ Civitas. Pulchro nitet Regis Academiâ gaudet, item Appellationis et Inquisitionis judicio, nec non Archiepiscopatu, cujus annui reditus 10000. Thaleros explent; Ei nunc ab A° 1717. summa gratiâ Cardinalis Alberonius præest. A° 1709. grassante peste plus quam 20000. hominum in hac Urbe abrepti sunt. Circumjacens Sevillano agro territorium in 4. partes dispescitur, quarum nomina Axarafa, Sierra, Colentina, Campiña vel Vanda Morisca, et Sierra d'Aroche. Hispani de hoc proverbium: qui Sevillam non vidit, nihil pulchrum vidit: quippe in ea ne somnia Palatia reperiuntur, et 120. Ptochotrophea numerantur.

SEVILIEN.

11. St. Ysidori Kirche.
12. St. Augustini.
13. die Königs-Pforte.
14. der Dom.
15. der Königl. Pallast.
16. der Silberne Thurn.
17. der Güldne Thurn.
18. die Xeres Pforte.
19. die Brücke Tripiana.
20. Wasser-Leitungen.
21. der Fl. Guadalquivir.

Haupt-Statt im Königreich Andalusien, am Fluß Quadalquivir, daselbst das aus West-Indien kommende Gold und Silber vermüntzet wird. Sie ist nach Madrit die größte und wichtigste Statt in gantz Spanien, und hat einen Königl. Pallast, eine Univerlität, ein Appellation, und Inquisitions Gerichte; wie auch ein Ertz-Bistthum, Welches jährlich 30000. Thaler einträgt, und vor A. 1717. der bekante Cardinal Alberoni besessen hat. Im Jahr 1709. sind durch eine ausgebrochene Lust-Seuche bonnen 3. Monath über 20000. Menschen in dieser Statt hingerafft worden. Das darum herum und zu Sevillien gehörige Gebiet, wird in 4. Theile abgesondert, welche sind Axerab. Sierra Constantina, Campine oder Vando Morisca. und d'Aroche. Die Spagnier pflegen Insgemein von diesem Ort zu sagen, wer Sevillien nicht gesehen, der hat nichts sehens gesehen: wie dann würcklich sich fast lauter Pallaste, und 120. Armen Häußer allhier befinden.

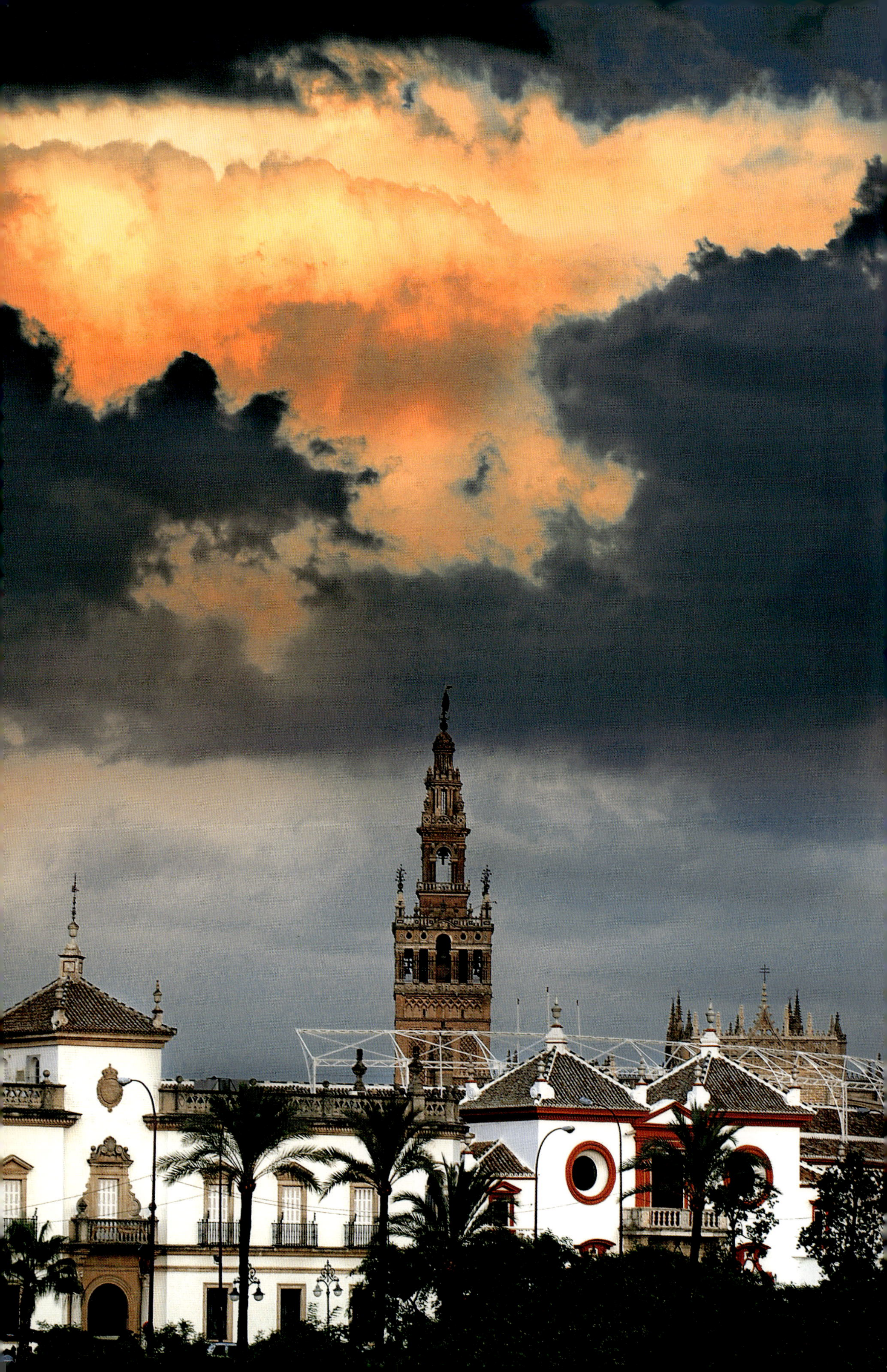

Then came the Christians and the Jews and the many diverse peoples who made the city their home in the centuries thereafter, crafting the traditions, the values, and the spirit that make today's Sevillians so unique in the world.

Almost as rich as the city's history is its mythology, a formidable canon led by a cast of characters including Figaro, Carmen, and Don Juan; even Hercules makes a cameo, with some legends tracing the original establishment of Ispal to the hero's voyage through the Strait of Gibraltar to the Atlantic. Of course, the city is also teeming with real-life legends—its matadors, national heroes like Juan Belmonte, Curro Romero, and Manolo Vázquez; its dancers, poets, and singers; its great artists, including Diego Velázquez and Bartolomé Esteban Murillo; and its modern-day elite, including the Duchess of Alba, and the fashion-design team Victorio y Lucchino.

For most people who come to Seville, though, it is the distinctive culture of the city that proves most seductive: the festivals and traditions, from Holy Week to the Seville Fair, that can be found nowhere else in the world; the incomparable art and delicious food; the vibrant flamenco music scene; the beloved architectural landmarks, like the colossal cathedral and the elegant, tranquil Casa de Pilatos; the winding streets, full of secrets; and, of course, the joy of its people.

Indeed, perhaps what makes Seville so unforgettable, more than anything else, is the special energy and spirit that surround the people of this city. Theirs is a very particular lifestyle, one in which relaxation is sacred and earthly pleasures are to be indulged fully. Time seems somehow to pass more slowly here—or maybe it's just that Sevillians know how to make the most of every moment; each night is an opportunity for an impromptu party with friends in the cobblestone streets, every sunny afternoon a chance to *tapear* on the banks of the Guadalquivir. For the people of Seville, life is filled with a special music, an unmistakably Sevillian rhythm that permeates the collective heartbeat of this place. They imbue the city with laughter, with tradition, with a symphony all their own. Theirs is a very particular sort of joie de vivre that visitors can't help but yearn for long after they've returned home.

•

A dramatic view of the Maestranza and the Giralda during a storm. *Following pages:* Italian marble bust of Alexander the Great, Archaeological Museum of Seville; Moorish and classical styles mix in the Patio de las Doncellas, one of the many courtyards within the Alcázar. *Pages 20–21:* Arcade overlooking the Plaza de España.

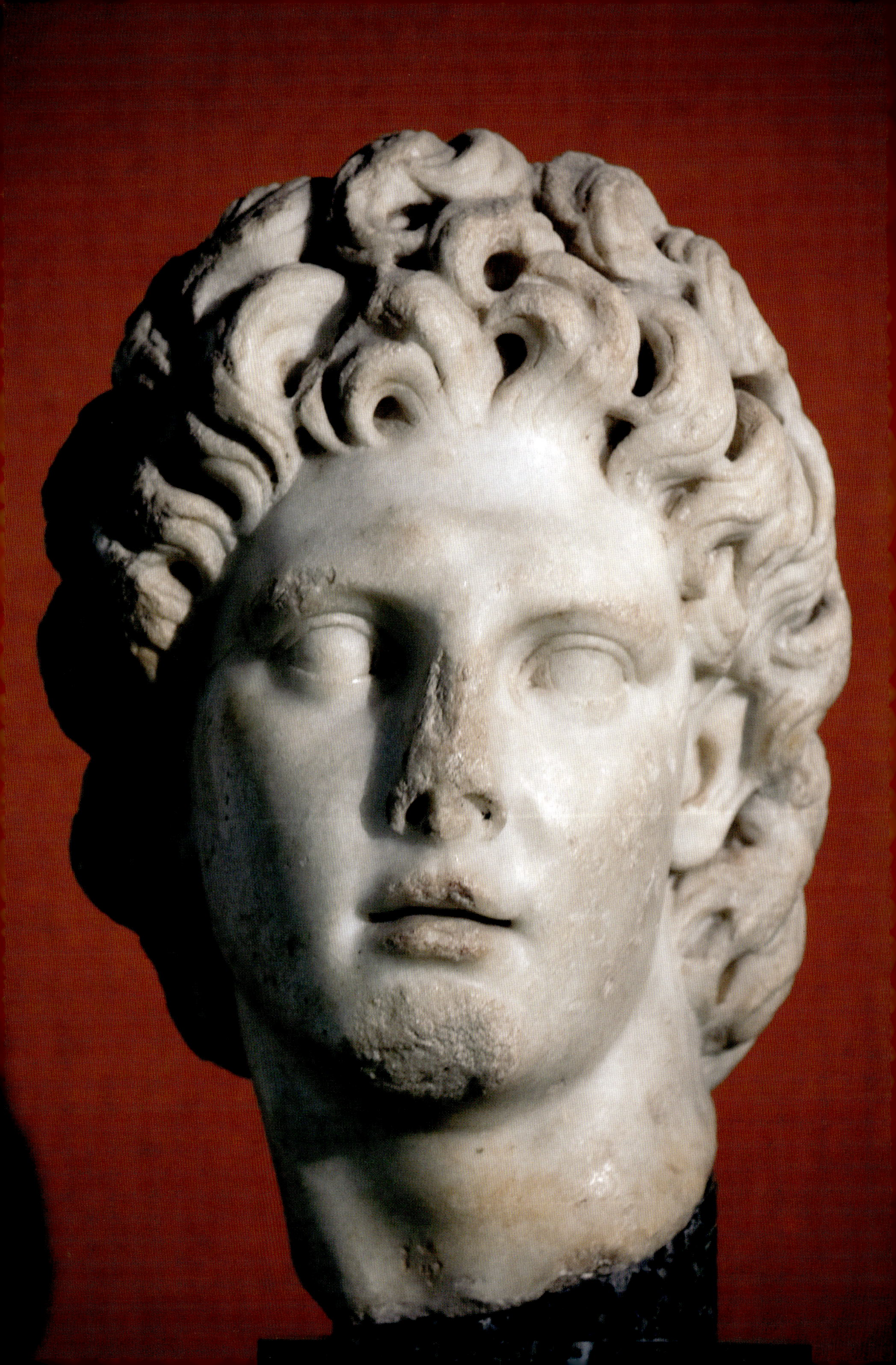

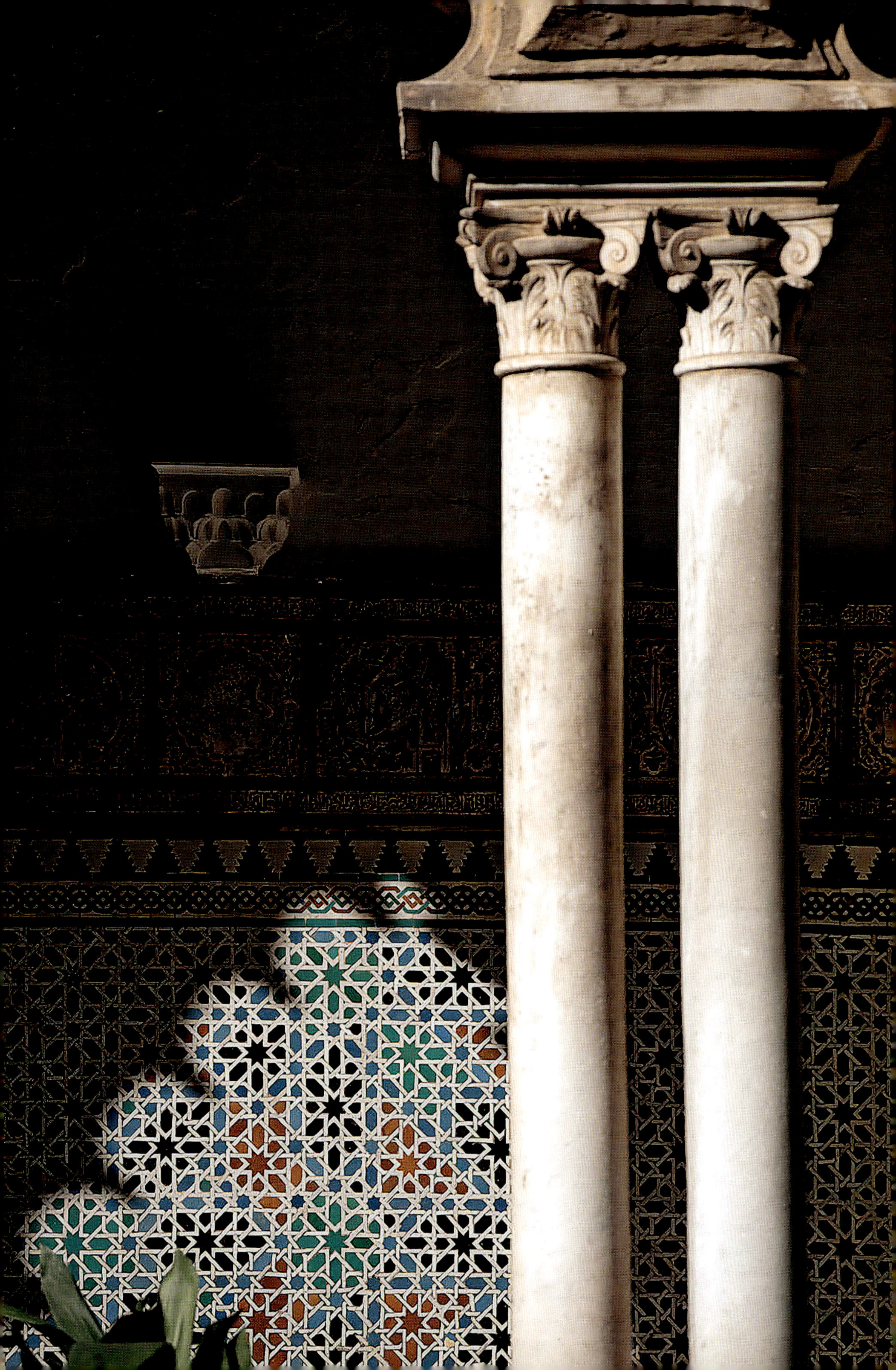

SEVILLA

TORRE DEL ORO
Ensayo de restauración y ornamentación

Inside the Royal Alfonsine Shipyards.
Right: Detail of a Sevillian coat of arms in the Plaza de San Francisco.

Left: Shield of the city on the Town Hall.

Right: Inscription on a window of the Alcázar.
Left: Eighteenth-century etching of the Gold Tower.

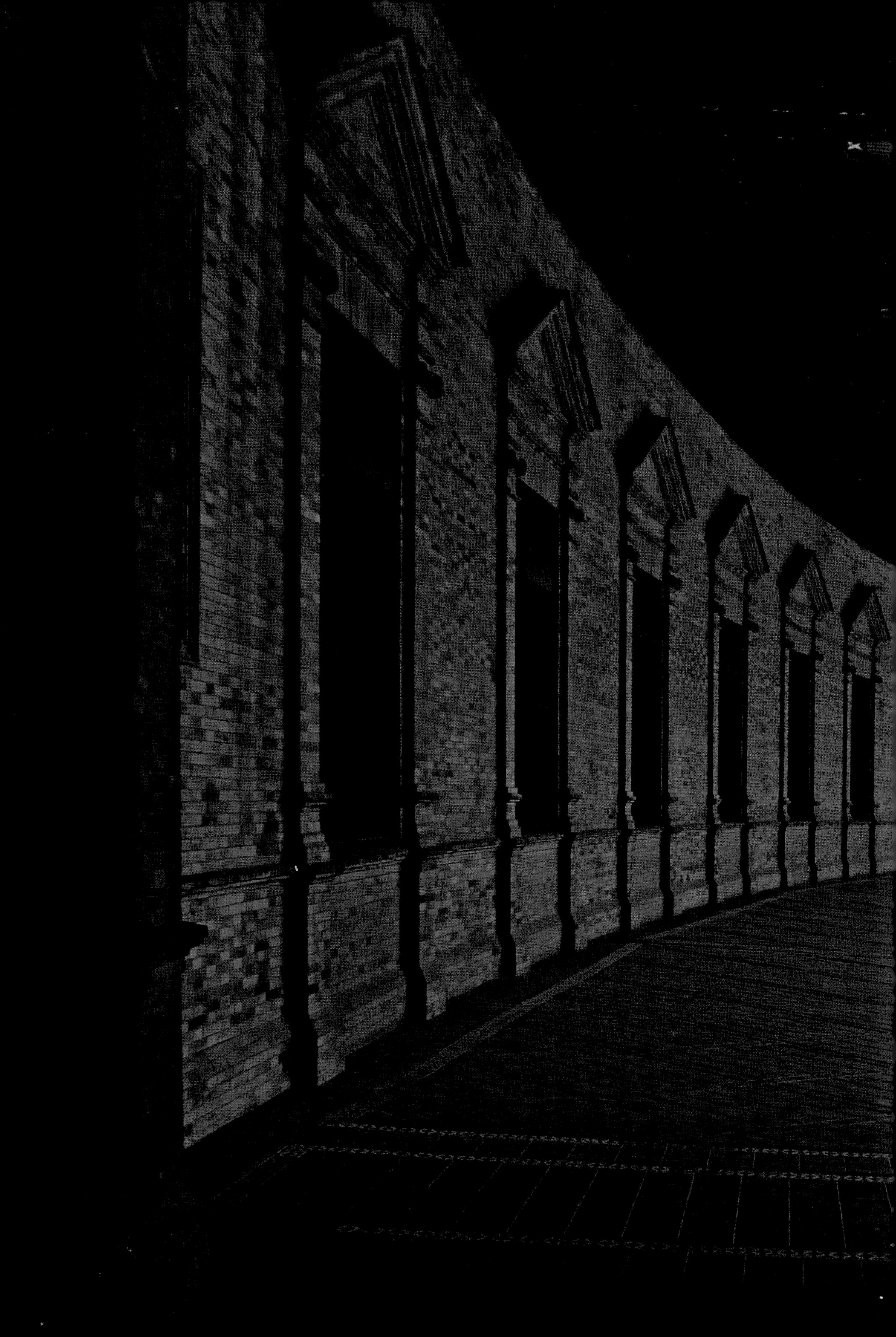

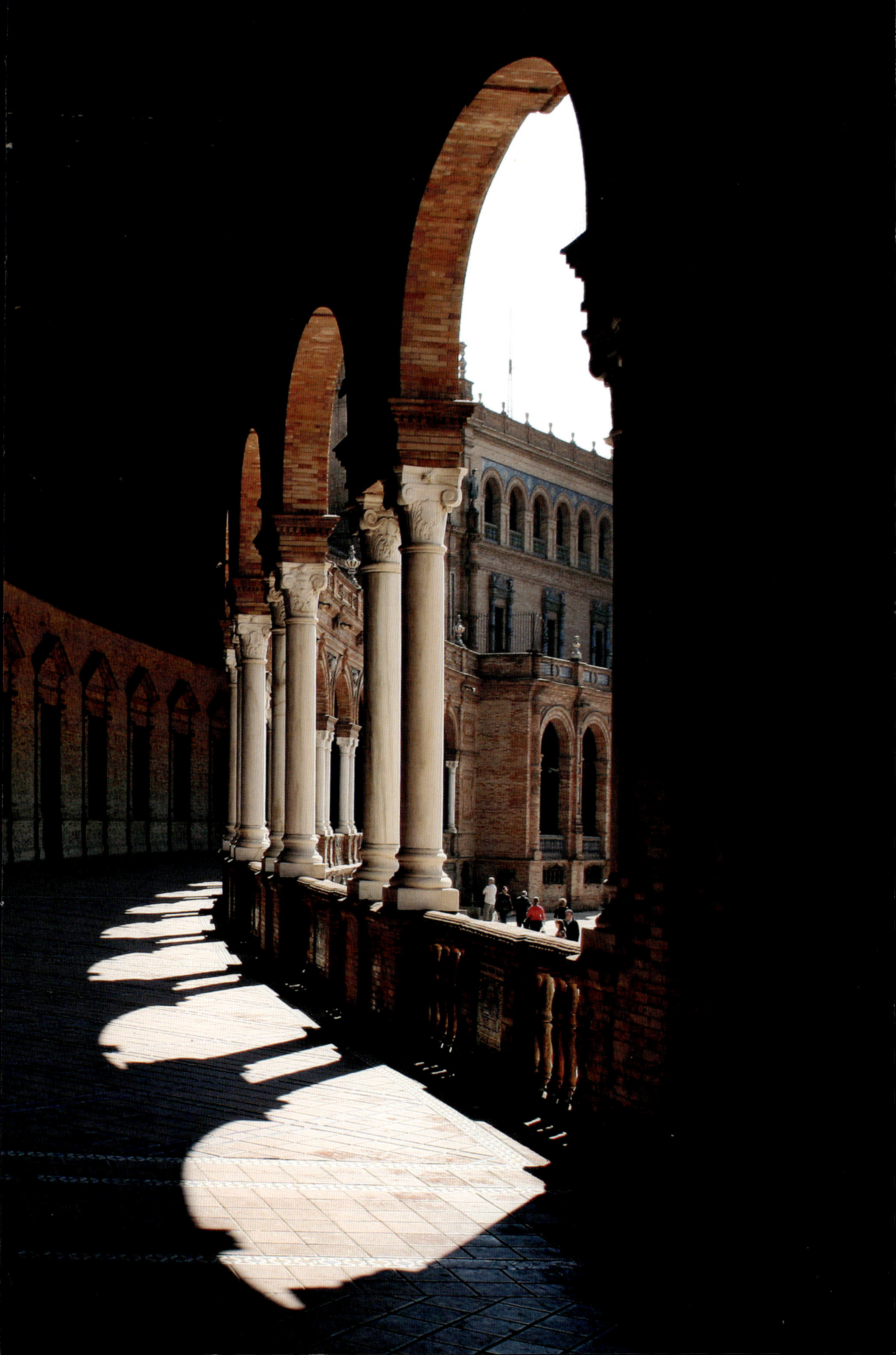

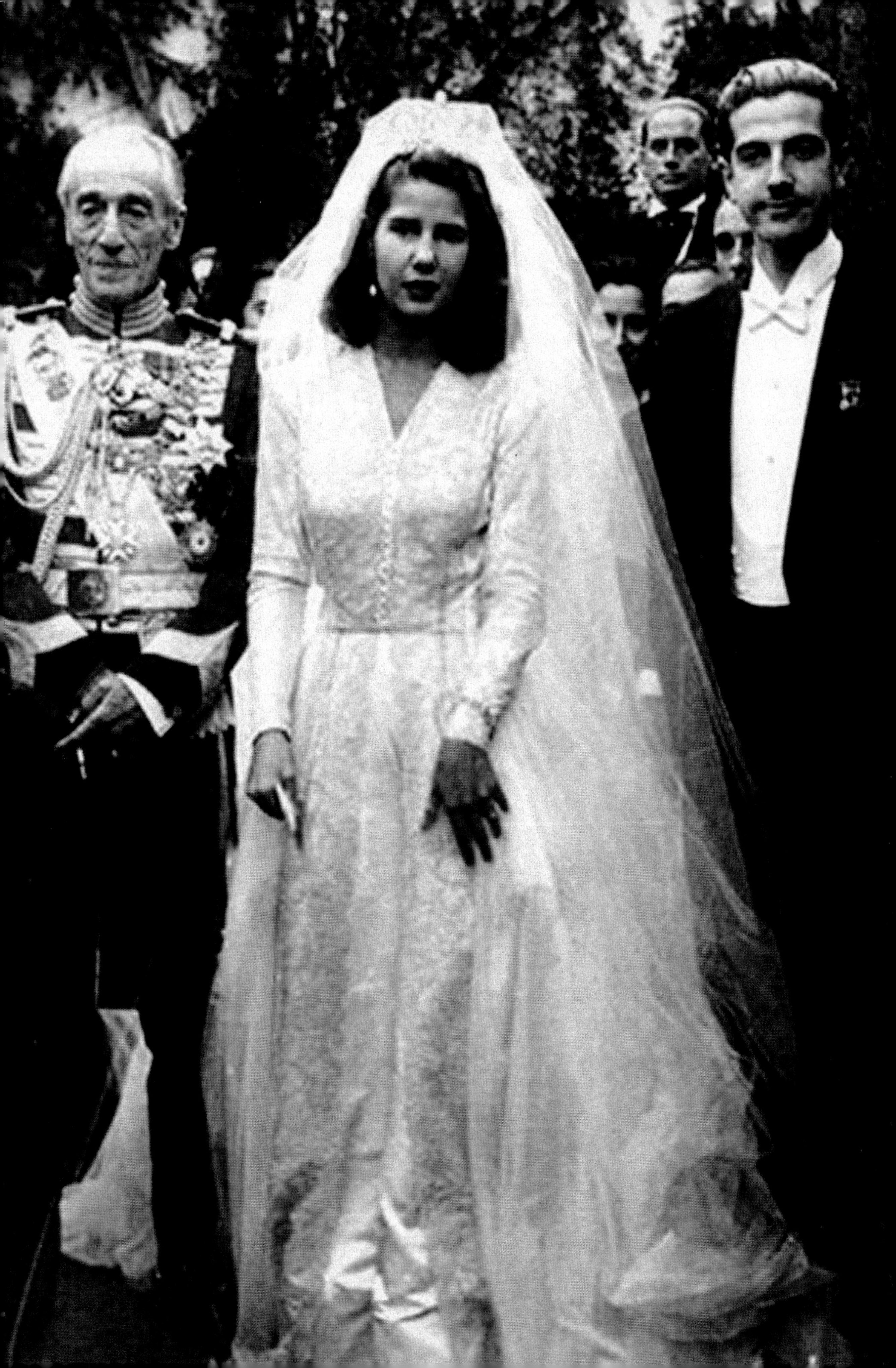

The Duchess of Alba

"Seville is not where I was born or where I spend the most time, but it's where I feel most at home. When I go to spend long periods at Dueñas, I'm not visiting; I go home."
—Cayetana Fitz-James Stuart y Silva, Duchess of Alba de Tormes

There is a famous saying in Spanish: "Genio y figura, hasta la sepultura" ("Character and looks, from the cradle to the grave"). There is, perhaps, no better way to describe María del Rosario Cayetana Fitz-James Stuart y Silva, the Duchess of Alba. She is adored and cherished by the Sevillians, and that affection is undeniably mutual.

Known as Cayetana de Alba or the Duquesa de Alba, she was born in Madrid, in the Liria Palace, on March 28, 1926. Cayetana is the eighteenth Duchess of Alba, head of the House of Alba, and holds more titles than any other noble in the world: five times a duchess; eighteen times a marquise; twenty-two times a countess, viscountess, and countess-duchess; and fourteen times a grandee of Spain. She is a distant relative of both King James II of England and Winston Churchill, as well as of Diana, Princess of Wales.

During her long stays in Seville, she lives in the Palacio de las Dueñas (the Palace of the Dukes of Alba), located in the heart of the city. Its interior is brimming with art (rumored to include works by Rembrandt, Goya, Rubens, and Velázquez) and other gifts from her countless friends and admirers—including Pablo Picasso, who once asked Cayetana to be his muse (she turned him down). Enchanting gardens perfumed with jasmine and paths of Seville's fine yellow soil, surround her magnificent Andalusian property.

In 2011, Cayetana married Alfonso Díez in an intimate ceremony at the Palacio de las Dueñas. The enormous crowd of Sevillians who gathered outside the gates of the residence was a true testament to how much Seville loves the Duchess. In fact, in 2011, the city erected a bronze statue of Cayetana, wrapped in a mantle, a Sevillian dress, in the Cristina Gardens, in front of San Telmo Palace.

Due to her busy social life and interest in art, Cayetana has opened her Seville home to the most interesting artists and personalities. This exclusive list includes Jacqueline Kennedy Onassis and Grace Kelly, among others. A major supporter of Spanish culture, she has also

The Duchess of Alba at her first wedding with groom Luis Martínez de Irujo and her father, the Duke of Alba, 1947.
Following pages: Cayetana dancing; Palacio de las Dueñas.

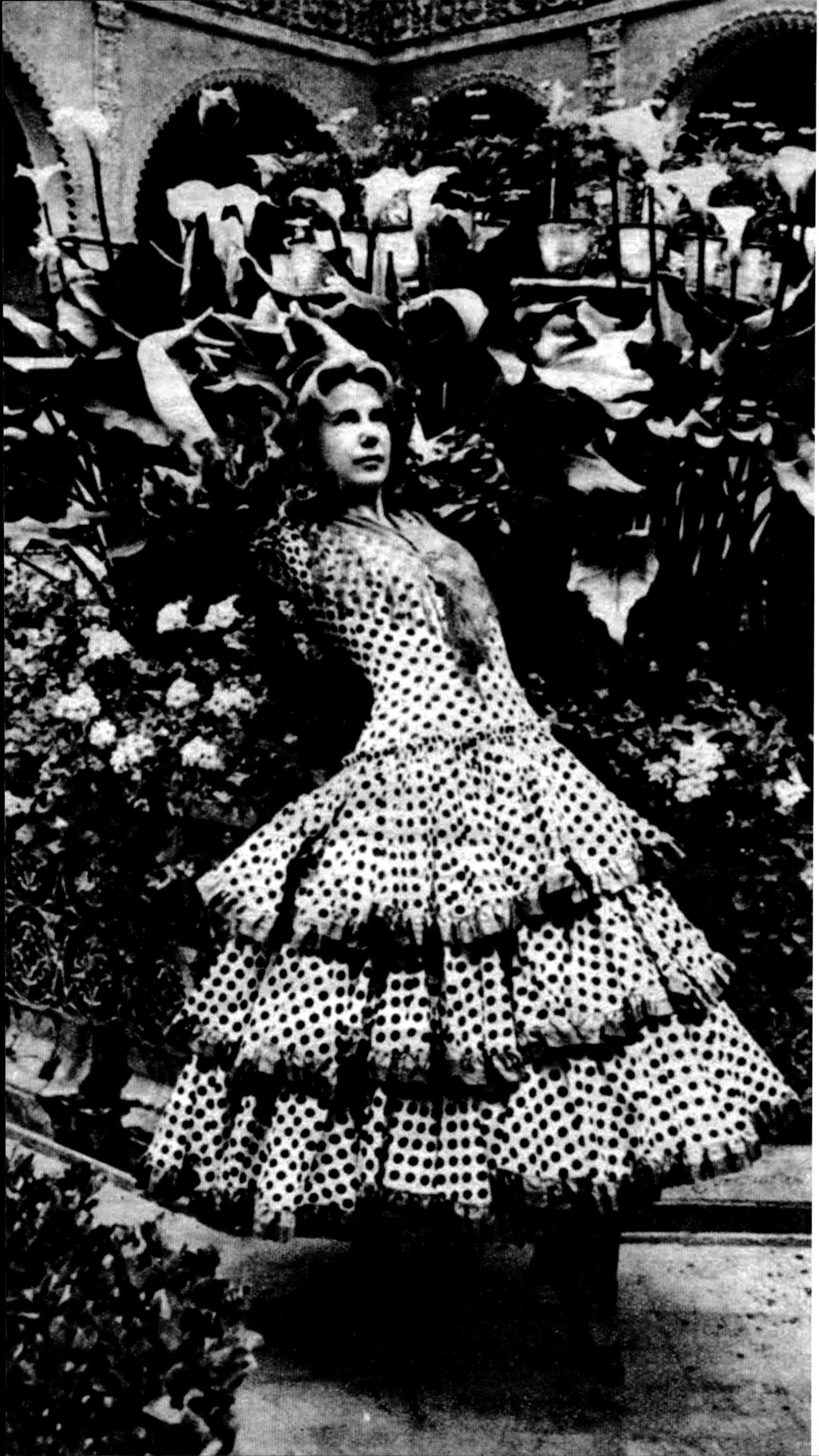

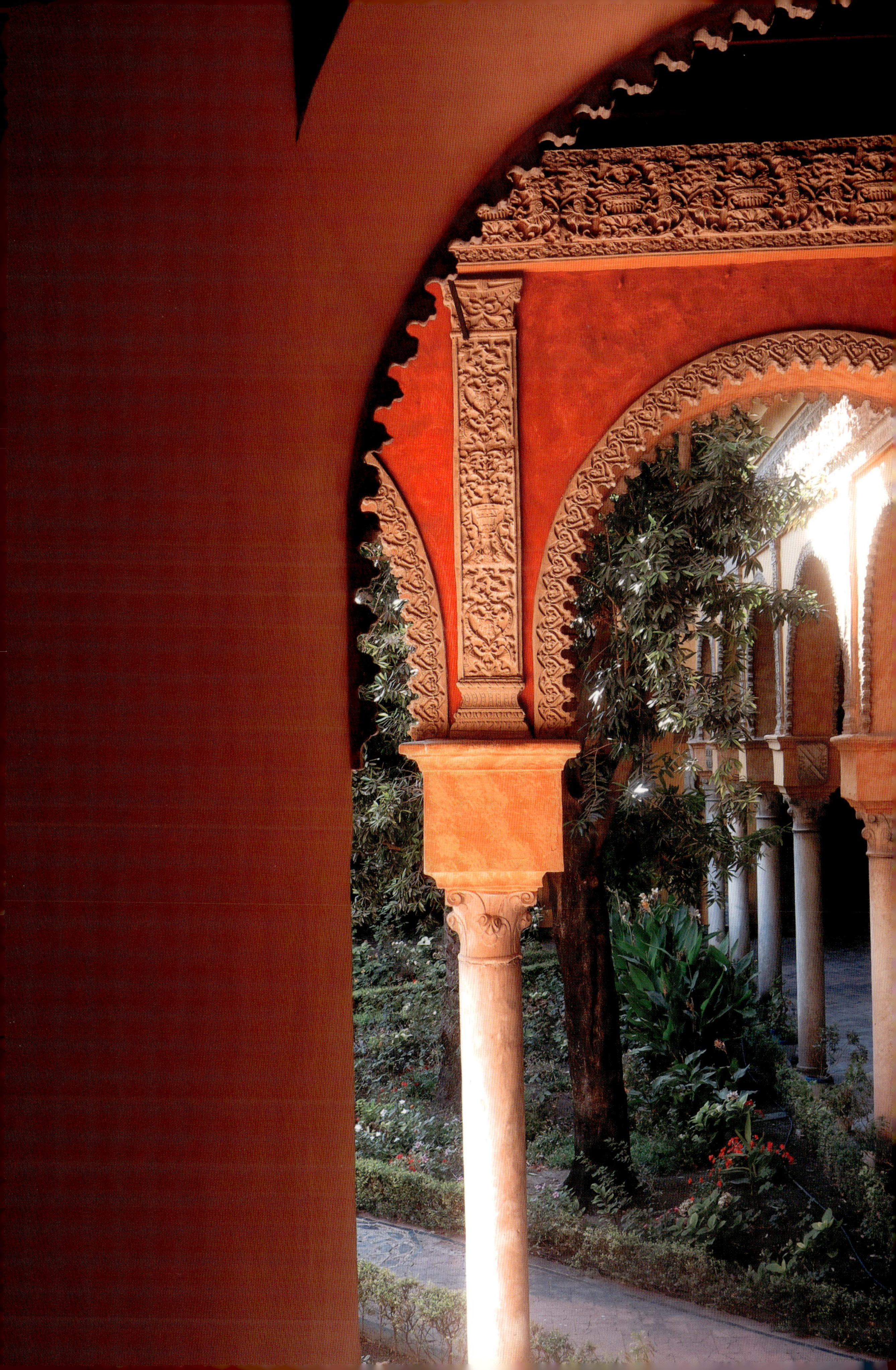

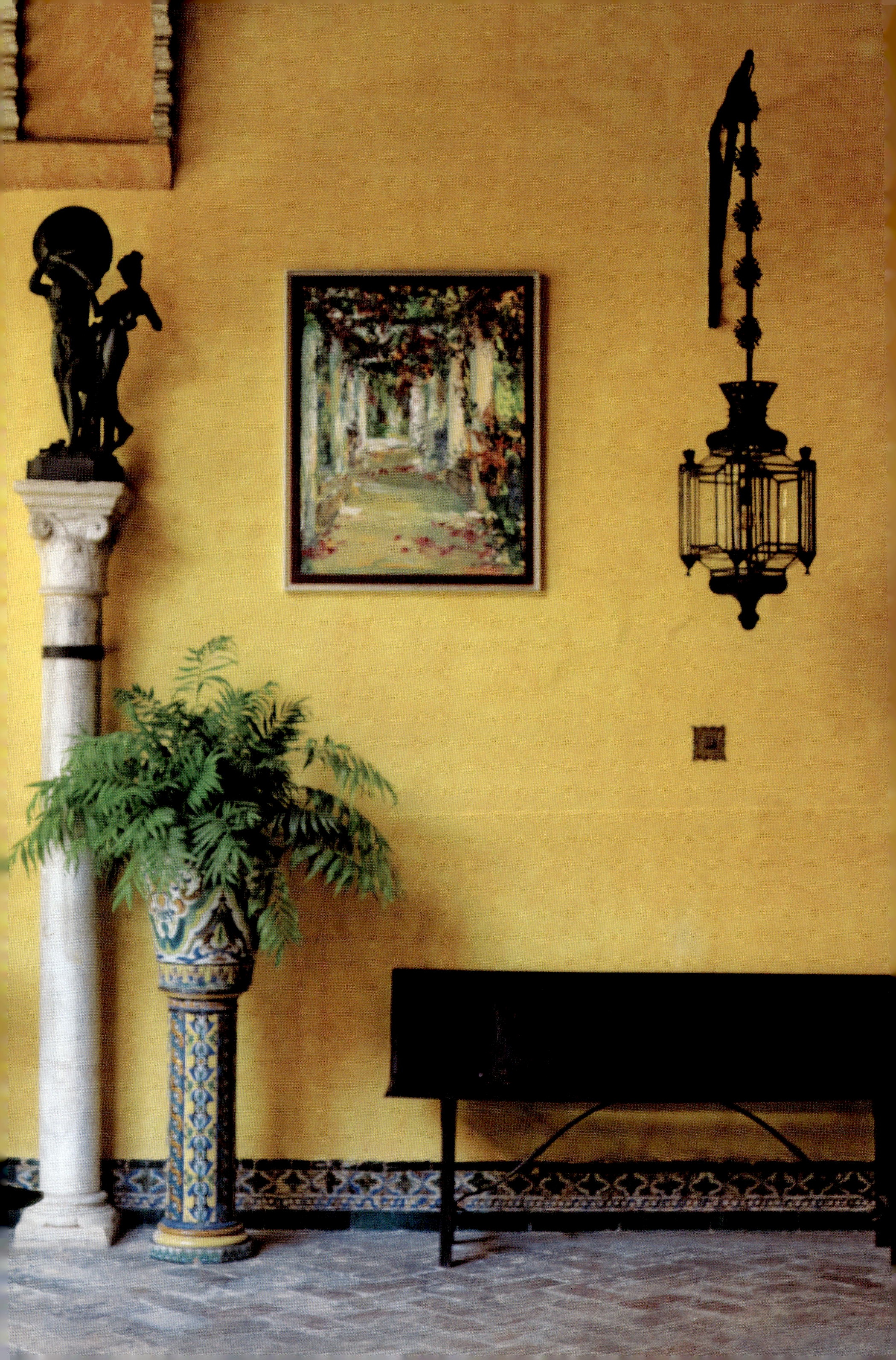

Clockwise from left: A patio within the Palacio de las Dueñas; *Duchess of Alba in White* by Francisco de Goya; Cayetana with her husband, Alfonso Díez; a loggia in the gardens of the Palacio de las Dueñas; poster of a fantasy portrait of Cayetana de Alba and the late Juanita Reina, with Cayetana's daughter and niece, by Reyes de la Lastra, for the 2010 spring festival; a secluded corner of the Palacio de las Dueñas gardens; portrait of the Duke of Alba, in Palacio de las Dueñas; Cayetana with her daughter Eugenia at the Maestranza.

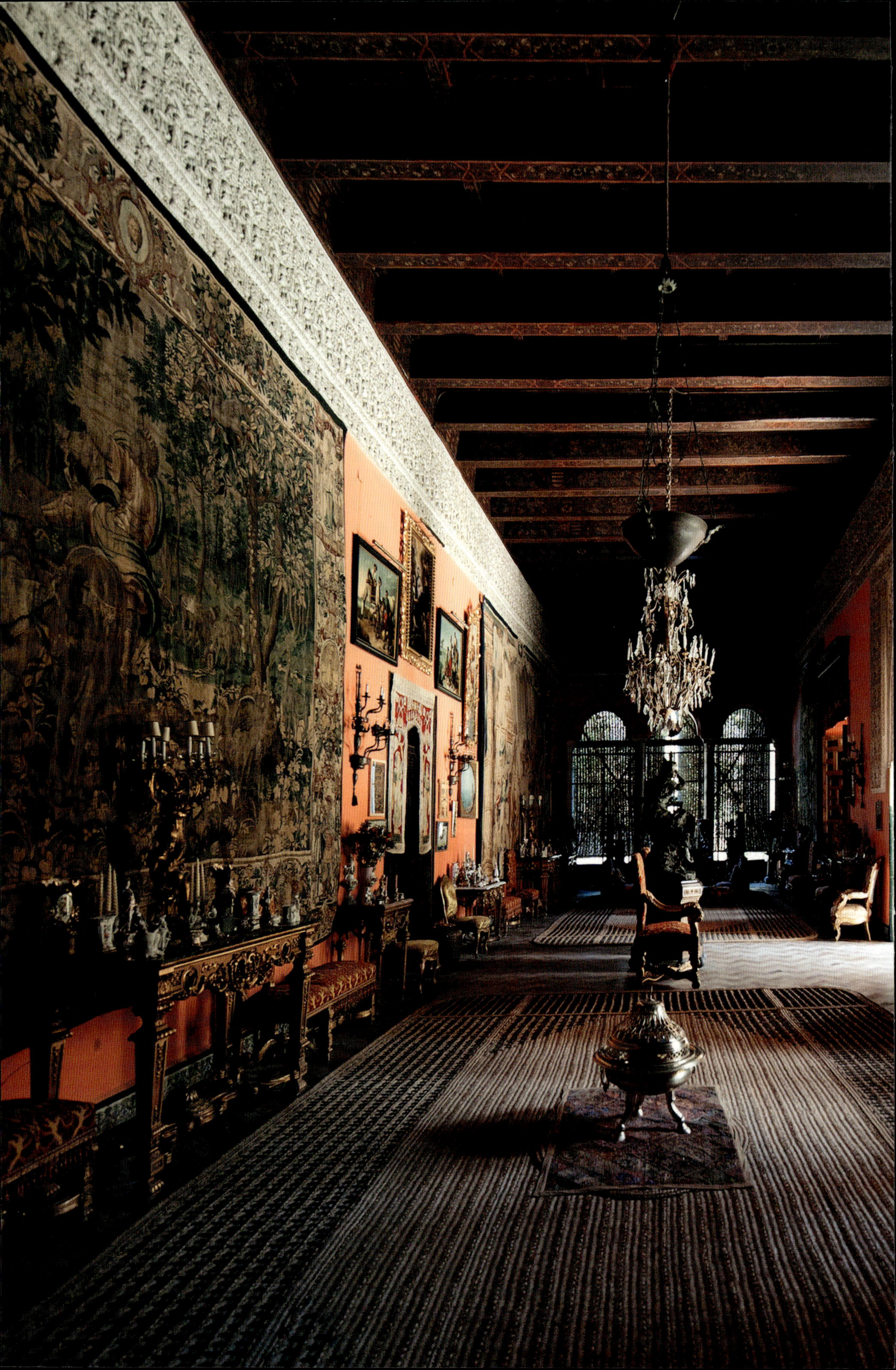

cultivated lifelong friendships in the worlds of flamenco and bullfighting. One of her best friends and most assiduous companions is none other than Carmen Tello, wife of the legendary matador Curro Romero; Tello served as the matron of honor at Cayetana's recent wedding to Alfonso Díez.

Although there have been many great *duquesas* of the Casa de Alba over the generations, Cayetana is known to be among the most influential, specifically for her generosity. Her status as the wealthiest woman in Spain has afforded her the opportunity to give back to the city she loves. According to her trusted friend and spiritual adviser, Father Ignacio Jiménez, her altruistic and positive nature, her desire to serve the community, and her patronage of her culture are so great and yet so discreet that, in most cases, no one knows about her benevolent contributions. She takes care of Seville in more ways than people know.

The Duchess is truly loved like no other in Seville. Active in the culture and life of the city, a philanthropist, and always elegant and glamorous, she is Seville's sweetheart.

A beautiful salon off the courtyard.
Following pages: The Duchess of Alba, surrounded by girls wearing mantillas, at a bullfight in the Maestranza.
Pages 32–33: Cayetana dancing with matador Fran Rivera inside the Palacio de las Dueñas after her third wedding, with the Siempre Así flamenco ensemble playing and singing Sevillanas.

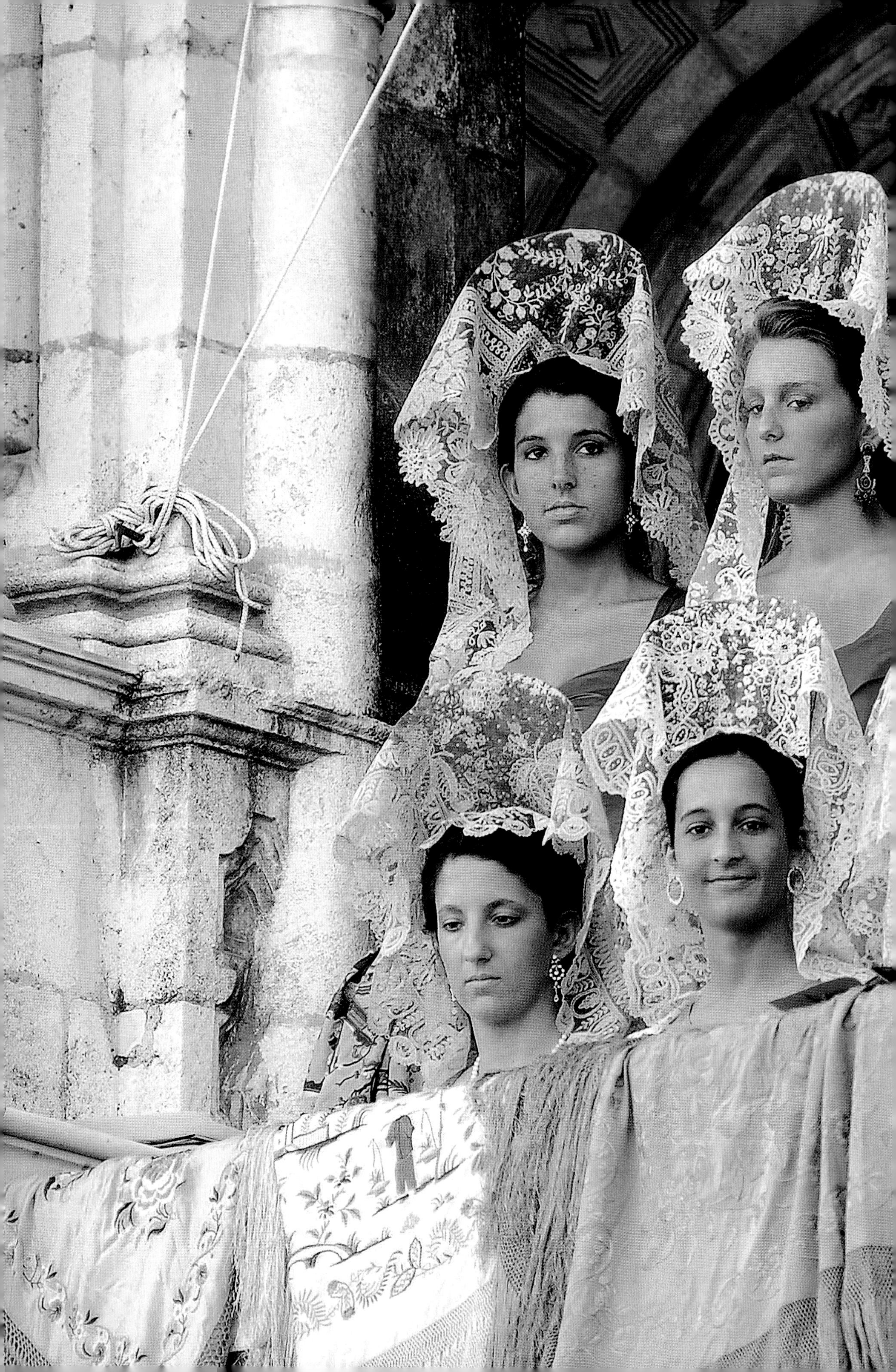

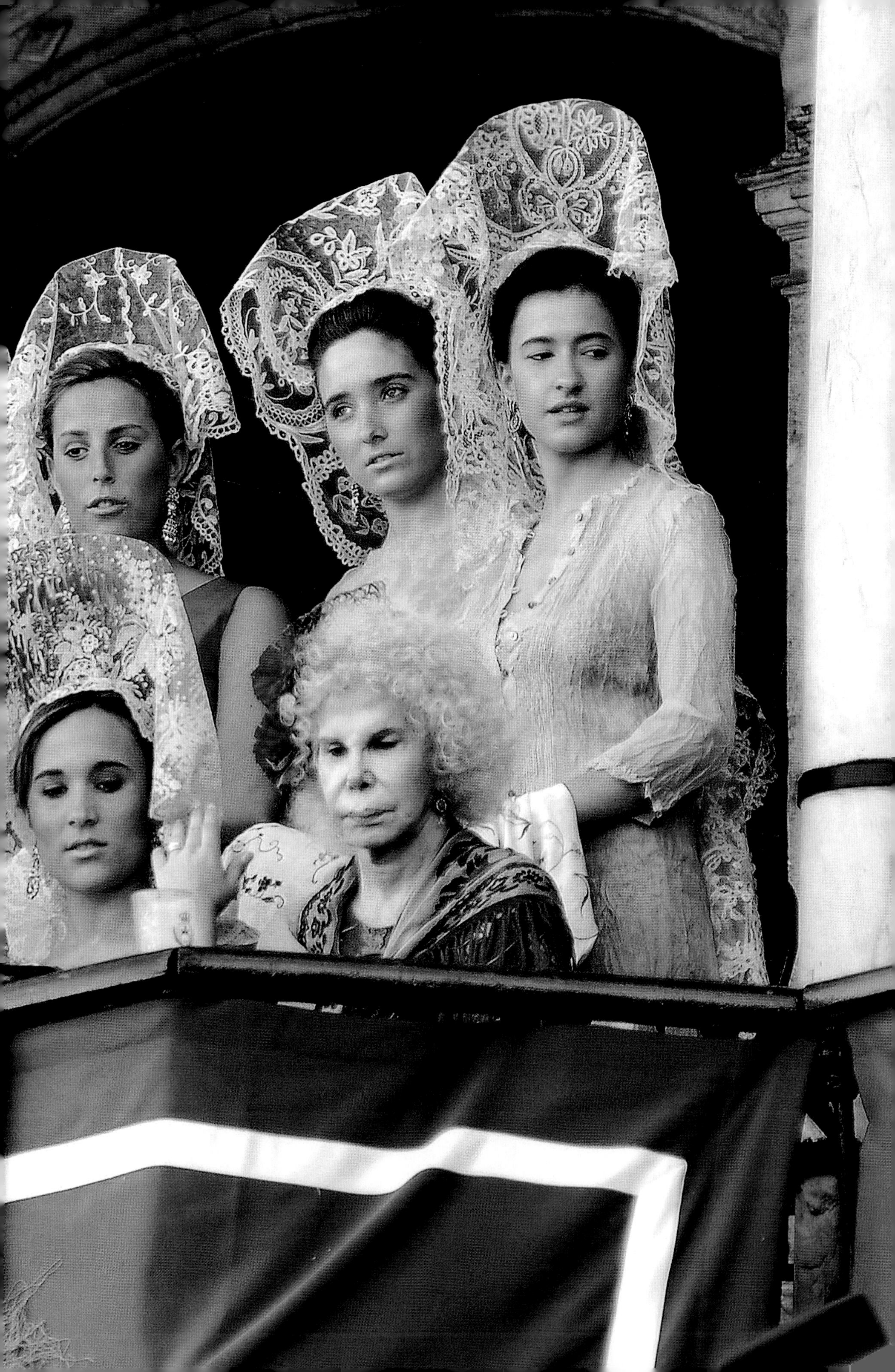

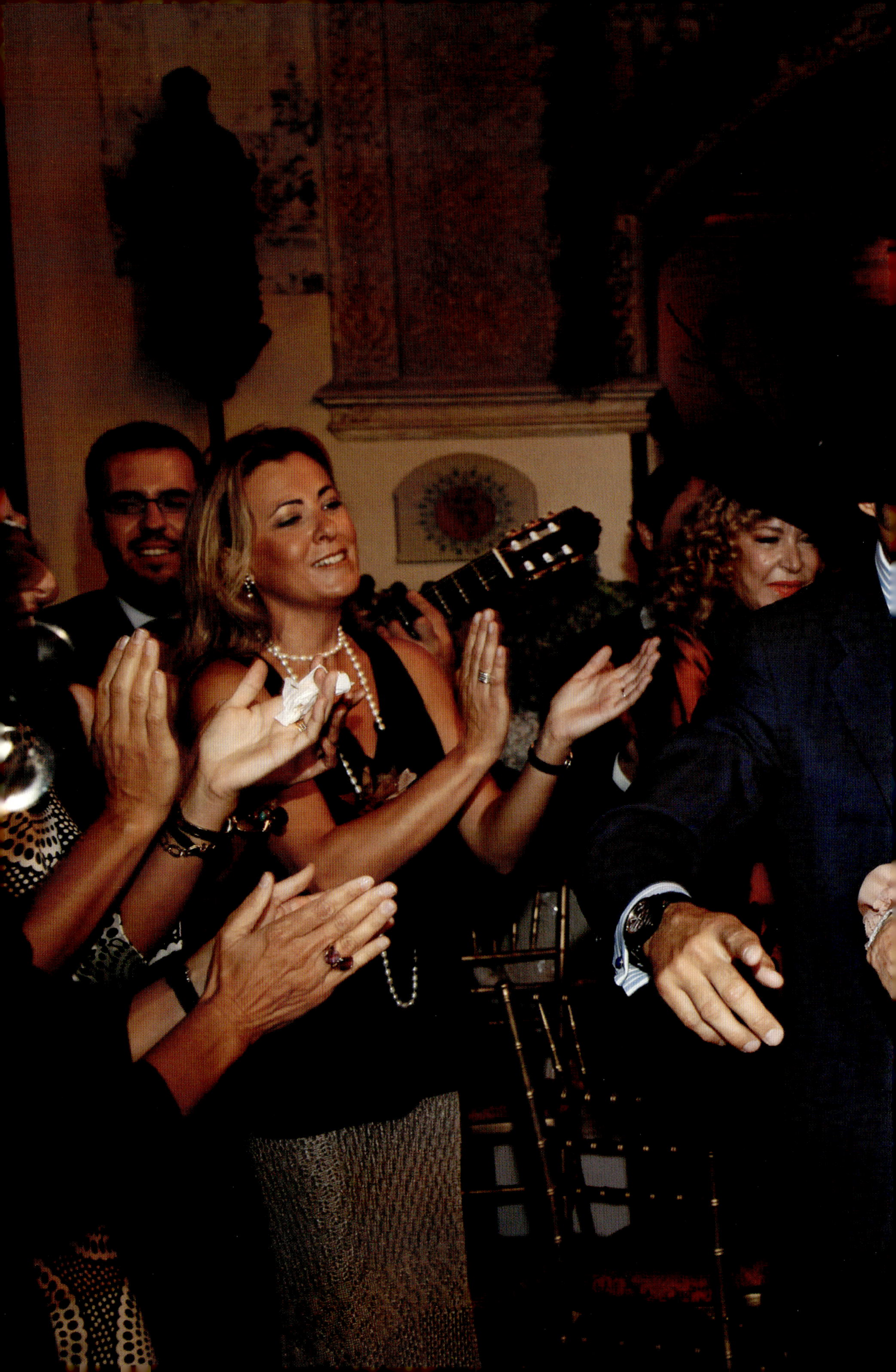

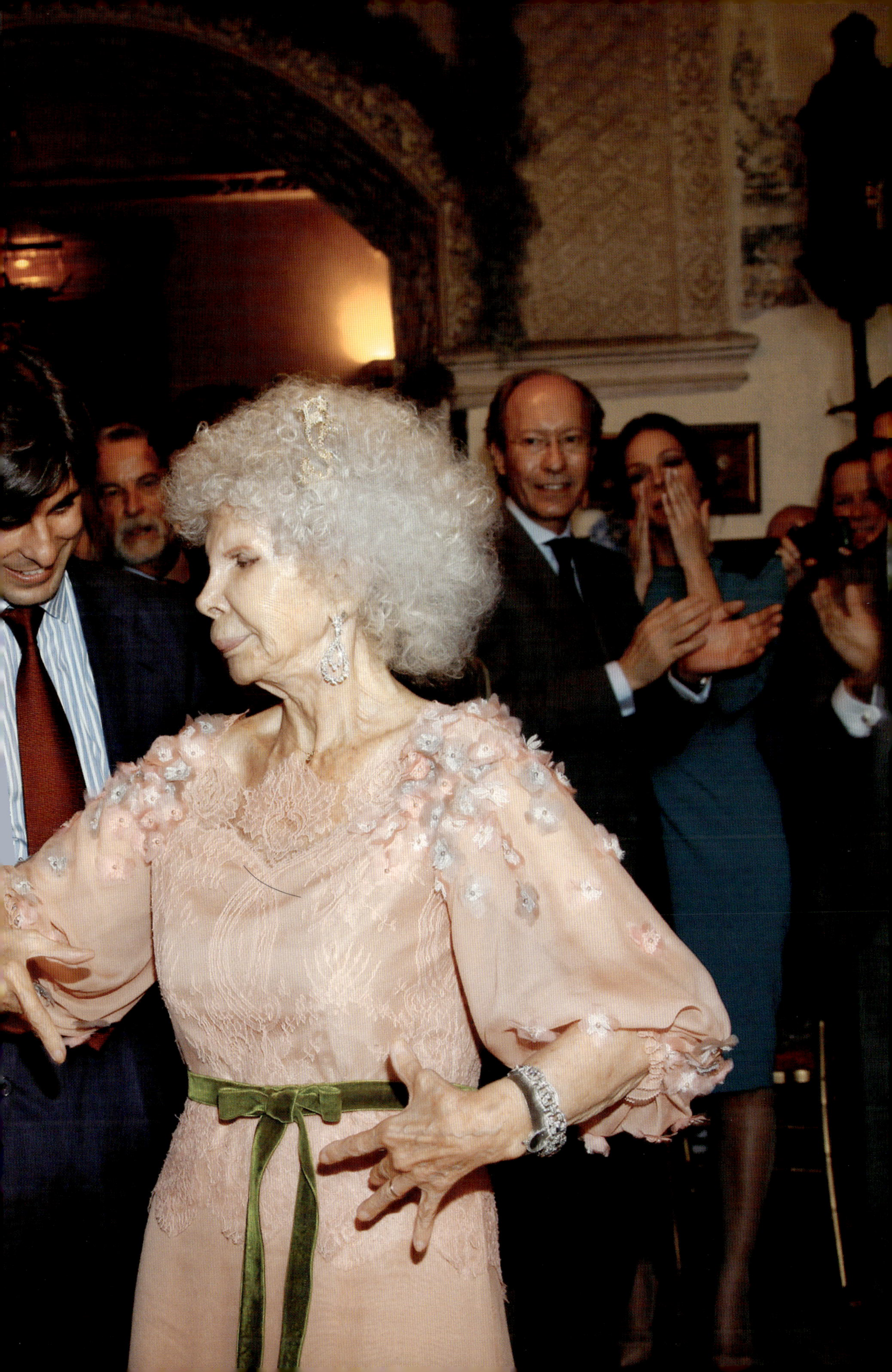

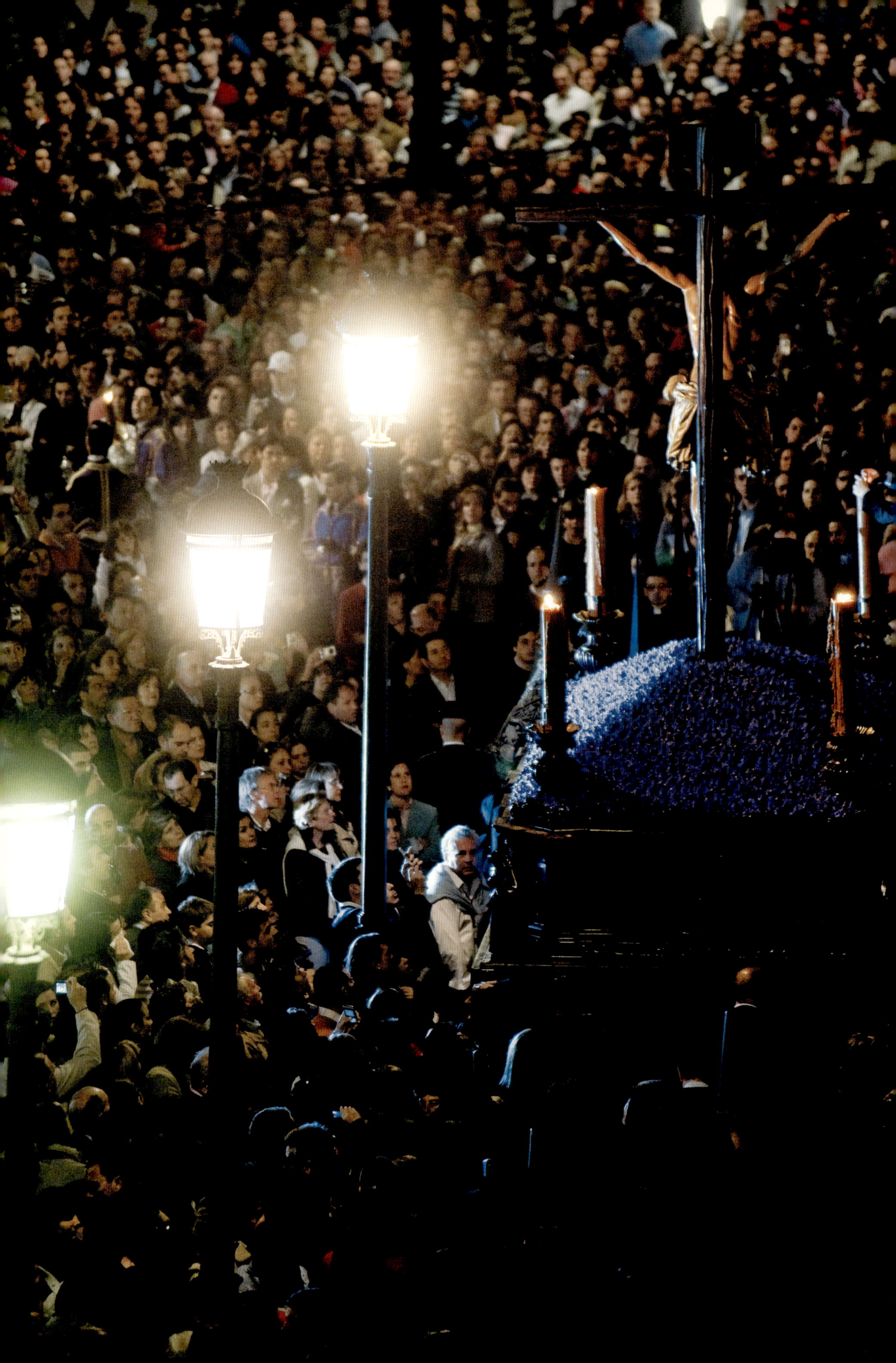

Holy Week

In Seville, April is not just the revival of spring; it is also the month when two extraordinary events occur: Holy Week and the Seville Fair (page 84).

The tradition of Holy Week officially began in the sixteenth century with the Via Crucis—processions of the Stations of the Cross. During the processions, sculptural representations of the events leading to the crucifixion of Jesus, built by religious brotherhoods, were carried approximately 1,000 yards from the Casa de Pilatos residential palace to the Cruz del Campo shrine (also known as the Temple) on the outskirts of Seville. As the tradition gained more and more followers each year, Cardinal Fernando Niño de Guevara decreed in 1604 that all processions must stop at the Seville Cathedral, and this remains part of the route today.

Starting the Wednesday before Easter (as decreed by Cardinal Niño de Guevara), the entire city transforms into an enormous stage with numerous processions crisscrossing through the streets, a chaotic ensemble of colors, chants, and celebrations. The processions are organized by the seventy-one brotherhoods, each of which has its own particular customs and style of dress—from the severe black robes of El Silencio to the white-plumed headdresses of La Macarena. These processions give Sevillians the opportunity to commemorate the Passion (the final hours of Jesus Christ's life) and the death of Jesus, by exhibiting pasos, or wooden floats, showing different scenes from the Passion. Each paso is sumptuously decorated with fabrics, candles, and flowers, often containing extraordinary sculptures overlaid in gold and silver. The Macarena and the Jesús del Gran Poder are the most famous and, artistically, the most revered. To witness the procession is an extremely moving experience, inspiring all, even the nonreligious.

From Thursday night to dawn on Friday, the climax of Holy Week, called La Madrugá, captures the attention of the entire city. The streets are jam-packed with Sevillians and thousands of penitents, including the members of each brotherhood, who accompany their paso in the Station of Penitence. The penitents dress in tunics in the traditional colors of their brotherhoods and cover their faces with cone-shaped hoods. The processions, with their highly individualized marching rhythms, are impressive and quite beautiful.

Today, Holy Week still remains a vital part of the Sevillian social and religious calendars, an important expression of a shared spiritual and cultural heritage.

Christ of the Good Death at the Confraternity of the Students. *Following pages:* Members of the Confraternity of the Love inside the Church of El Salvador; The Virgin of the Kings entering the Seville Cathedral after the procession. *Pages 38–39: Figure of Christ*; a depiction of *Christ of the Good Death*, illuminated by candlelight.

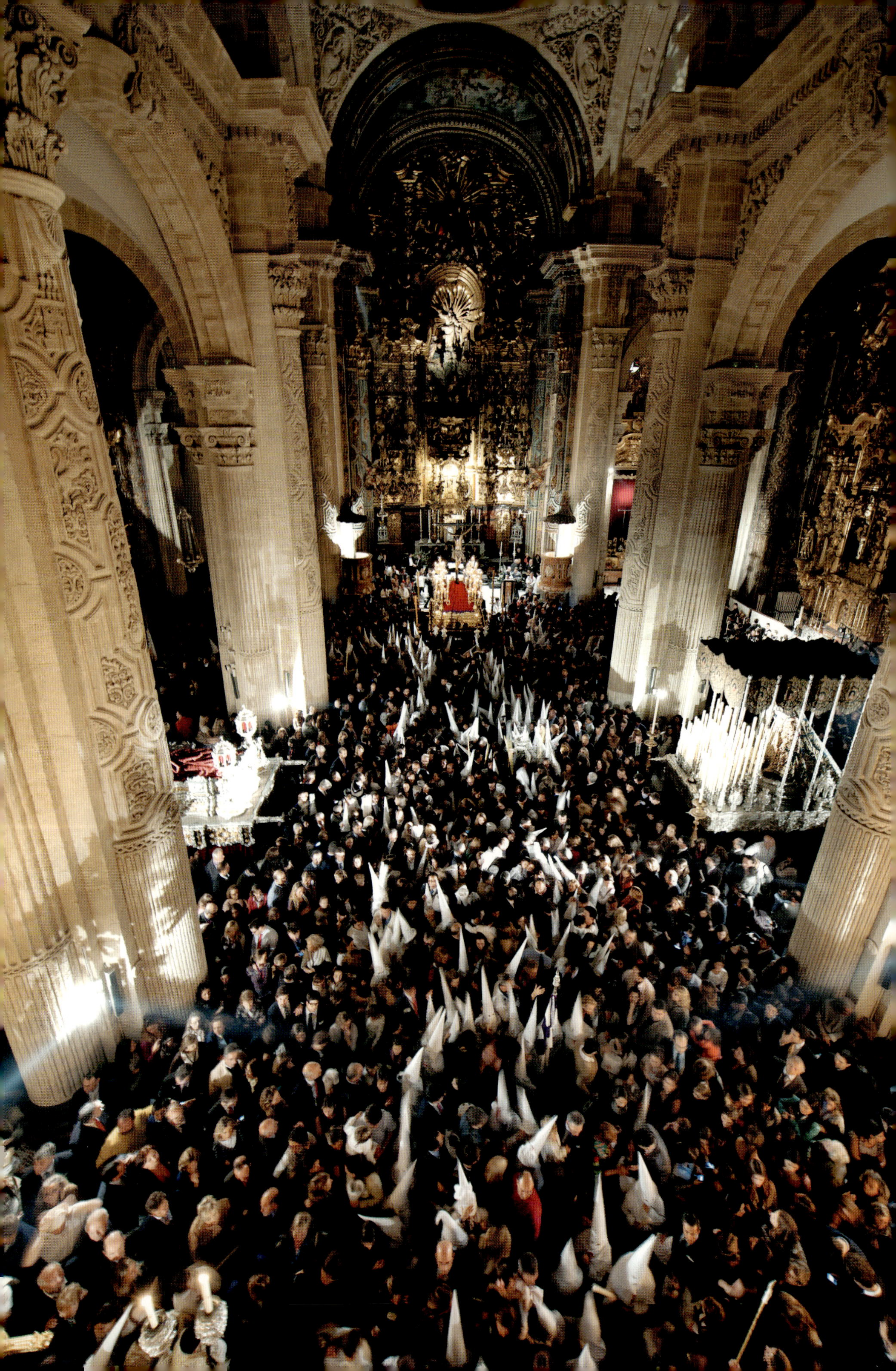

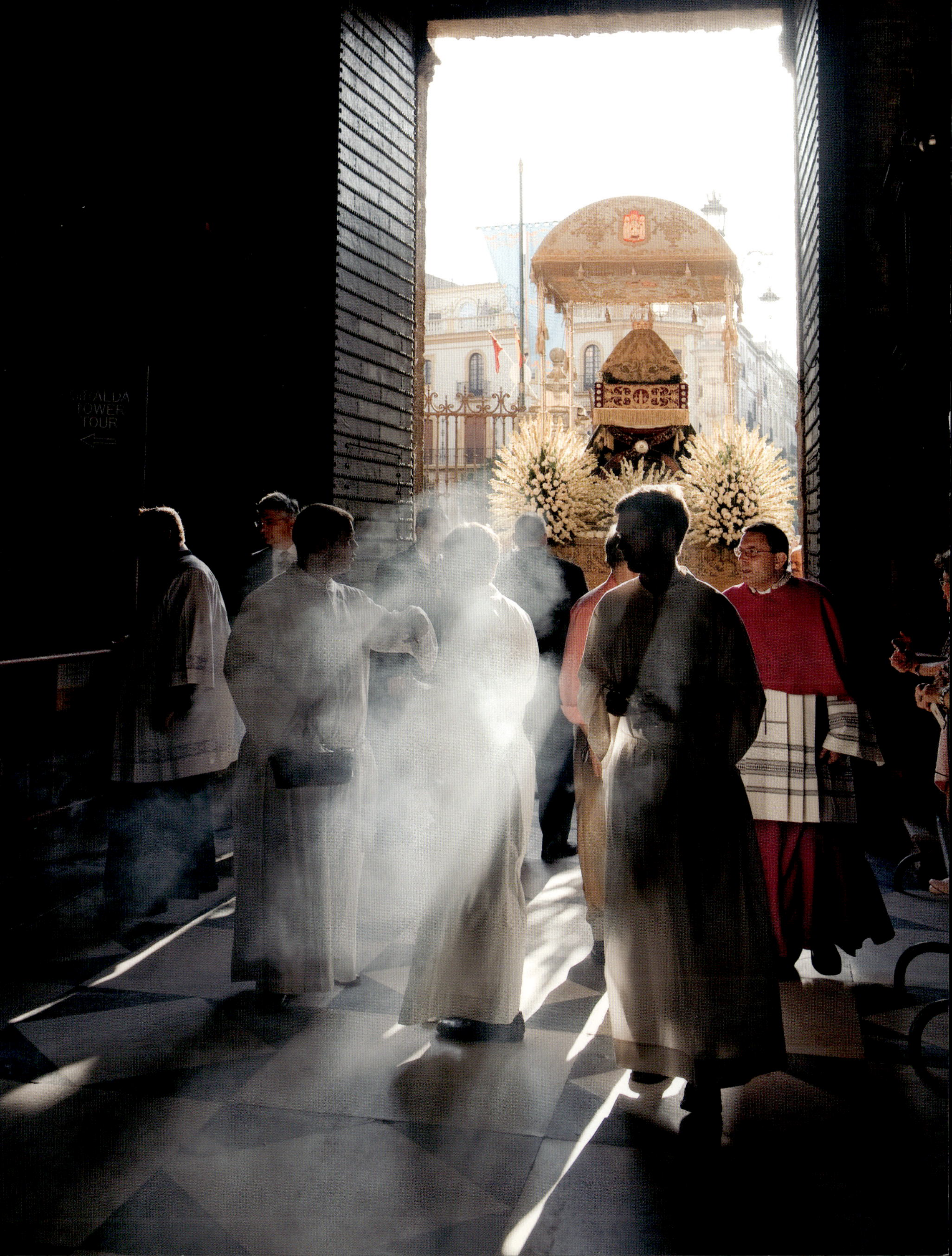
TOUR

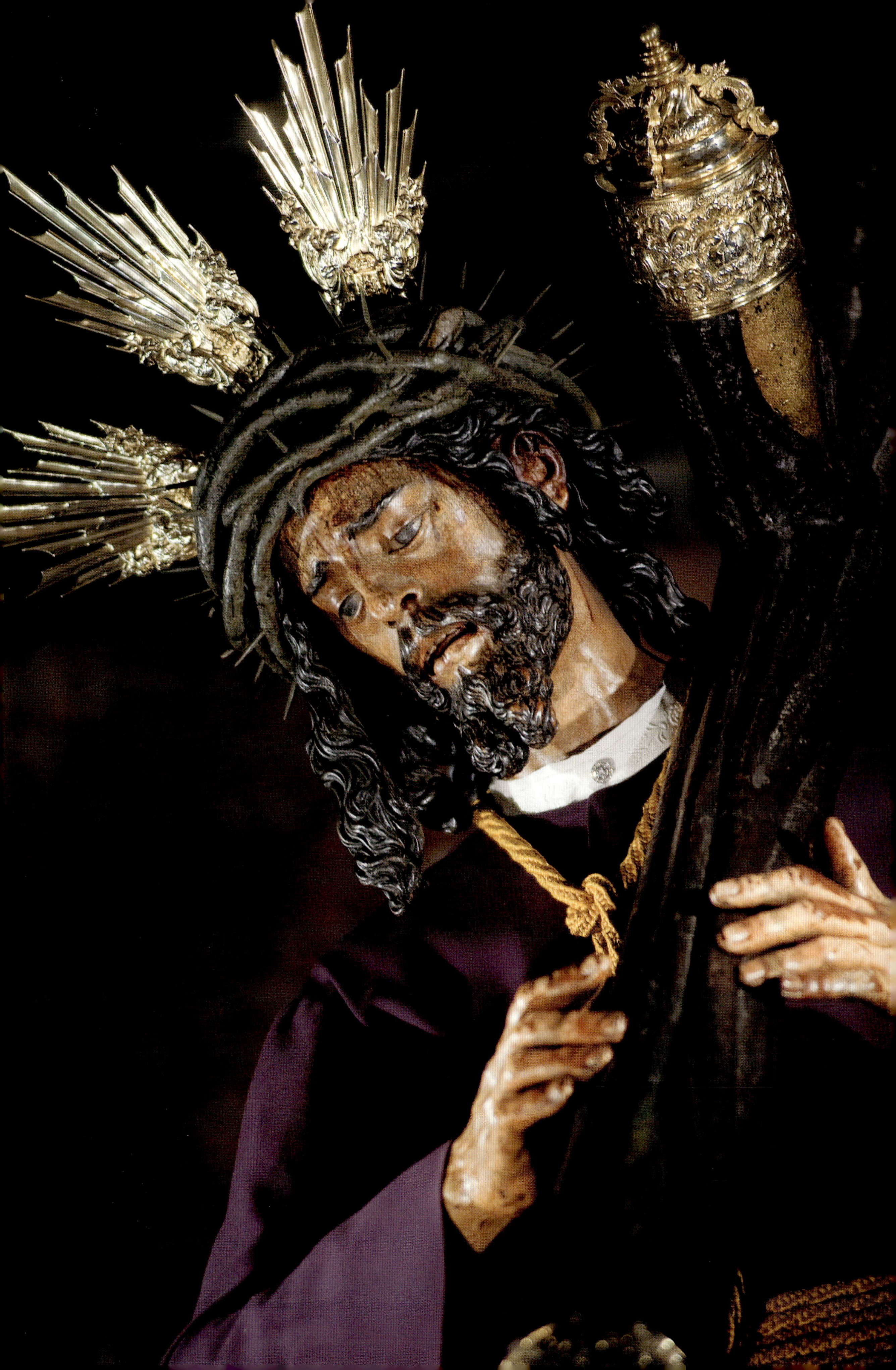

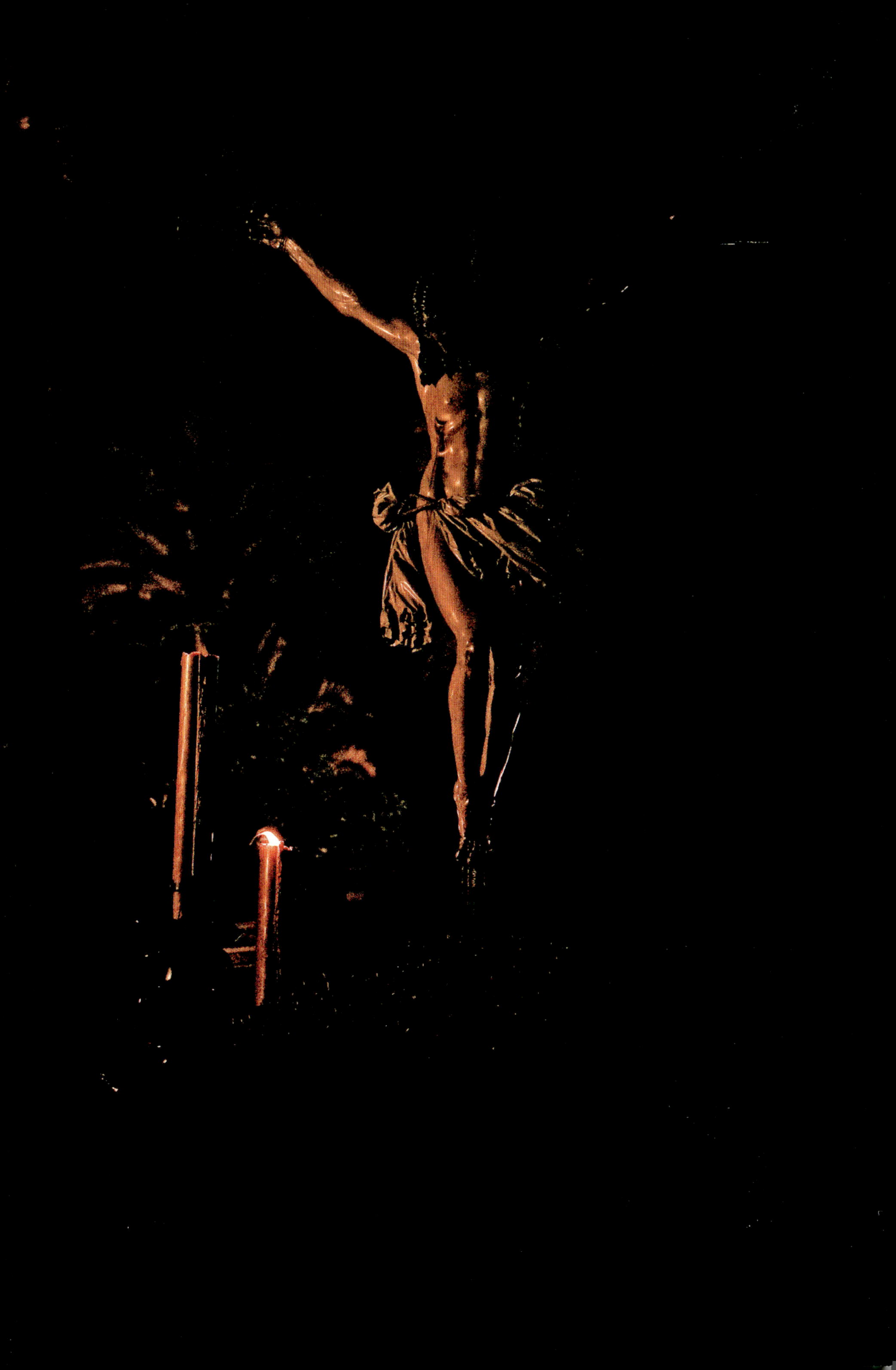

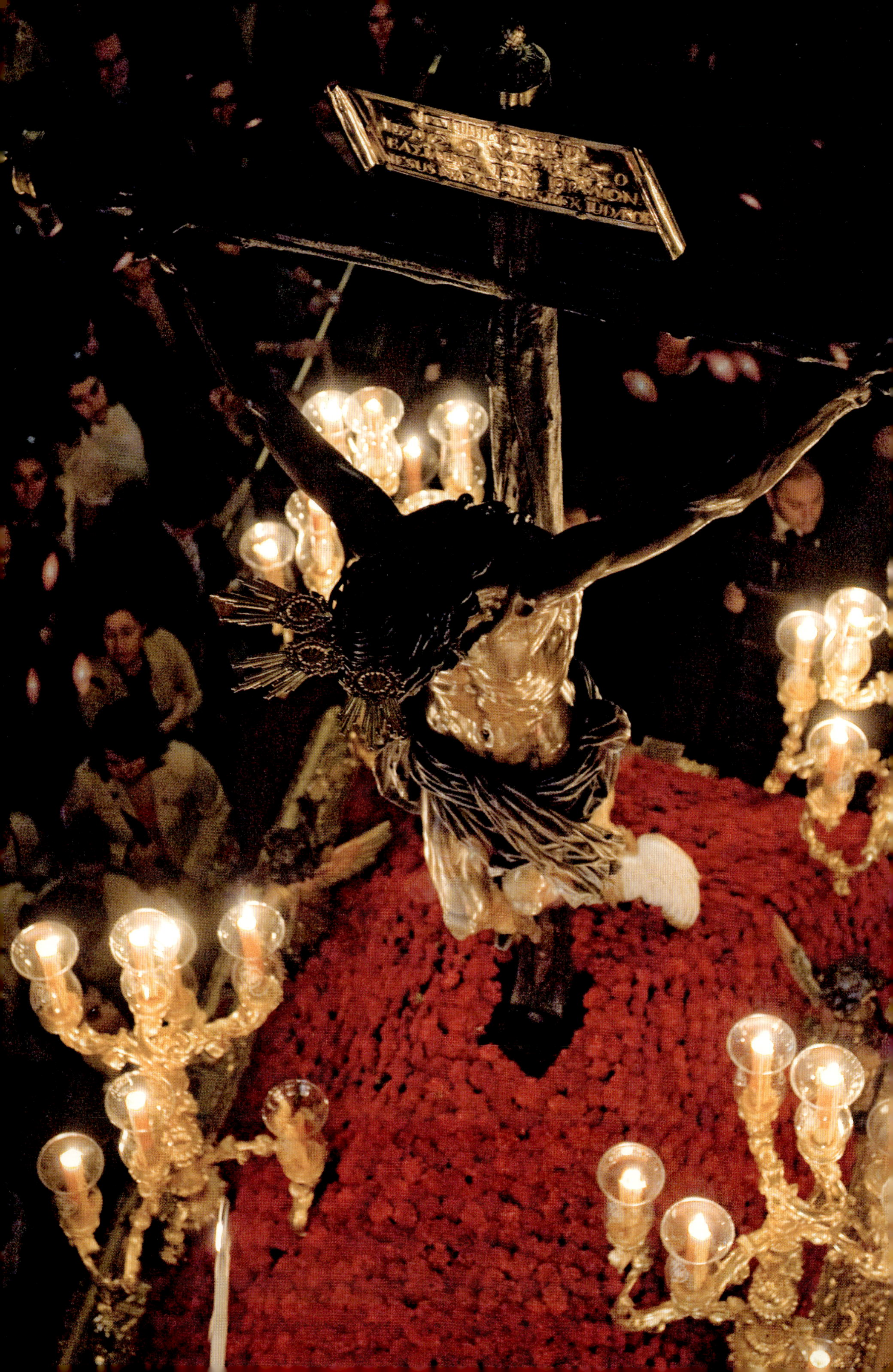

Clockwise from opposite: The *Cristo del Amor* from the clerestory of the Church of El Salvador, dressed for Holy Thursday; *Christ of Santa Cruz*; inside the Basilica of Jesus of the Great Power; the *Virgin of Macarena* dressed in black after the death of the matador Joselito; mosaic of the *Cristo del Amor* in the Cuesta del Rosario; penitents of the Confraternity of San Bernardo entering the cathedral traditionally dressed in Holy Week garb; members of the Confraternity of Santo Entierro, seen from the top of the cathedral; a child dressed as an altar boy watching the Virgin's *salida* from a balcony.

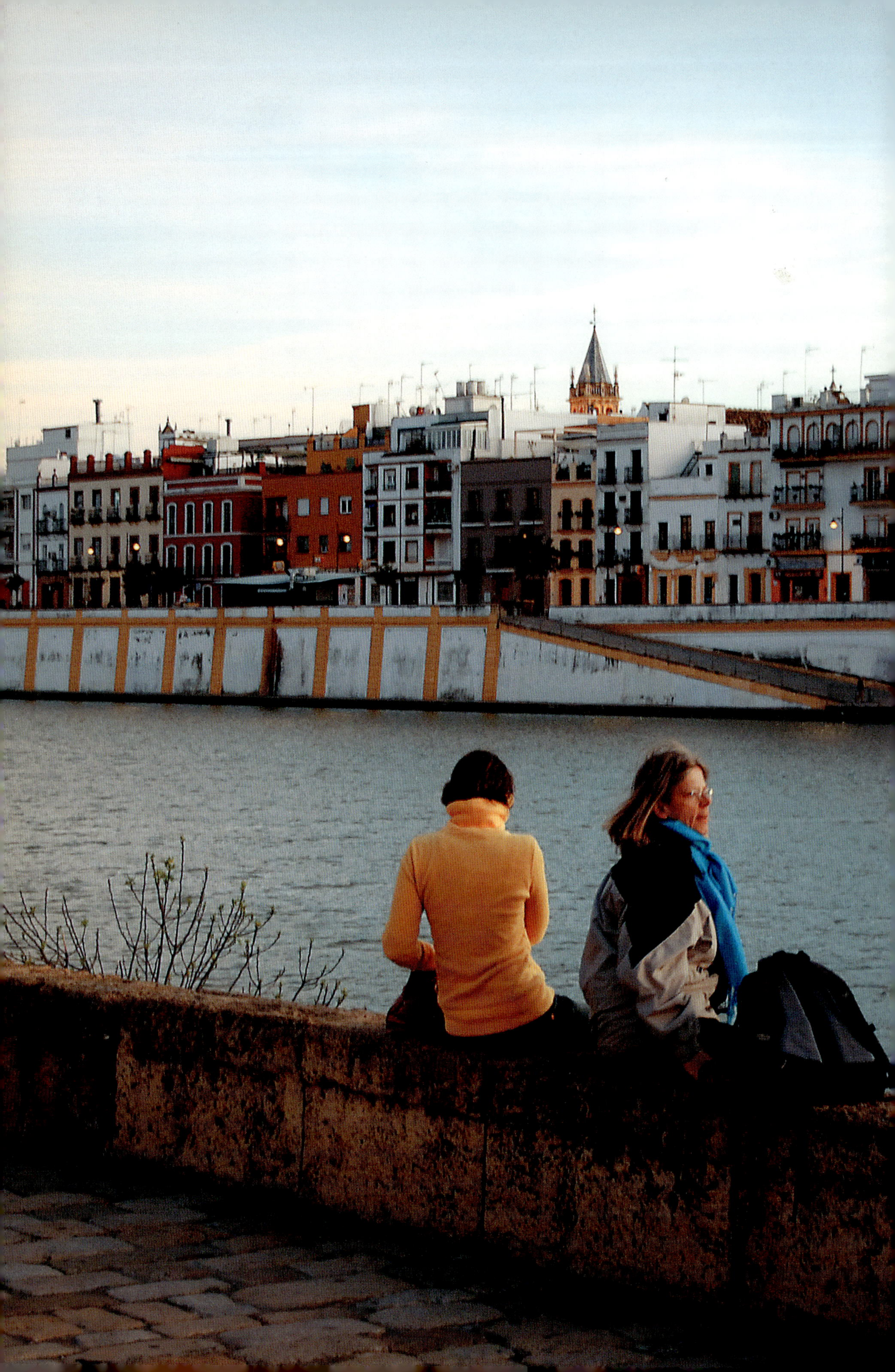

The Guadalquivir

From Seville to Sanlúcar,
From Sanlúcar to the sea,
In a boat made of silver
With oars made from coral,
Wherever you go, sailor,
You'll take me with you.
—Antonio Machado, early-twentieth-century poet

Seville exists because of the Guadalquivir River—al-Wadi al-Kabir, the Great River. Born on the Guadalquivir's banks, Seville continues to grow today.

The river is Seville's Main Street, the avenue that leads to the sea, and Spain's only navigable river. Serving as the port and the doorway to the Spanish West Indies for centuries, the river was the commercial axis between Europe and the Americas.

The Guadalquivir's importance traces back to ancient times, when its waters harbored Phoenician sailboats, Roman galleys, Arab xebecs, caravels of Christian troops during the Reconquest of Spain, and the longships of fearsome Vikings, who fell in love with its shores and created settlements that endure even today.

These are the same banks on which the Almohads, a Moroccan Berber-Muslim dynasty, built the Torre de Oro in the thirteenth century. The Torre de Oro, or Gold Tower, named for the golden sheen its bricks cast on the water, was erected to protect the city from attacks via the river. An immense chain was fastened to the tower, and slung across the Guadalquivir to secure a pontoon bridge and connect to its sister tower to provide an additional barricade—though it didn't stop Admiral Bonifaz from breaking it with his flagship during the siege of Seville in around 1247.

Watching the sunset from the banks of the Guadalquivir. *Following pages:* A detail of an etching, *The Golden Tower,* by Reverend Samuel Manning, circa 1870; the Alamillo Bridge, designed by the renowned architect Santiago Calatrava, at twilight.

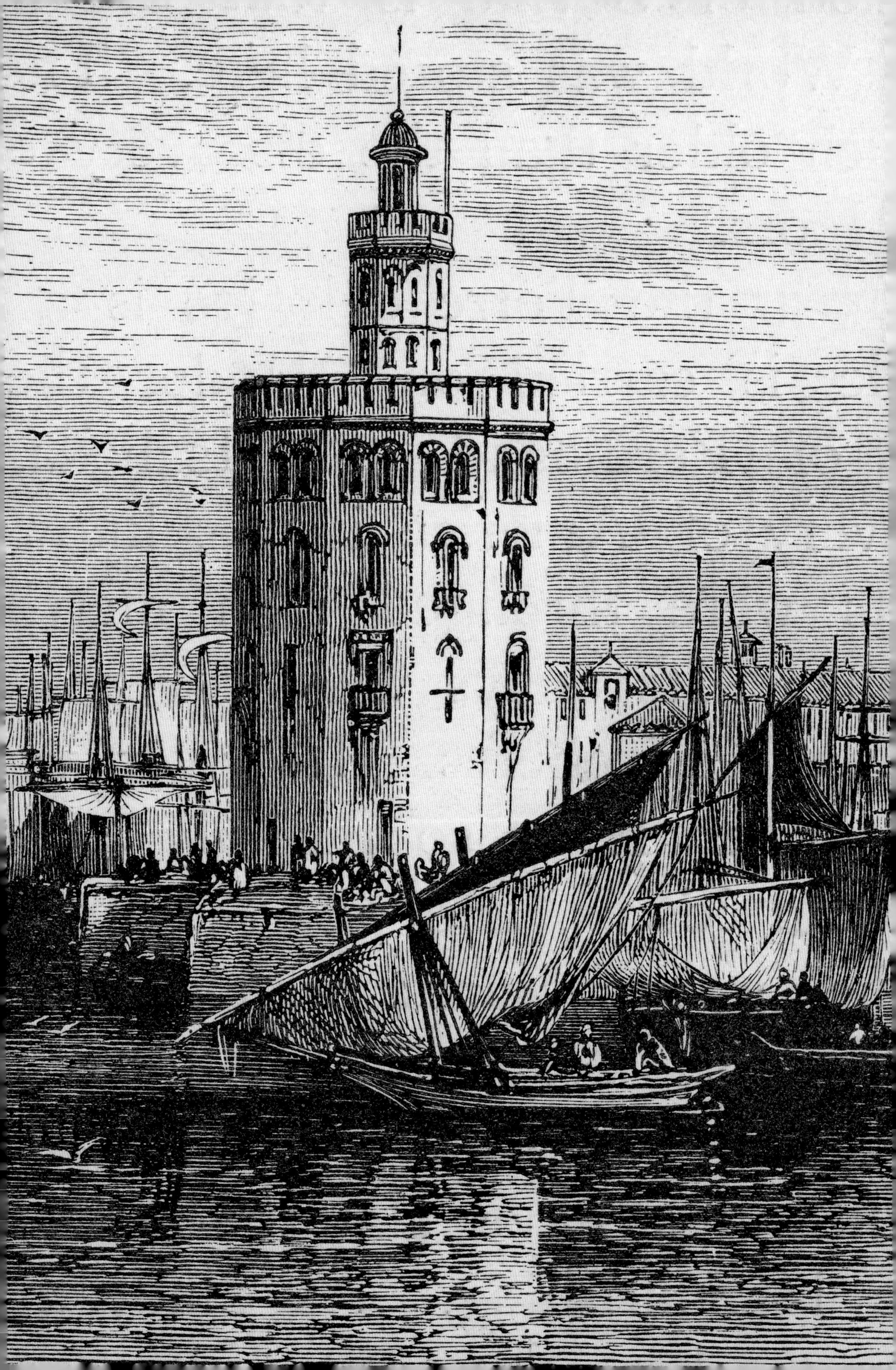

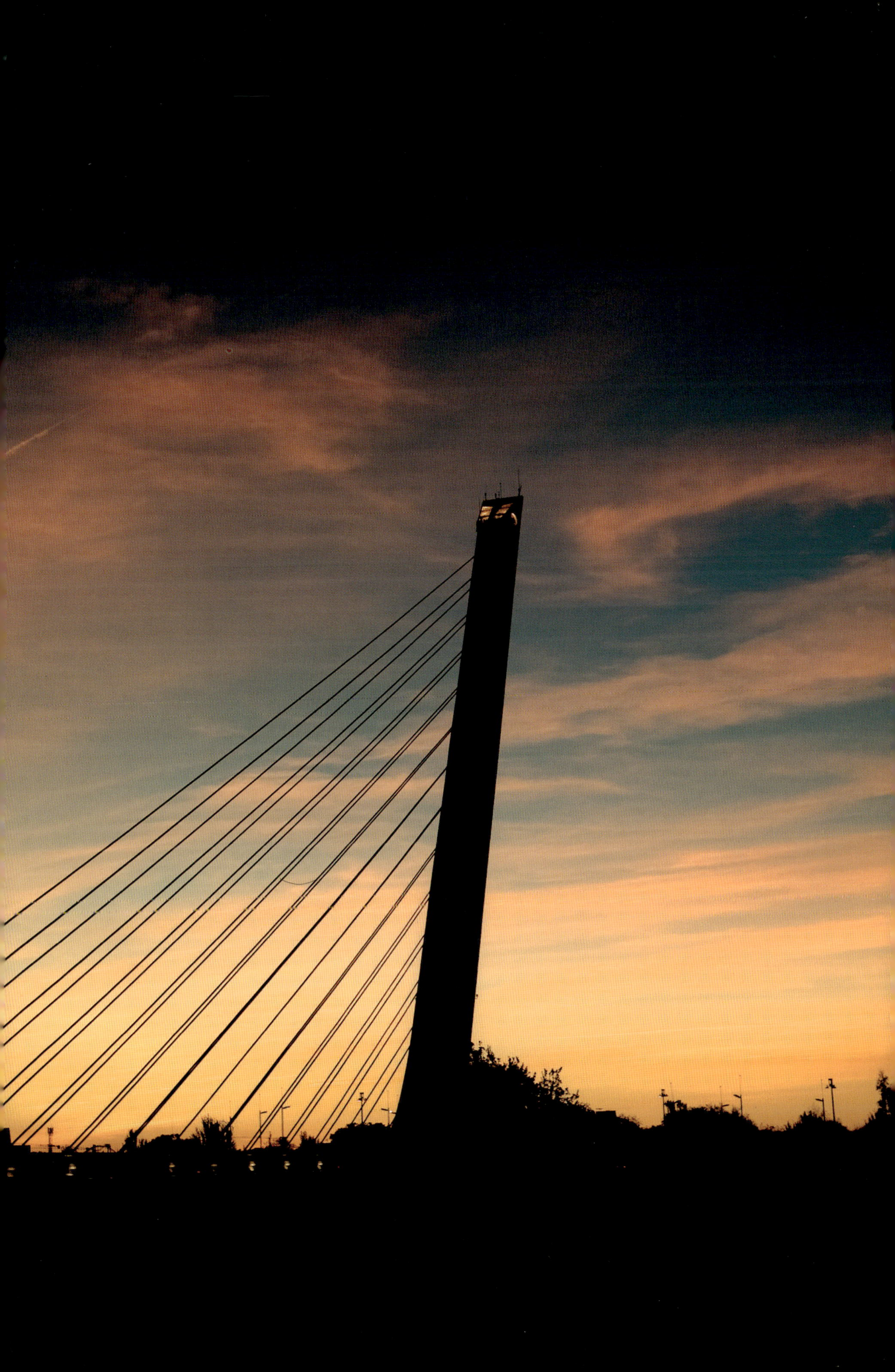

A nineteenth-century photograph of the Torre de Oro, the river, and Betis Street in Triana. *Right:* Betis Street today.

It was this very port that also saw the departure and arrival of Juan Sebastián Elcano and his weary seamen after completing their three-year journey around the world in 1522, thereby empirically proving that the Earth was indeed round.

Also floating on this river were the ships constructed in the Royal Shipyards, a cathedral of infinite arches on the banks of the Guadalquivir, commissioned by King Alfonso X in around 1252. And on this same waterway, from 1402 to 1506, the enormous stones that were used to construct the Seville Cathedral were brought from Sanlúcar on huge barges pulled by men along the shore.

The Guadalquivir is also the link between Seville and its surrounding neighborhoods and districts on the opposite shore: the outskirts of Triana, Aljarafe, and Huelva. For more than seven centuries, the only way to access these areas was via a bridge of ships constructed, in 1171, by the Almohad caliph Abu Ya'qub Yusuf. This bridge was merely a structure of planks that rested upon a row of thirteen ships, arranged perpendicular to one another, tied together, and anchored to the river bottom. Much upkeep was required: The boards and the ships were constantly being replaced due to dampness and decay.

Following pages: The Argentina Pavilion, one of ten pavilions built for the Ibero-American Exposition of 1929, seen from the river.

Then, circa 1852, the Bridge of Isabel II, or as it's commonly known, the Triana Bridge, was finally born, located beside the Saint George Castle. French engineers Gustavo Steinacher and Fernando Bernadet designed the bridge, which would become a historic monument and, most important, the only link between Seville and Triana.

Later, a number of bridges, ten of which still exist today, spanned the Guadalquivir River. The most recent addition, the Alamillo Bridge, was completed in 1992 and provides access to La Cartuja island; it was designed by the internationally celebrated Spanish architect and engineer Santiago Calatrava.

Today, the river's wharf is a destination for tourists arriving on immense, fifteen-story cruise ships, once again converting the Guadalquivir into a port of entry for thousands of travelers. And here on the banks of the iconic Guadalquivir, life is good—from the numerous tapas bars and flamenco and dance halls to the more serene places to take in the scenery, such as Alamillo Park. For the most beautiful views of the Triana Bridge and Seville, Betis Street, famous for its riverfront nightlife, is the place to go, second to the iconic Colón Promenade, all along the beautiful Guadalquivir River.

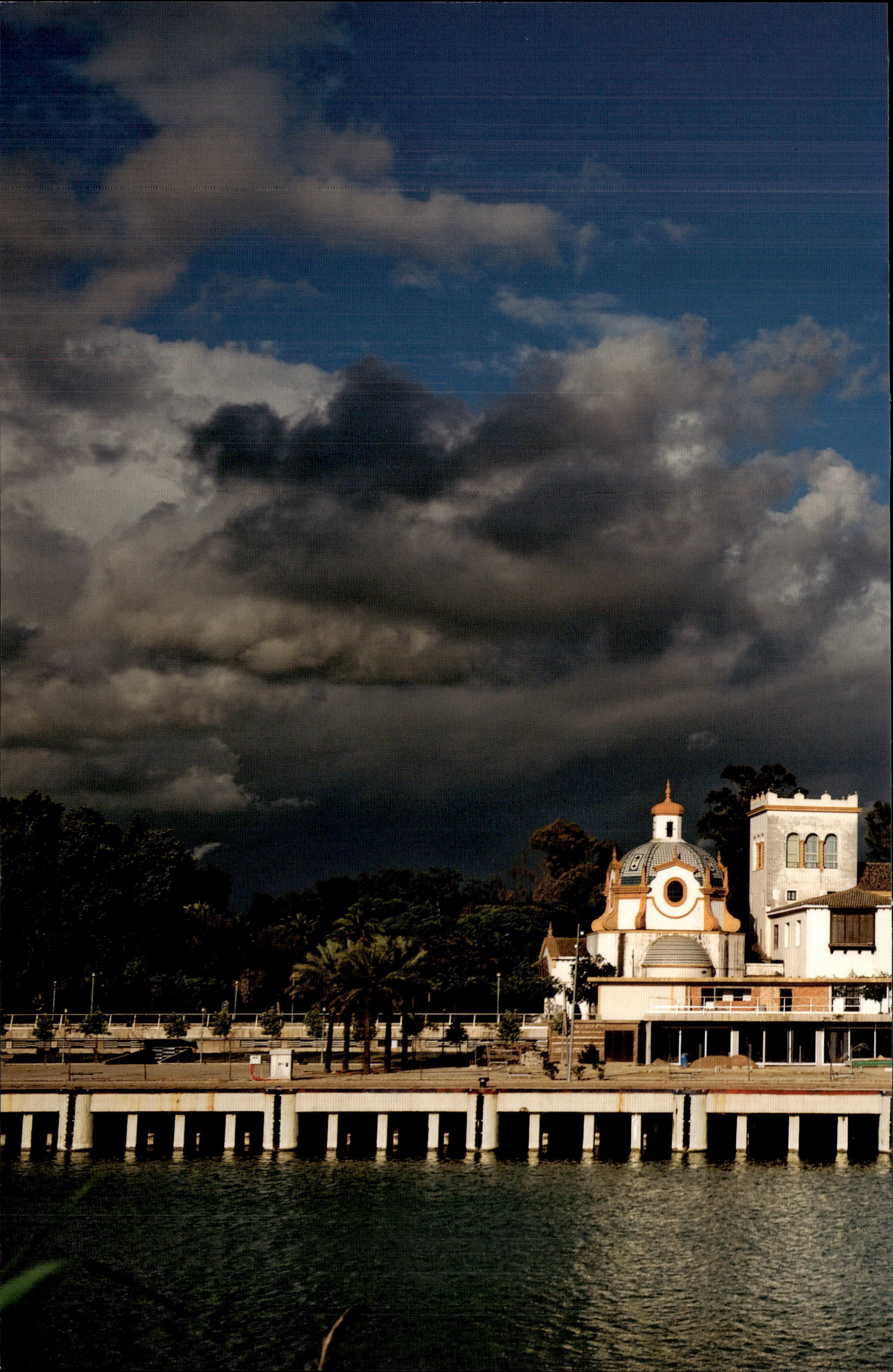

FALTAN
1 9 1
DIAS Para la MADRUGA

HERMANDAD DE LA MACARENA

HERMANDAD MACARENA

Cruzcampo
Bodega Hnos.

Waterfront dining at Abades restaurant in Triana.
Below: A tapas bar at Casa Román, in the Santa Cruz neighborhood.

Above, left: A bowl of gambas al ajillo, a staple at Seville's tapas bars. Left: Cruzcampo, a popular Spanish brew, with a dish of Spanish olives.

A typical tapas bar in Triana. Left: An antique cash register at a bar on Feria Street.

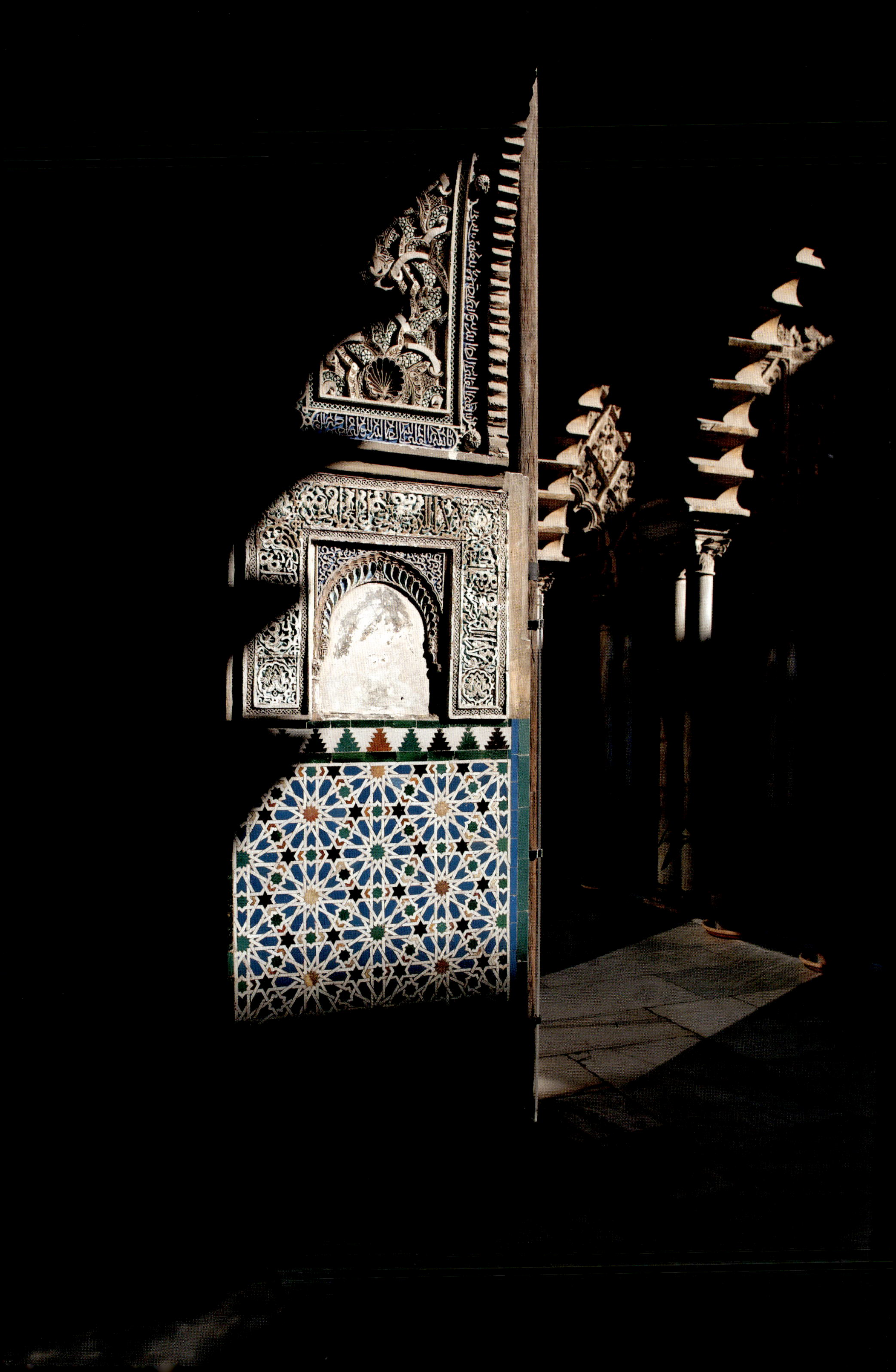

The Alcázar

I cried at the passing of the partridges,
when they flew above me, free,
unhindered by neither cages nor chains.
—Al-Mutamid, Caliph of Ixbilia. Poems from the Alcázar, 15th Century

The Alcázar, one of the oldest inhabited royal palaces in the world, is Seville's most precious treasure. Surrounded by the wall of Seville, it is comprised of a series of fortresses and lovely gardens.

Within the Alcázar, marble sculptures and majolica pottery abound, and the sweet scent of jasmine drifts through the many arches and the fountains, with their crystal green waters. Orange trees intermingle with lemon trees, boxwood with myrtle hedges, blackbirds with doves, cypresses with laurels. Visitors can't help but be moved by the serenity and peace contained within these palace walls.

The Alcázar was built eleven centuries ago from the ruins of an ancient Roman fortification constructed on the remains of the Tartessian Kingdom.

At the start of the eighth century, when Seville was called Ixbilia, Abd-al-Rahman III ordered the construction of a new government fortress on the present Alcázar site. Later known as the Palace of al-Mubarak, or "the Blessed Palace," this fortress would become not only the center of official and administrative life but also the cultural, artistic, and especially the literary heart of the city, where, in the eleventh century, the caliph al-Mutamid himself dazzled listeners with his poetry.

Over the next century, the Almoravids, who ruled much of North Africa and the Iberian Peninsula between 1040 and 1147, continued to extend the foundation of the Alcázar all the way to the Guadalquivir River, in an effort to be closer to the source of economic power, which at the time was tied to transportation and fluvial trade.

In the twelfth century, the Almohads completed the construction of the Palace of al-Mubarak, some of which still remains today, including the Patio del Yeso (Plaster Courtyard), and the garden of the neighboring Casa de la Contratación (House of Trade), where one can gaze over the treetops to the horizon.

The Patio de las Doncellas. *Following pages:* The Alcázar's Mercury Fountain at night; inside the Hall of Ambassadors.

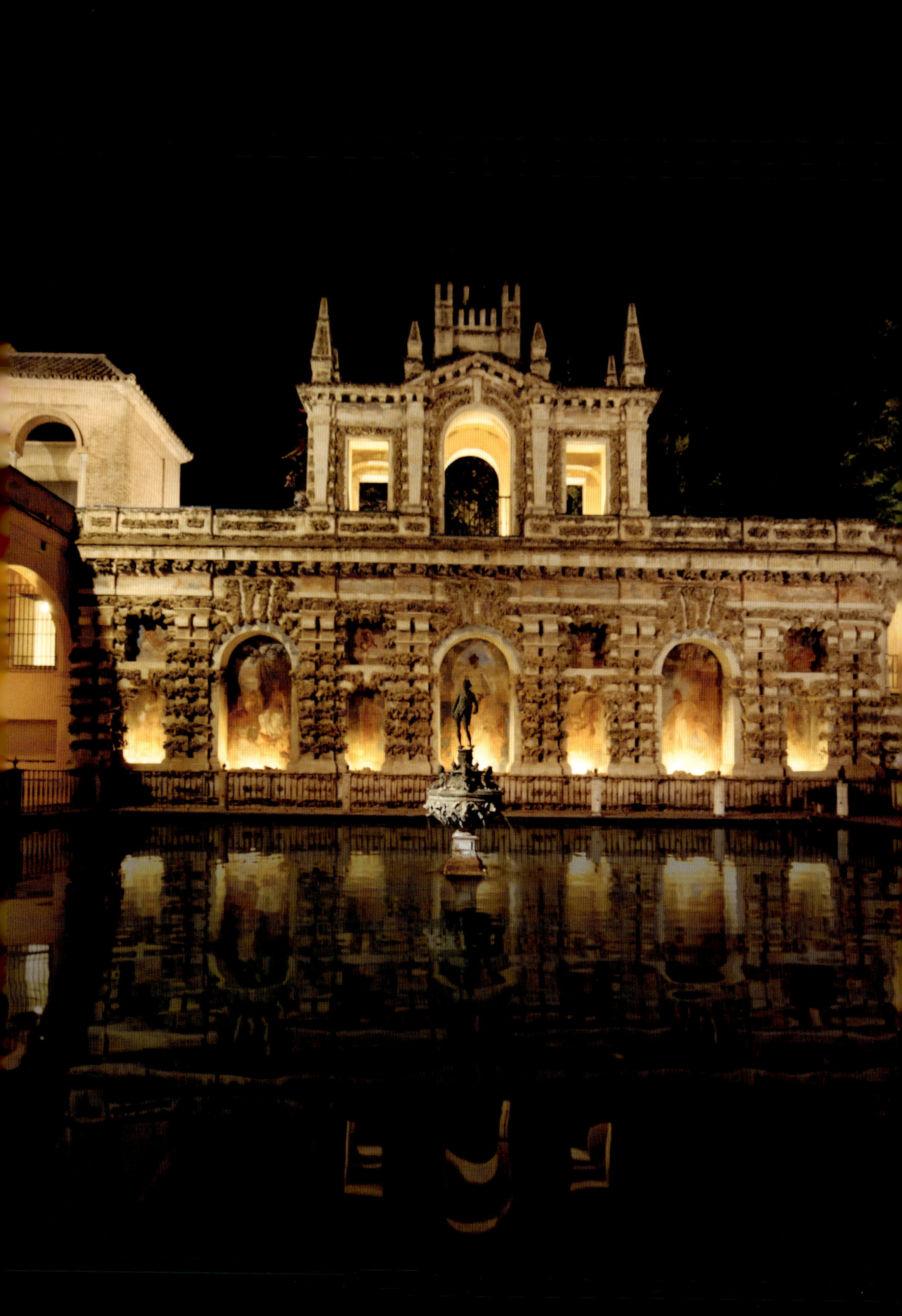

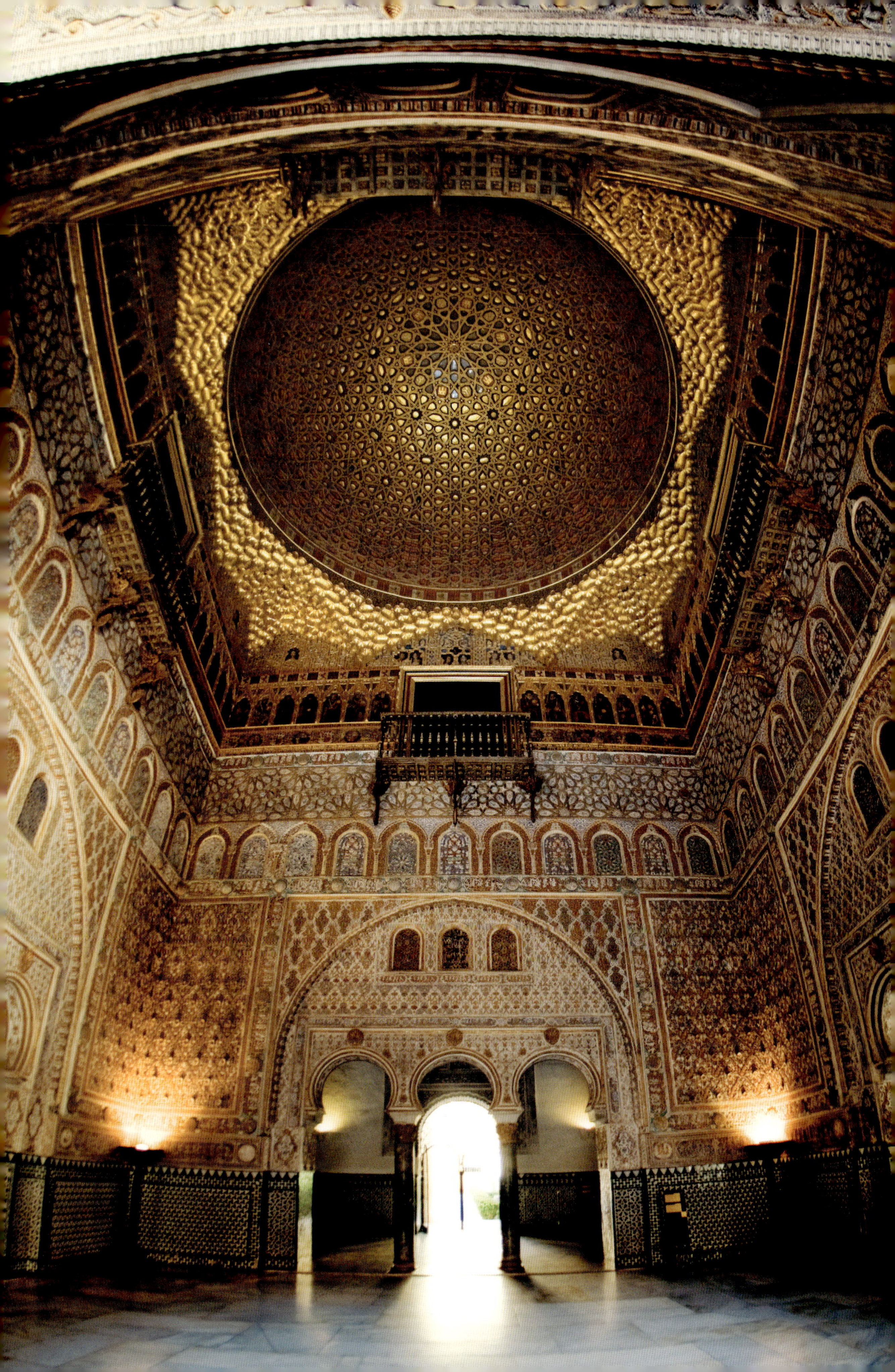

Windows line the façade of the Palace of Pedro I. *Right:* Painting of a scene at the Alcázar, by Manuel Wssel de Guimbarda, 1872.

In 1248, the Christian conquest of Ixbilia converted the Royal Alcázar into what it is today: the headquarters and residence of the royal family, and the seat of municipal power in Seville.

Since that time, around nine mansions have been built in the Alcázar, resulting in the sort of melding of cultures and styles that makes Seville's urban landscape so unique—from the Alfonsine Gothic Palace, where King Alfonso X (1221–1284) encouraged an intellectual golden age in the city, to the Mudéjar Palace, built by King Pedro I in the fourteenth century. Pedro I was a Castilian king, but he was enamored with Arabian aesthetics; Moorish architectural touches were integrated into the design of the palace, such as a labyrinth of courtyards and rooms filled with forests of columns built by artisans from the Alhambra of Granada. Pedro's additions also included the Patio de las Doncellas (Courtyard of the Maidens), a tranquil open space with a reflecting pool and sunken gardens surrounded by two levels of dark, cool arcades and archways featuring ornate Moorish motifs carved in wood and stucco; the lower level contains Arabic references to Pedro as "sultan." The gardens of the Alcázar are as impressive as the buildings, especially the beautiful, baroque-style Mercury Pond and fountain, nestled in the center of the lush grounds.

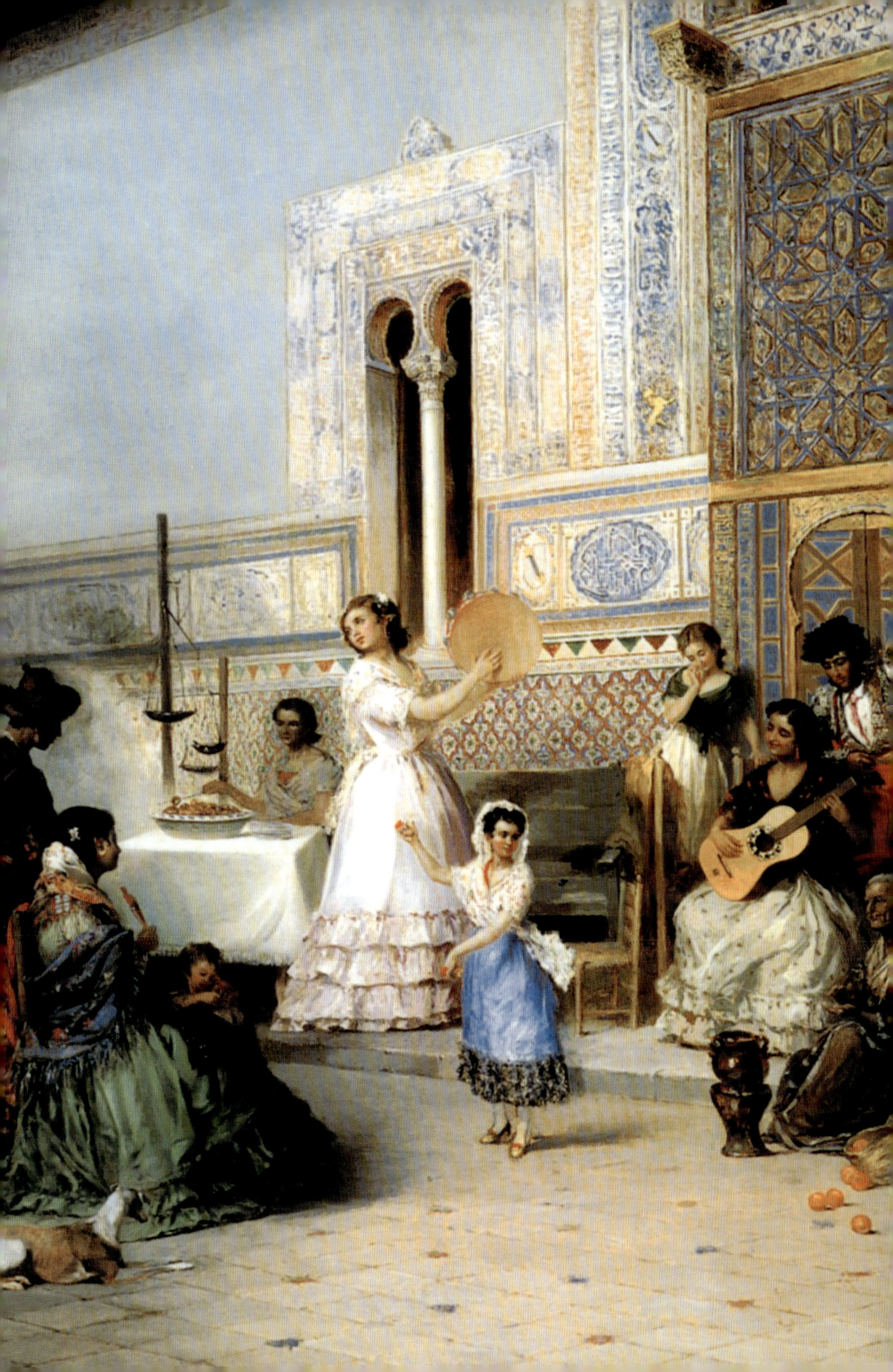

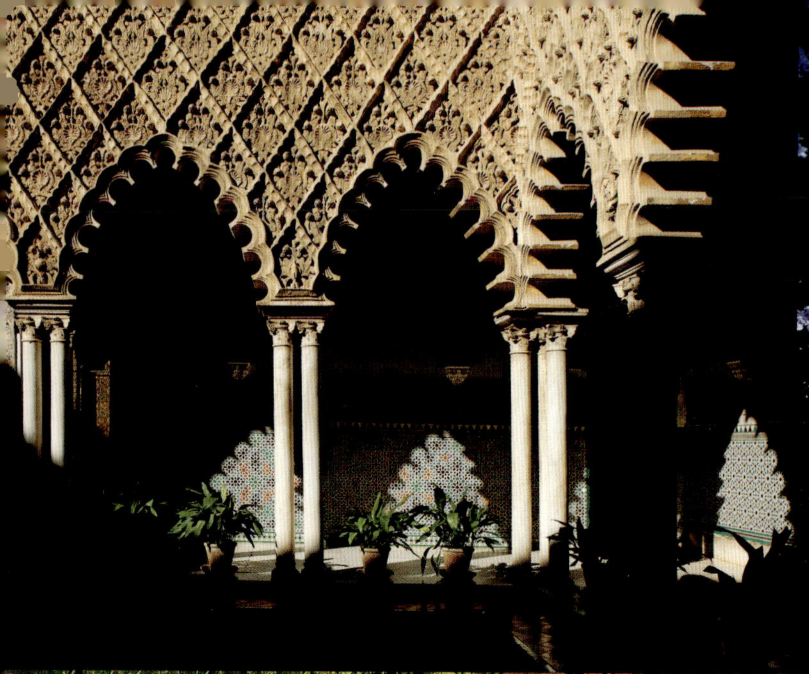

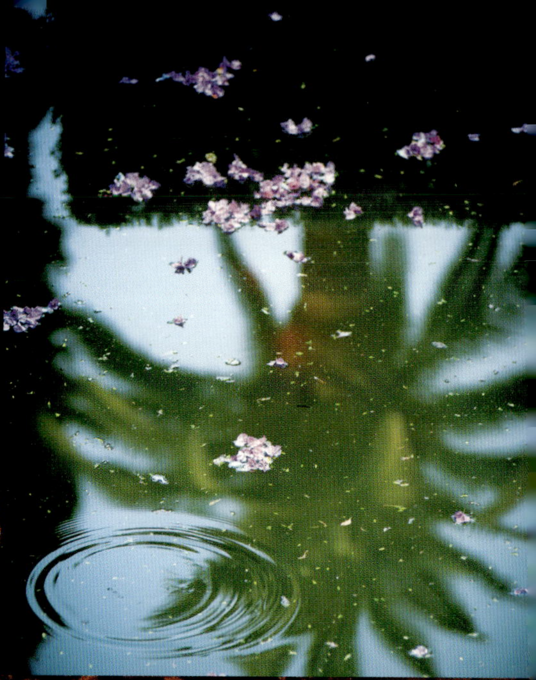

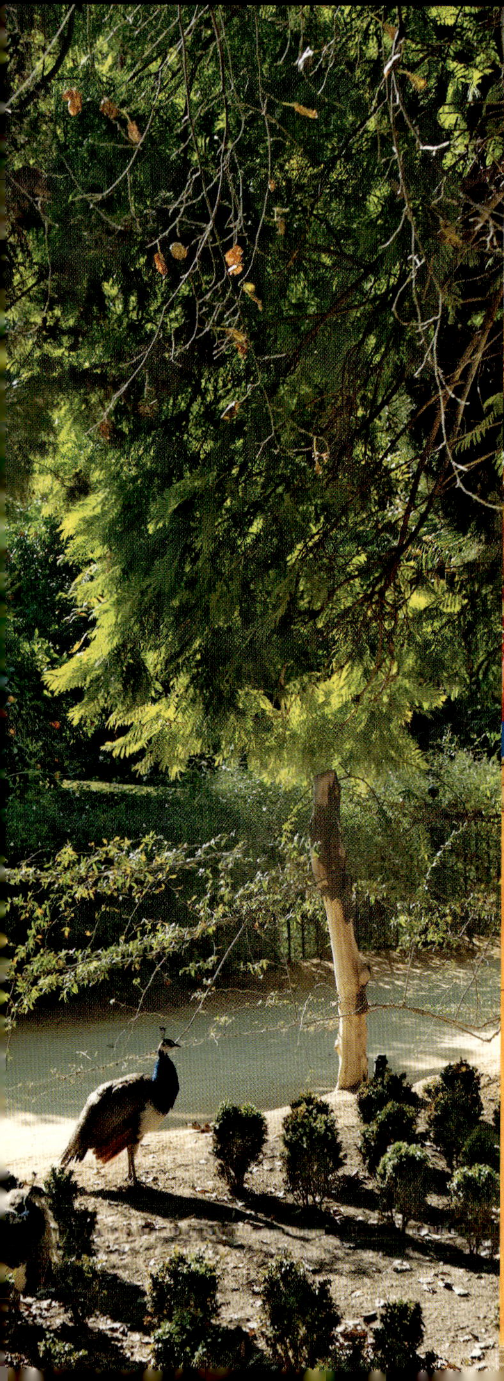

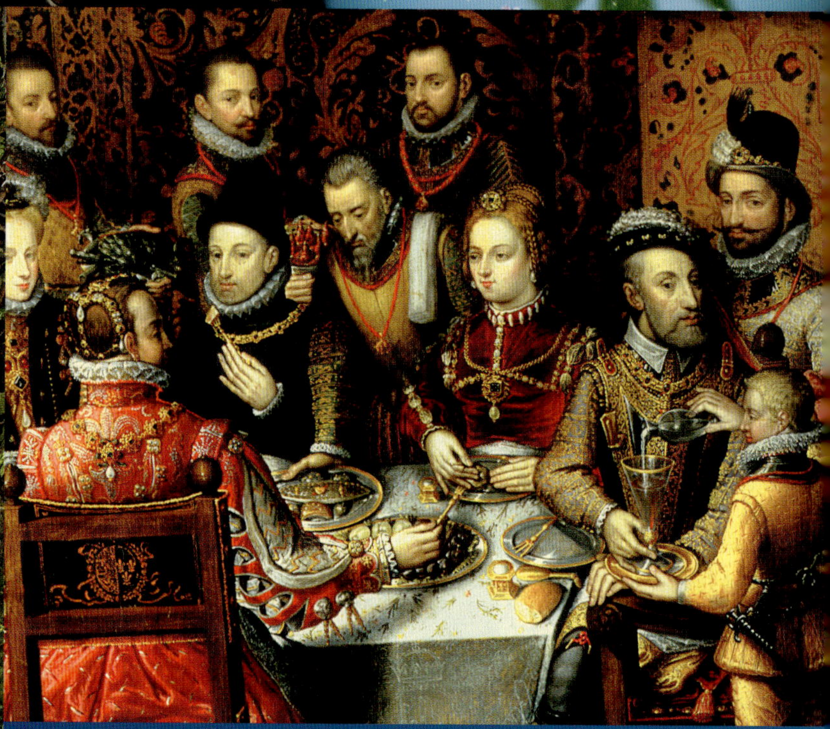

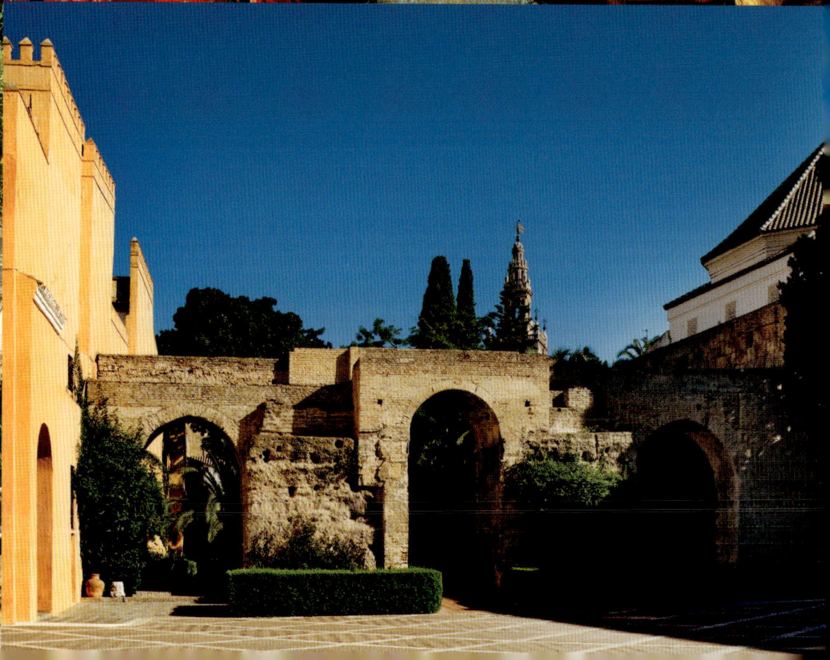

Clockwise from opposite, top left: Ornately carved loggias form a perimeter around the Patio de las Doncellas; reflection in a fountain outside the Alcázar; Patio de las Doncellas; oil painting of a Sevillian garden; an enchanting creature at home at the Alcázar; tile design in the Cenador de la Alcoba; Patio de la Montería; peacocks roam free in the gardens of the Alcázar; *The Banquet of the Monarchs,* by Alonso Sanchez Coello, circa 1579.

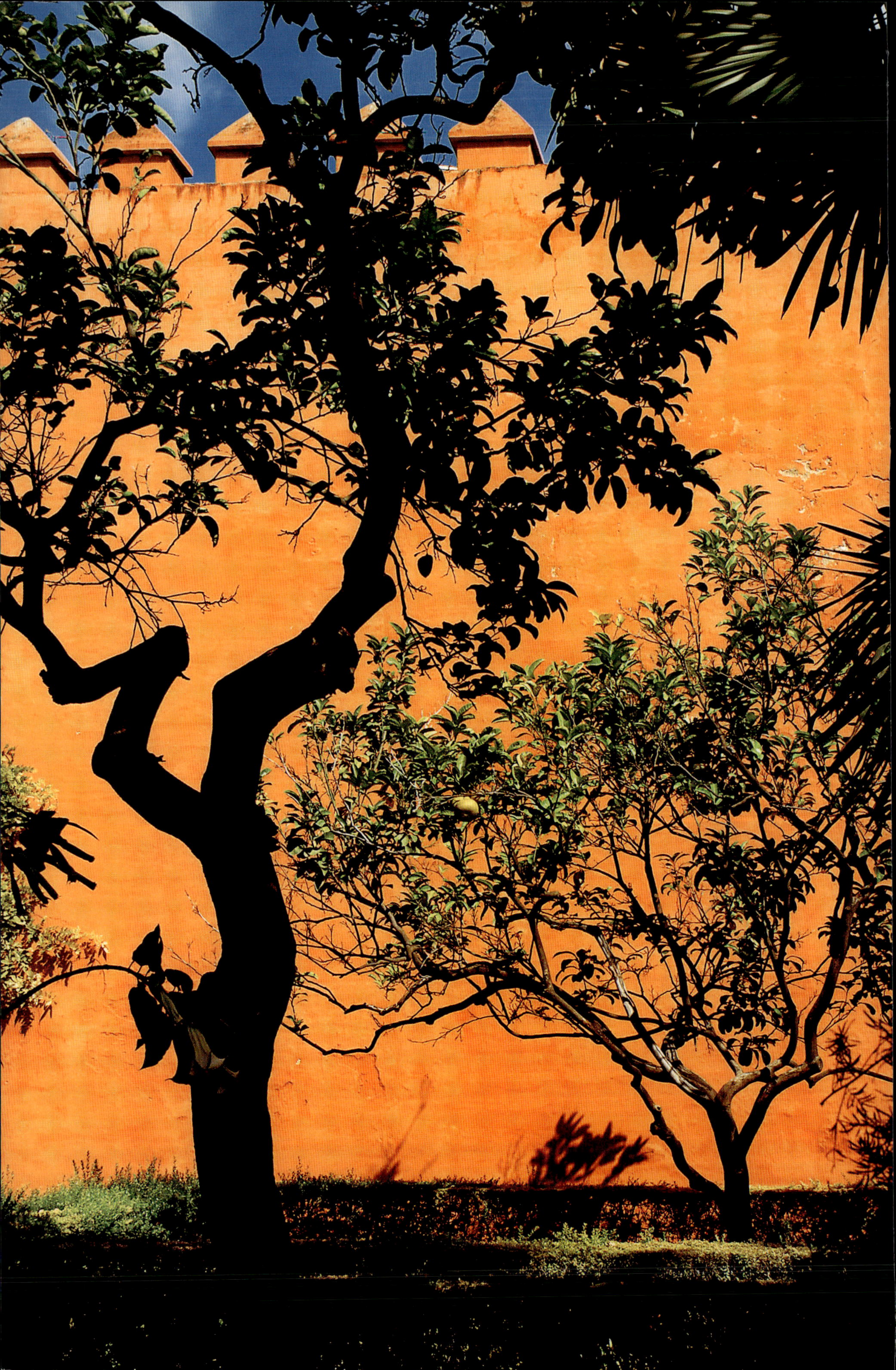

Over the course of history, the Alcázar has hosted various important ceremonies and events. In 1477, Spain's Catholic monarchs Ferdinand V and Isabella I arrived in Seville and lived in the fortress; one year later, in June of 1478, their second child, Prince Juan, was born in the palace.

In 1526, Carlos V wed his cousin Isabella of Portugal in the Alcázar. The bride's court arrived at the palace late in the evening prior to the wedding to rest before starting the next day's preparations. Since they were both royalty, the wedding would be a splendorous affair, with thousands of guests from all over Europe expected to attend. As the story goes: Upon meeting his bride, who was very beautiful, Carlos V wanted to consummate the marriage as quickly as possible. He sent for the bishop, who was asleep. When Carlos V learned that the bishop's servants refused to wake him at that hour, he sent for the priest who was reciting Mass at the cathedral (at the time, Masses were held at the cathedral all day and night). Carlos V forced the priest to marry them that very moment in the Patio de la Montería (Courtyard of the Hunt). Immediately thereafter, the king took his new wife in his arms and they locked themselves in the Mudéjar Palace. They weren't seen again until five days later, exhausted but happy. It is said from chronicles of the time that the queen didn't stop smiling for several months.

The Alcázar has hosted many kings: Ferdinand III (now known as Saint Ferdinand); Alfonso X ("the Wise"); Alfonso XI; Pedro I ("the Cruel"), with his love, María de Padilla; Isabella I ("the Catholic"); Carlos V and Isabella of Portugal; Felipe II and all of the Hapsburgs; Isabella II; Alfonso XII and his son Alfonso XIII; and today, Juan Carlos I, his wife, Sofía, and their family when they come to Seville.

Registered by UNESCO as a World Heritage Site in 1987, the Alcázar continues to be one of the most celebrated, and visited, landmarks in Spain, if not the world.

Grapefruit and mandarin trees can be found in the gardens.

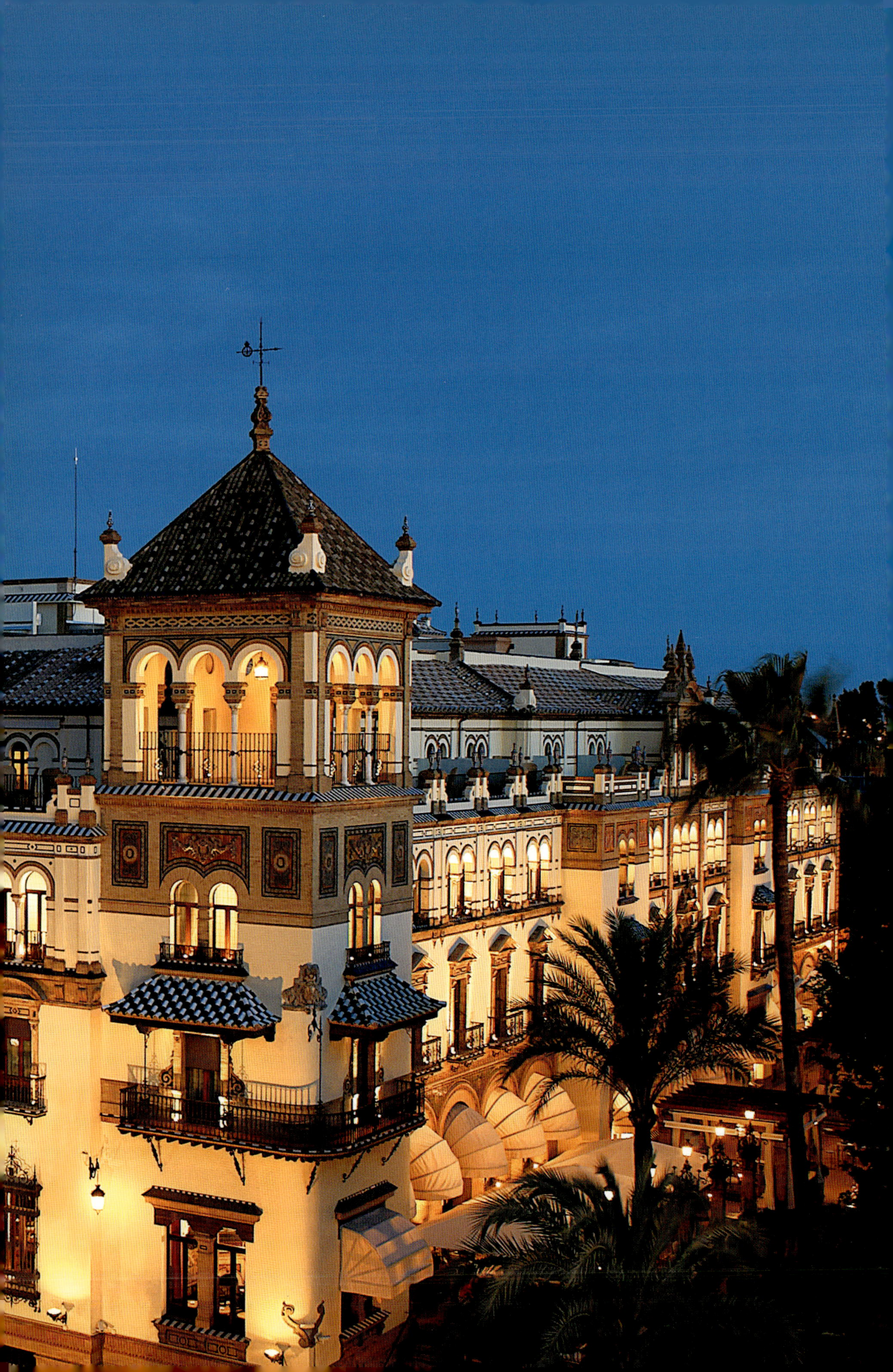

Alfonso XIII

"I love Seville greatly and all that is within my power I will do in obsequiousness of this beautiful city. There have been other kings who were great lovers of Seville and I shall try to do for this city everything I can."
—His Majesty Alfonso XIII, at the inauguration of the World's Fair of 1929.

Alfonso XIII was the king of Spain from the day he was born in 1886, until 1931; his father, King Alfonso XII, had died before his son's birth. Although Alfonso XIII was nicknamed "the African" because of his neo-imperialistic decision to conquer and incorporate the land inhabited by the Rif and Jibala tribes in northern Africa, he was widely beloved, especially in Seville.

During the years of preparation for the Ibero-American Exposition (World's Fair) of 1929, King Alfonso XIII frequently visited Seville to supervise the construction of new facilities for the international event. The monarch unconditionally supported the capital of the south, and his commitment and attention to the city greatly contributed to the success of the exhibition.

It was perhaps because of this mutual affection between the king and Seville that the beautiful and grand Hotel Alfonso XIII was named after him. Many luminaries and heads of state traveled to the city for the World's Fair, and in order to accommodate them accordingly, the king himself ordered the construction of this regal hotel. Ever since, for more than 85 years, it has retained its renowned status, welcoming celebrities and dignitaries from around the world.

Hotel Alfonso XIII was inaugurated in 1928 by the king, and since then Sevillians and elite world travelers alike have been known to visit the Hotel Alfonso XIII for some of the world's most luxurious accommodations.

This celebrated landmark is centrally located in the Puerta de Jerez plaza, between the Royal Tobacco Factory and San Telmo Palace, facing the walls of the Alcázar. It is also a short walk to the main sites in the city such as the Seville Cathedral and the Giralda Tower.

Designed by the architect José Espiau y Muñoz, the hotel exhibits a neo-Mudéjar architectural style—impressive, sweeping arches; ornamental towers; and magnificent works of cast iron and ceramic—giving it a royal and unique character. After an extensive $25 million restoration project in 2012, the property remains a fitting testament to its grand legend with

View of the Hotel Alfonso XIII. *Following pages:* One of the hotel's grand ballrooms.

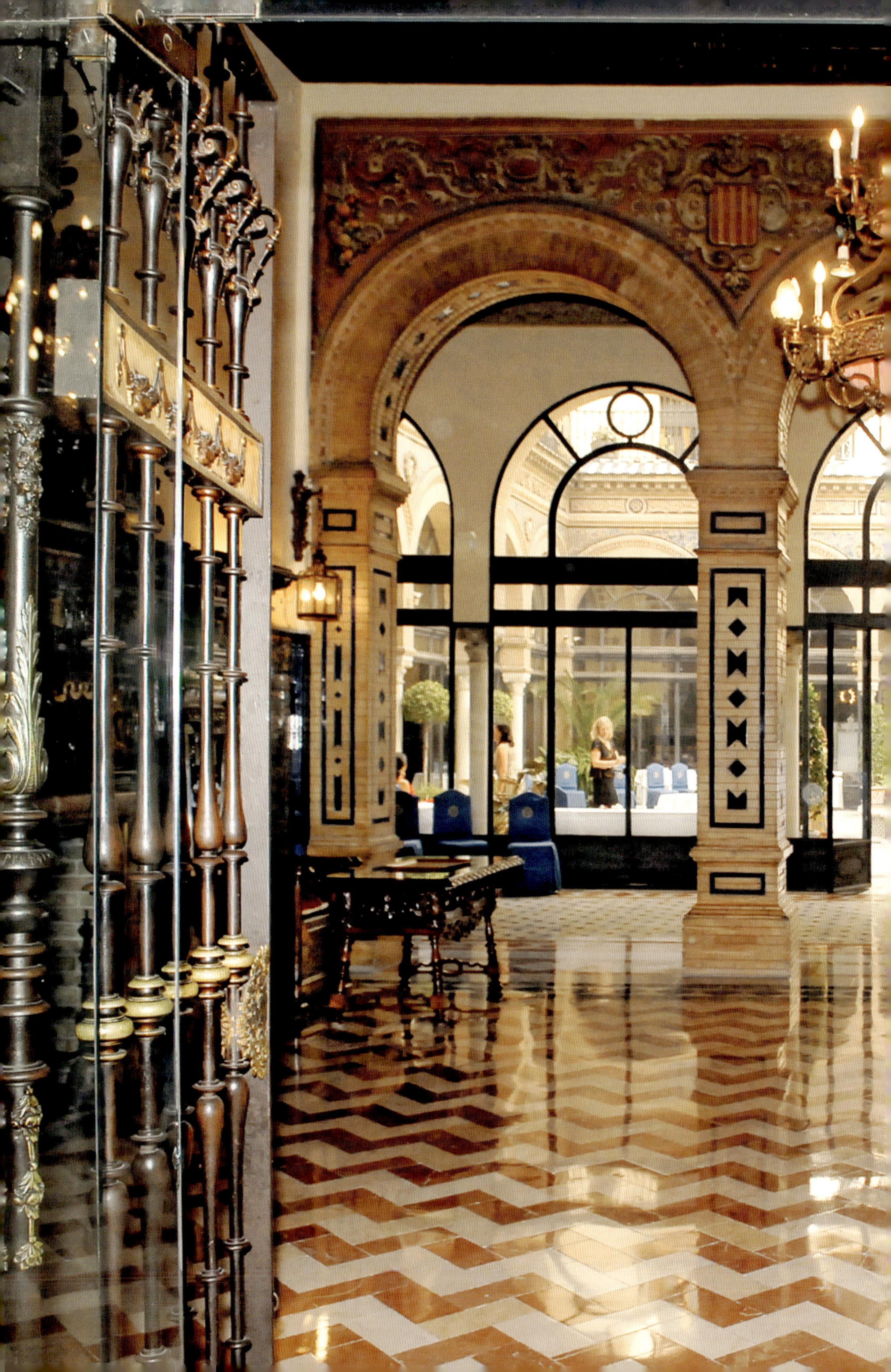

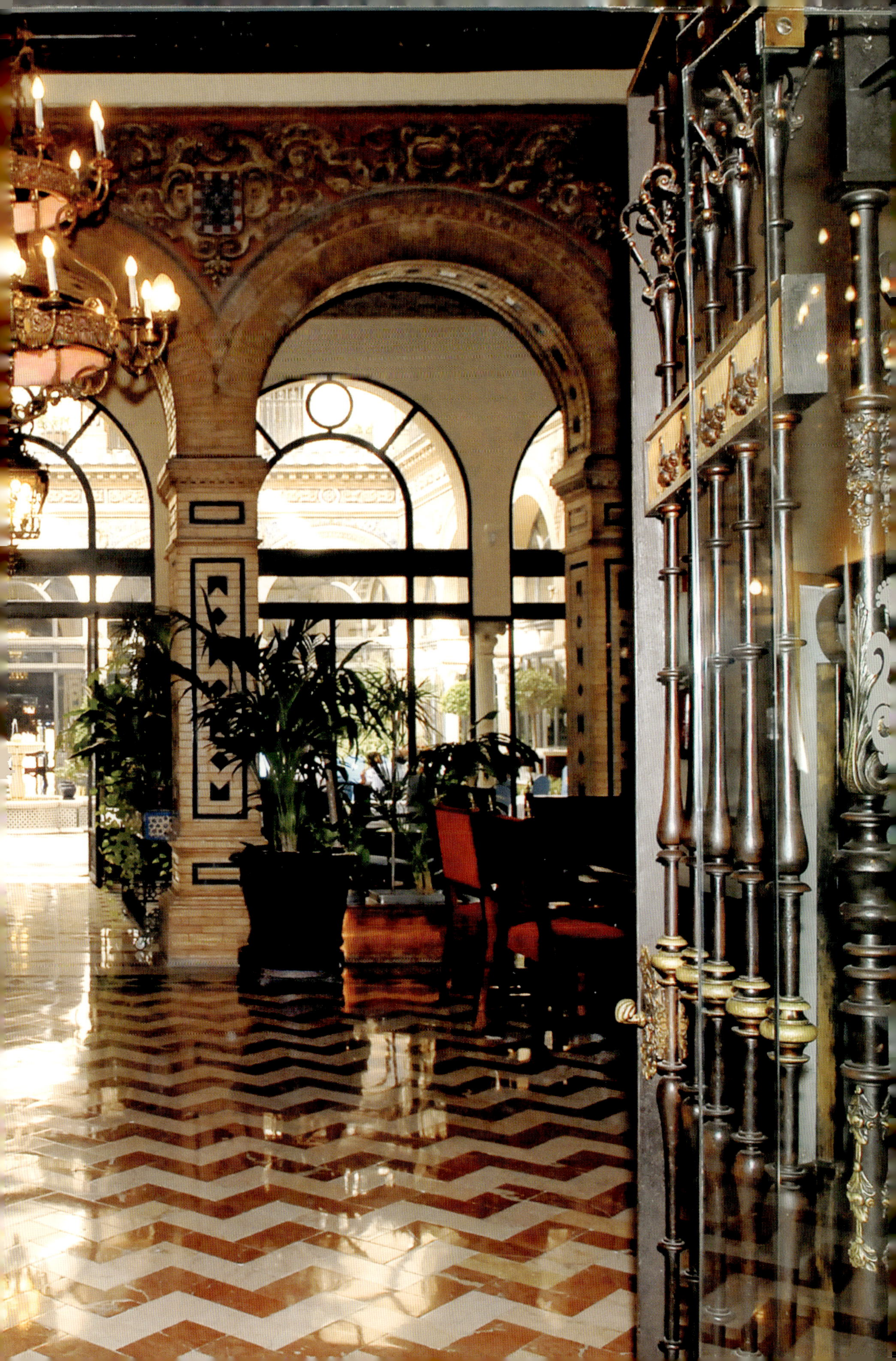

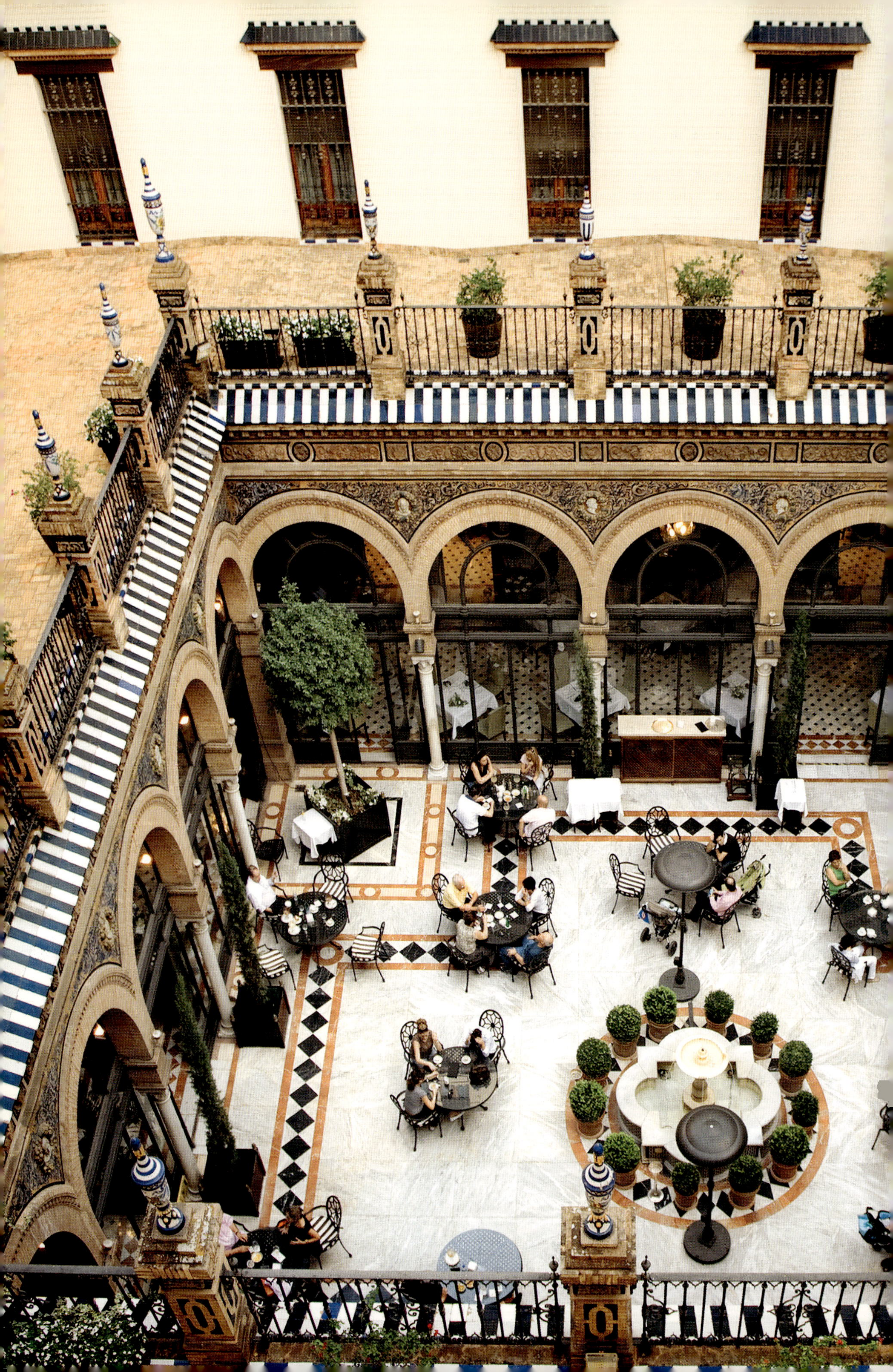

more than 150 rooms. It is a paragon of luxury and comfort that rivals any hotel in Paris, New York, or London.

Starting with Alfonso XIII and his wife, Victoria Eugenie of Battenberg, the most prominent people of their times—among them: Ernest Hemingway, Orson Welles, Henry Kissinger, Audrey Hepburn, Prince Charles and Princess Diana, Ava Gardner and Luis Miguel Dominguín, Prince Rainier and Princess Grace of Monaco, Jacqueline Kennedy Onassis, the cast of the film *Lawrence of Arabia* (which featured the hotel), including Peter O'Toole, which featured the hotel, Plácido Domingo, Tom Cruise, Cameron Diaz, Brad Pitt, and Angelina Jolie—have graced this iconic palace.

An outdoor courtyard at the Hotel Alfonso XIII.

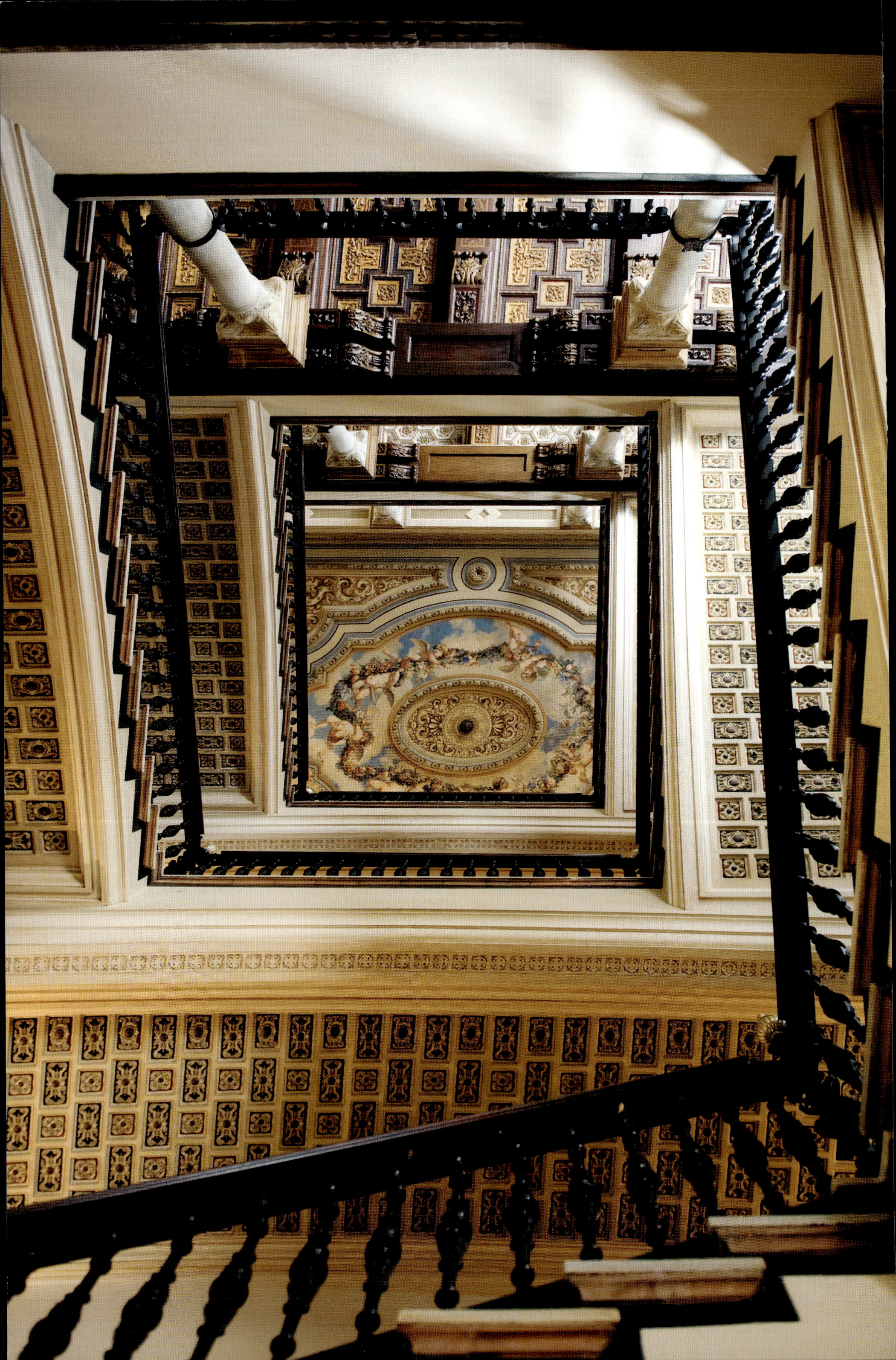

Clockwise from opposite A stairwell in the hotel; King Alfonso XIII, circa 1914; photograph of the Hotel Alfonso XIII soon after its completion; Sevillian woman at the hotel; at the bar of the hotel; young groom and friend of the author Juan Carlos Millán in one of the ballrooms; stained-glass window; Prince Charles and Princess Diana leaving the hotel; ceramic tile coat of arms; exterior of the Hotel Alfonso XIII.

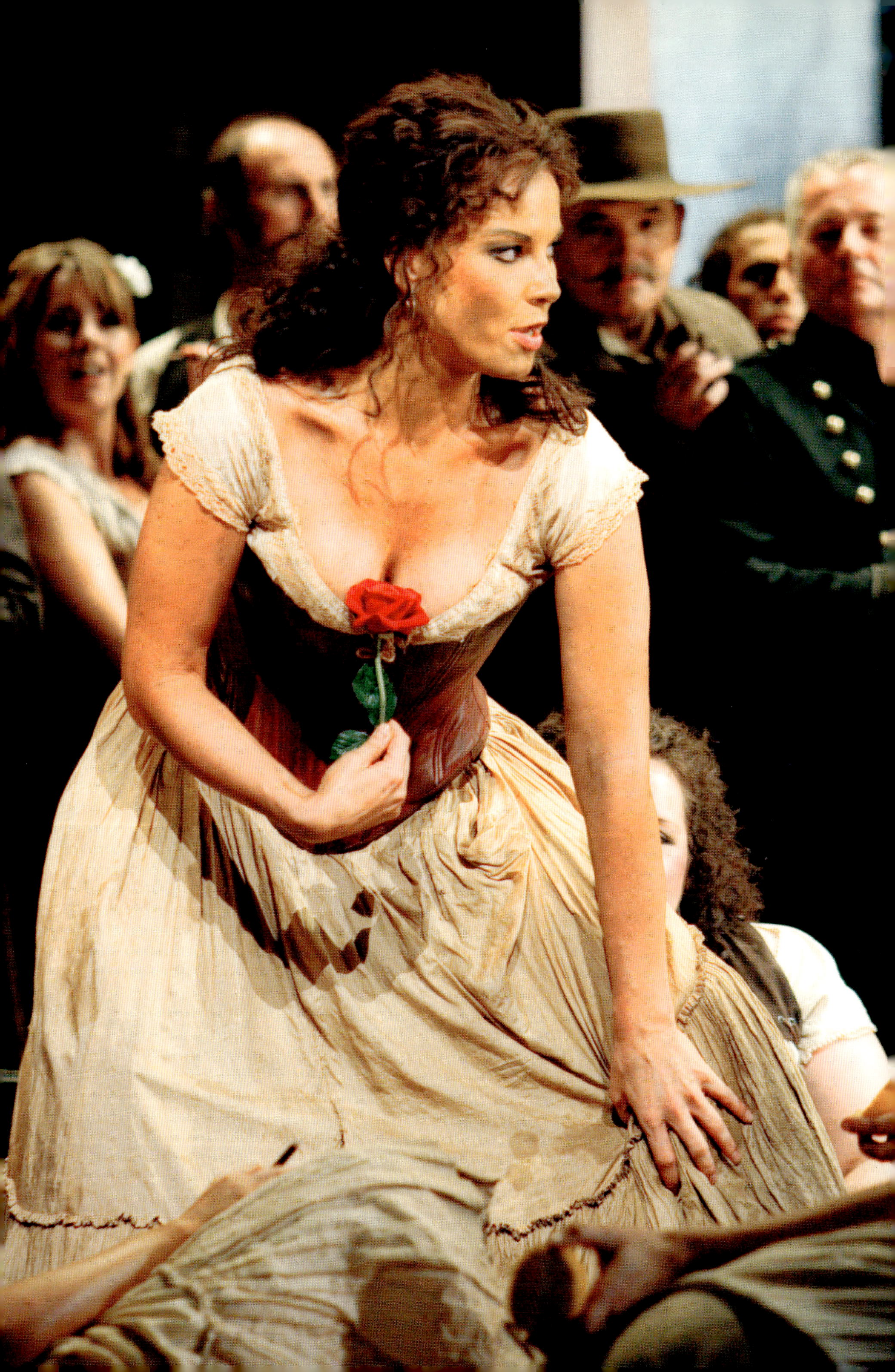

Don Juan, Carmen, and Figaro

Of the many contributions that Seville has made to our contemporary cultural canon, three characters rise to the top of the list for their originality and their enduring appeal. Don Juan, Carmen, and Figaro, the barber of Seville, have all become symbols of the city.

The influence of these three figures has been so great that they have inspired more than a hundred operas, novels, plays, and other works, with Bizet's *Carmen*, Mozart's *Don Giovanni*, and *The Marriage of Figaro* being the most famous among them.

The figure of Don Juan dates to the early seventeenth century, with Tirso de Molina's play *The Trickster of Seville*. About 150 years later, Lorenzo Da Ponte wove the drama into the libretto for Wolfgang Amadeus Mozart's *Don Giovanni*, remembered today as one of the composer's most extraordinary operas.

The character of Don Juan represents a complete break from all preestablished rules and norms of the era. Neither the morality of the Church nor the justice of mankind holds any value for him; he is a man who sees life as a game. The seduction of women, even cloistered nuns like Doña Inés, is what gives his life meaning.

In Seville, the infamous Don Juan remains an icon, an integral part of the city's collective heritage. On November 1, All Saints' Day, it is traditional to stage José Zorilla's 1844 play *Don Juan Tenorio* in churches, schools, plazas, and other public spaces, re-creating the atmosphere of Don Juan's sixteenth-century Seville, illuminated with torches and candles as it would have been back then. The Santa Cruz neighborhood fills up with groups of youths dressed as rogues, who act out short scenes from the Don Juan legend.

The myth of Carmen, the sensual gypsy woman who worked in the Royal Tobacco Factory of Seville and fell in love with an officer named Don José, remains just as powerful to audiences today. Inspired by a tragic story of star-crossed love recounted to him by the Countess of Montijo,

Illustration of the Archivo de Indias, formerly known as the Consulate. *Left:* Elina Garanca as Carmen, 2009.

Prosper Mérimée wrote the novella *Carmen* in 1845. It was from this text that Georges Bizet drew to compose his legendary opera thirty years later.

Many clichés surround the saga of *Carmen*: the passion and sensuality of Sevillian women; the quarrelsomeness of its men; the excitement of the bullfighting world; and the beauty of Seville's dances, music, and songs, and of this land. And although the site of Carmen's tobacco factory now houses the University of Seville, visitors can still go there and experience the splendor and spirit that animated this unforgettable story.

The legend of Figaro, the barber surgeon of Seville, began with a series of three plays written in the late 1700s by Pierre Beaumarchais: *The Barber of Seville* (which informed Rossini's classic opera of the same name), *The Marriage of Figaro* (on which Mozart based one of his most revered masterpieces), and *The Guilty Mother*. In each play, Figaro, the comically cynical surgeon, steals the show as the moral compass in the then-corrupt world of the Spanish aristocracy. He serves as the lovable everyman, relatable and full of the soul of the Spanish people.

As a visitor, it is easy to see why the city inspired so many truly memorable characters. Walking the streets of Seville and speaking with its inhabitants are an exercise in fantasy, an invitation to dream.

A scene from a production of *Carmen* at the Royal Opera House in London, 2009.

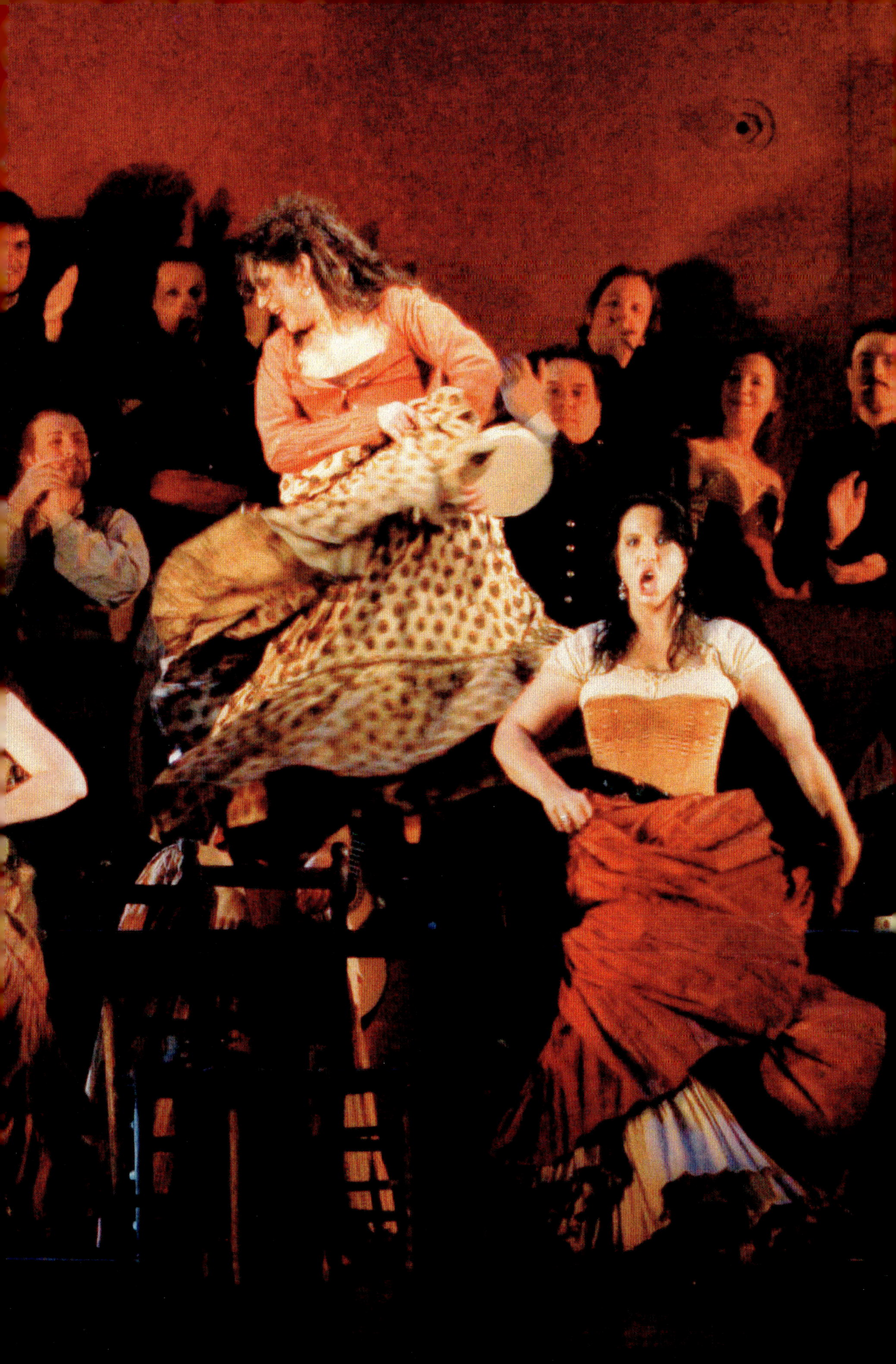

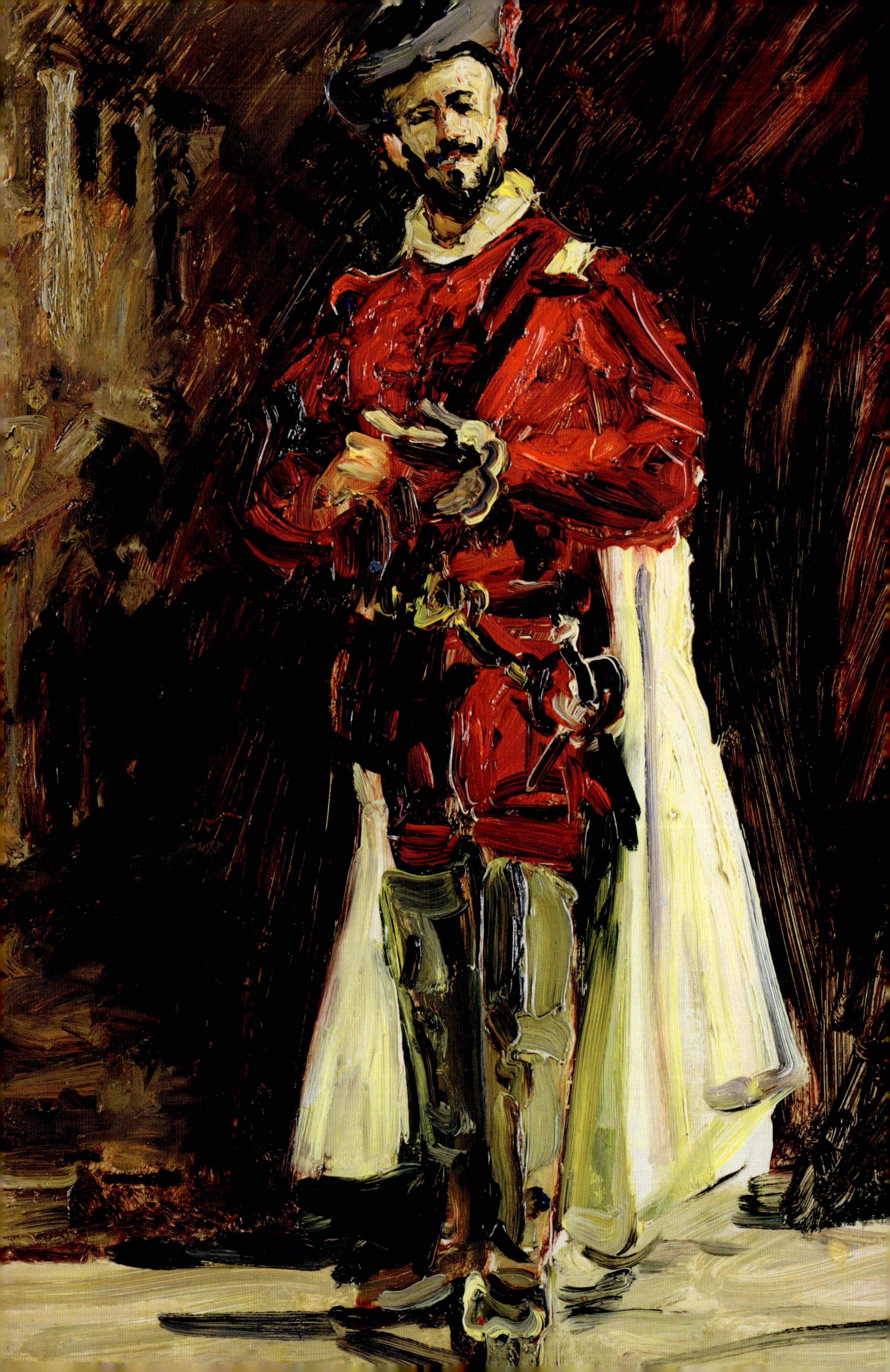

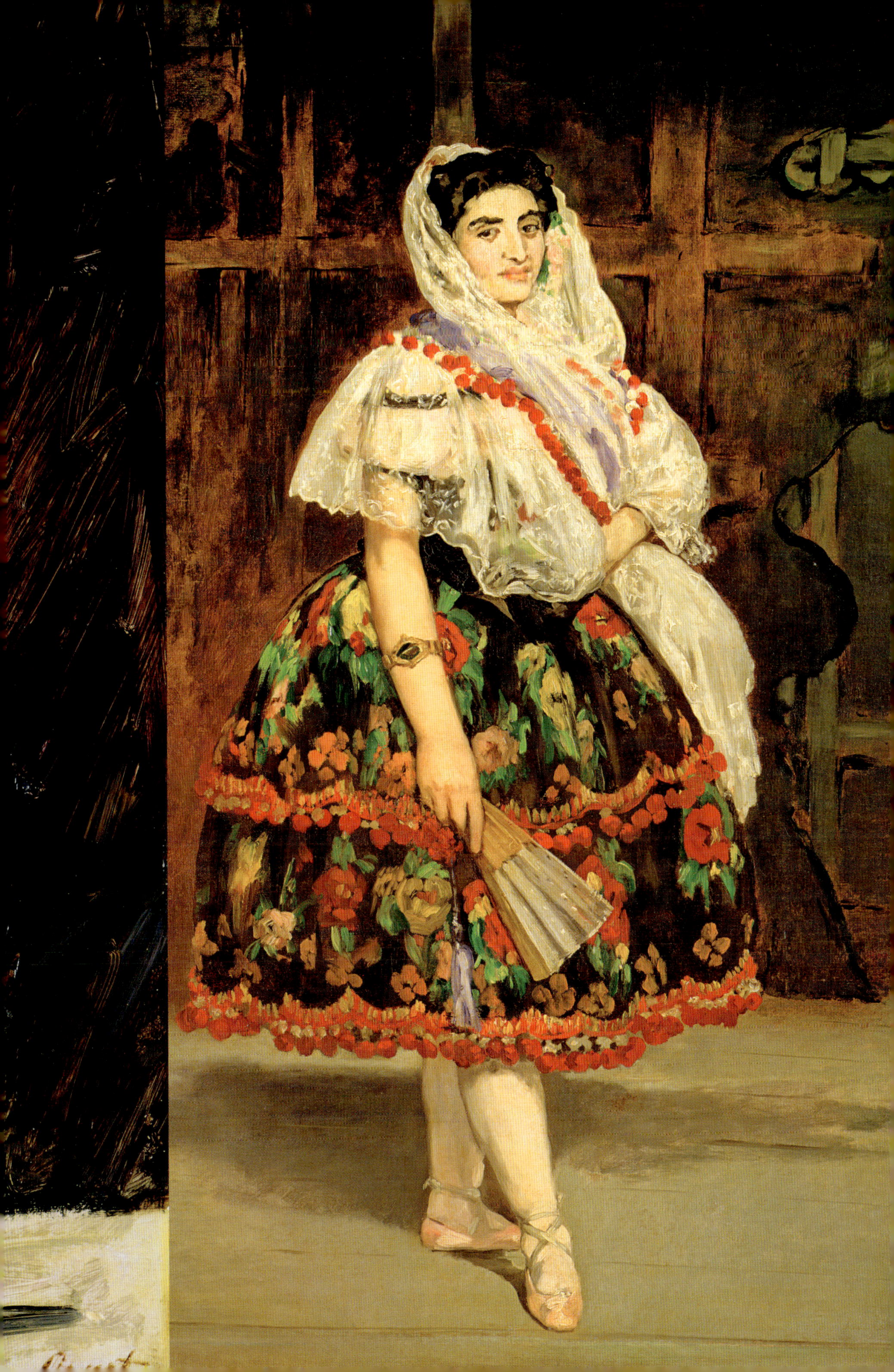

" There are only four questions of value in life, Don Octavio. What is sacred? Of what is the spirit made? What is worth living for, and what is worth dying for? The answer to each is the same: only love."

JOHNNY DEPP IN DON JUAN DEMARCO

Johnny Depp in *Don Juan DeMarco*, 1995. *Previous pages:* Painting of singer Francisco D'Andrade portraying Don Giovanni, by Max Slevogt, 1912. *Lola de Valence*, a ballerina at the time of *Carmen*, by Edouard Manet, 1862. *Following pages:* Carmen and the Cigarreras lived in Triana. They crossed the Triana Bridge to go to work at the Royal Tobacco Factory of Seville. *Pages 82–83: Signing of the Marriage Contract*, from *The Marriage of Figaro*, by Viniegra y Lasso.

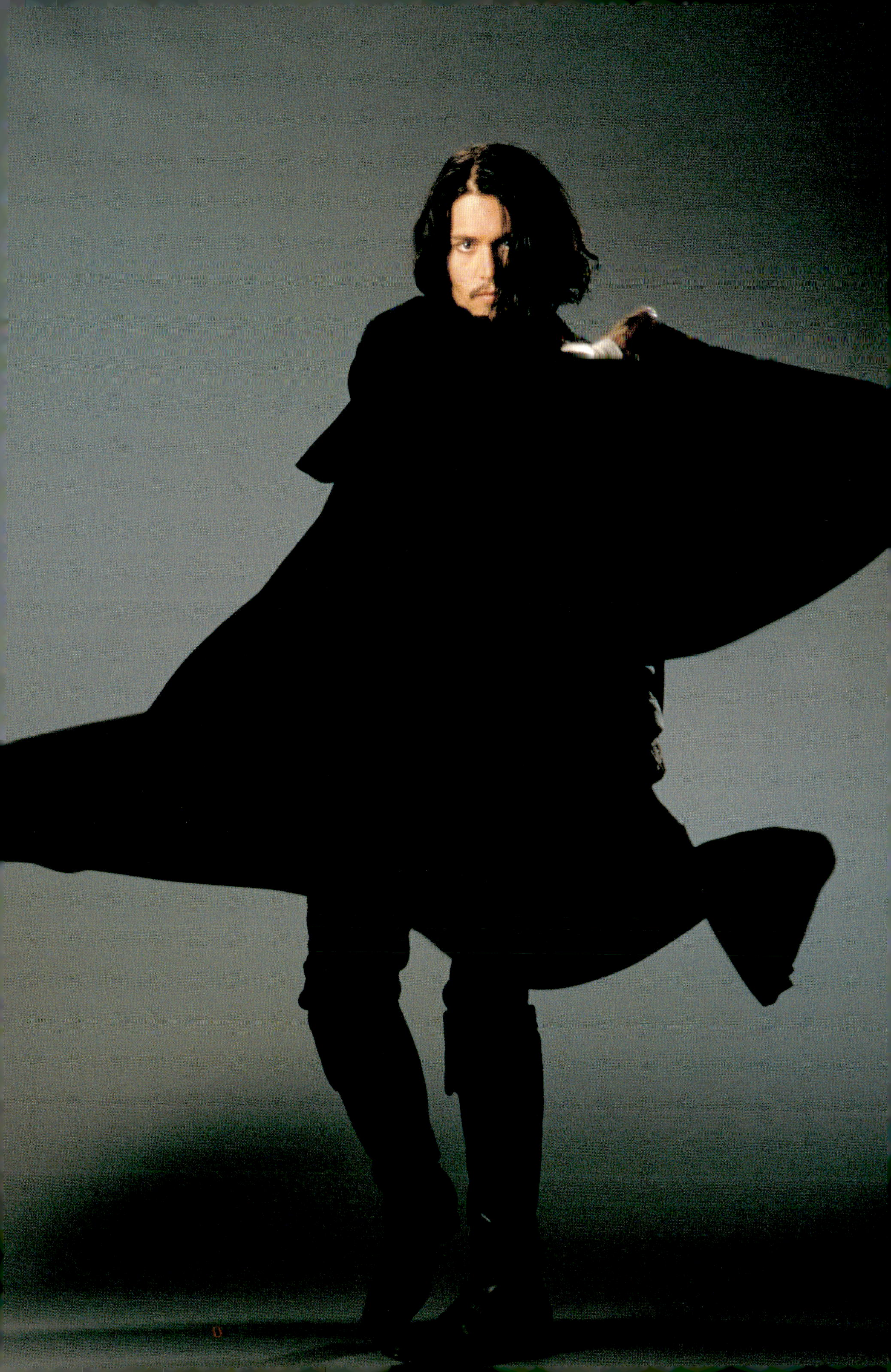

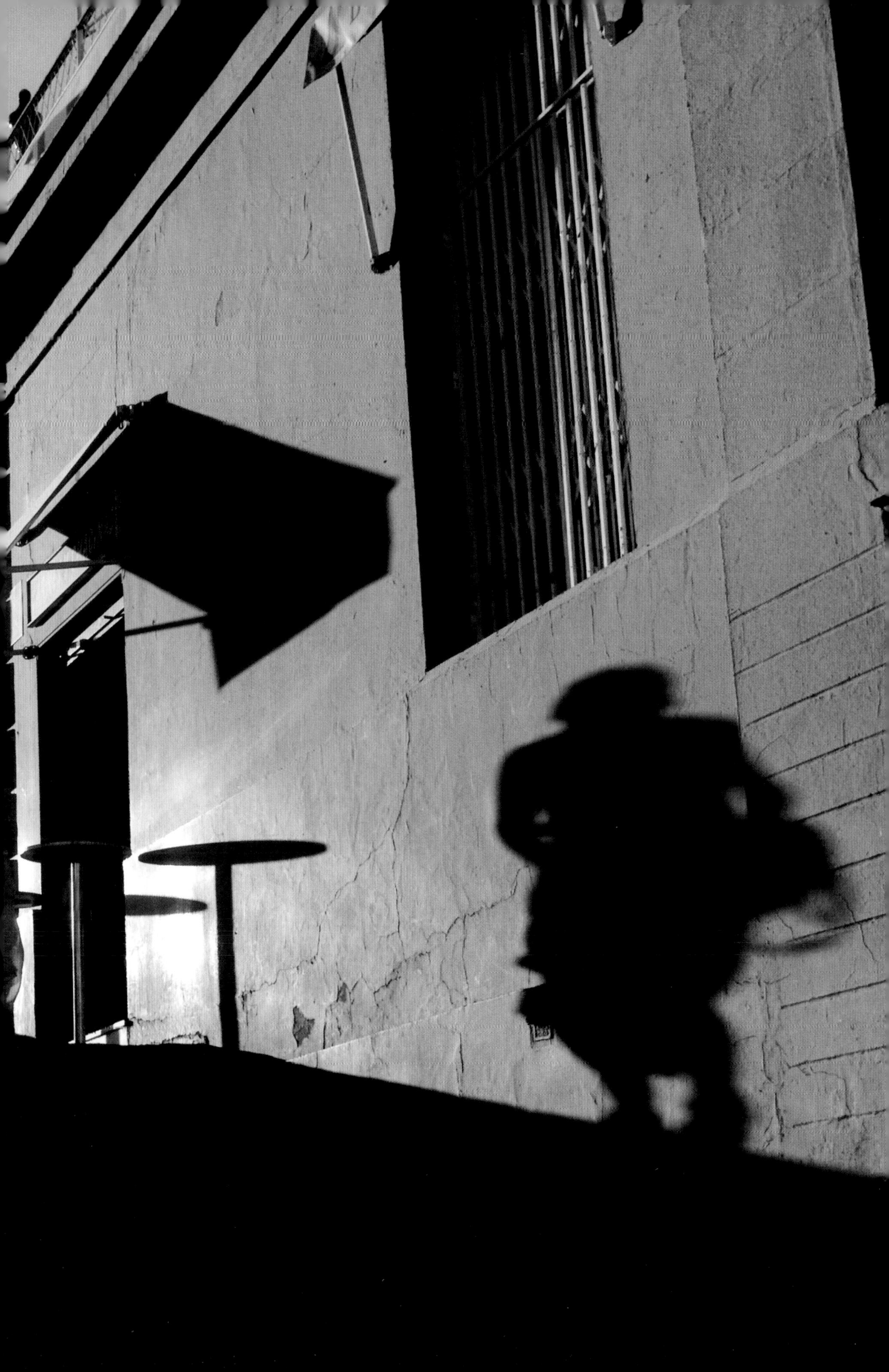

PRIX DE LA MEILLEURE CONTRIBUTION ARTISTIQUE CANNES 83
Emiliano Piedra et Gaumont présentent

Un film de
CARLOS SAURA

CARMEN

Clockwise from opposite, top left: Flamenco dancer Cristina Hoyos; painting of actor Thenard playing Figaro, by Henri-Pierre Danloux; illustration of the Royal Tobacco Factory of Seville, by Gustave Doré, circa 1862; portrait of matador and painter John Fulton at the Torre de Oro; opera singer Julia Migenes-Johnson; matador Luis Miguel Dominguín, a "Don Juan" of his time; *Portrait of a Spanish Woman,* by Heinrich Wilhelm Schlesinger; poster for the 1983 film adaptation of *Carmen.*

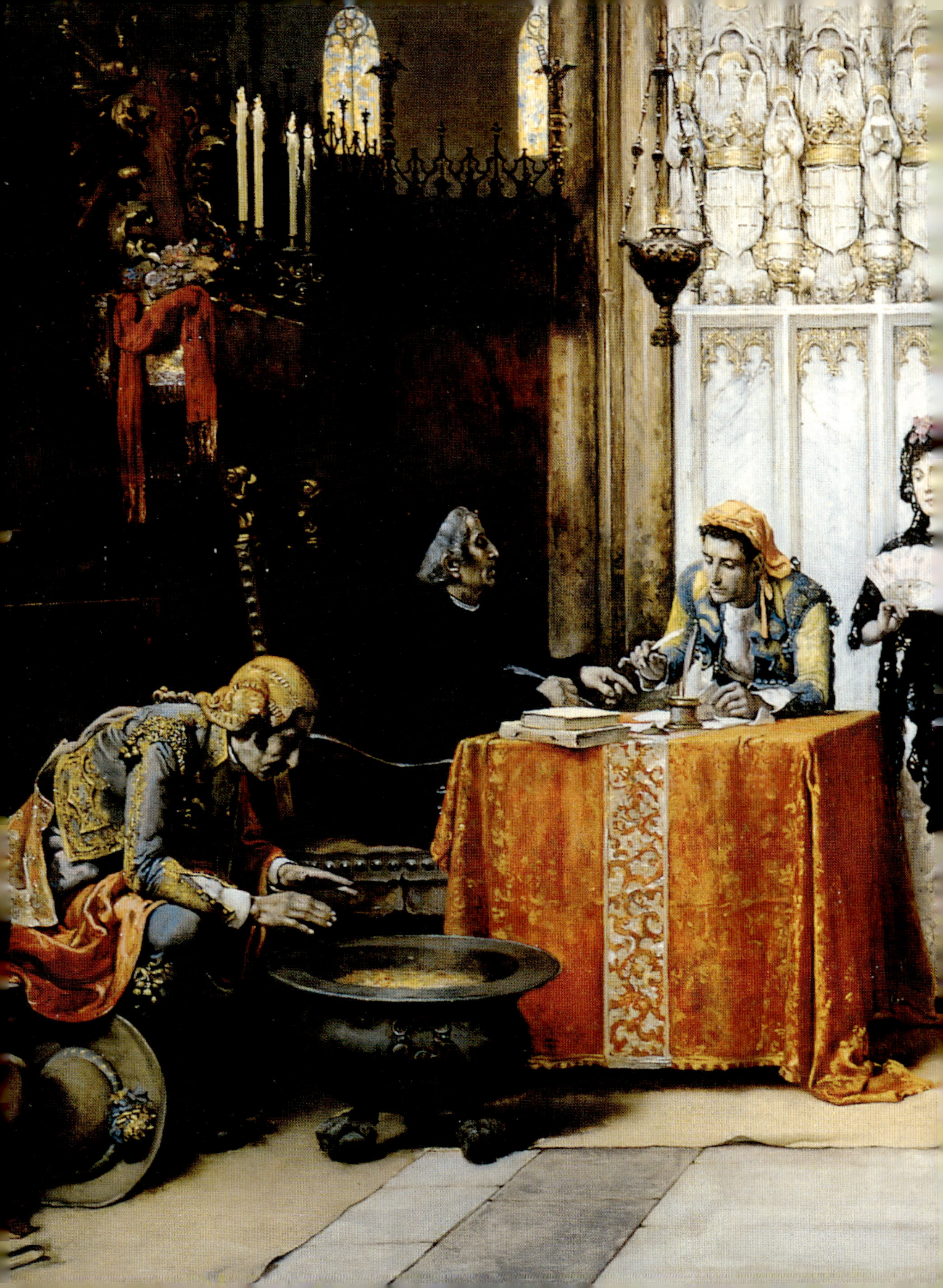

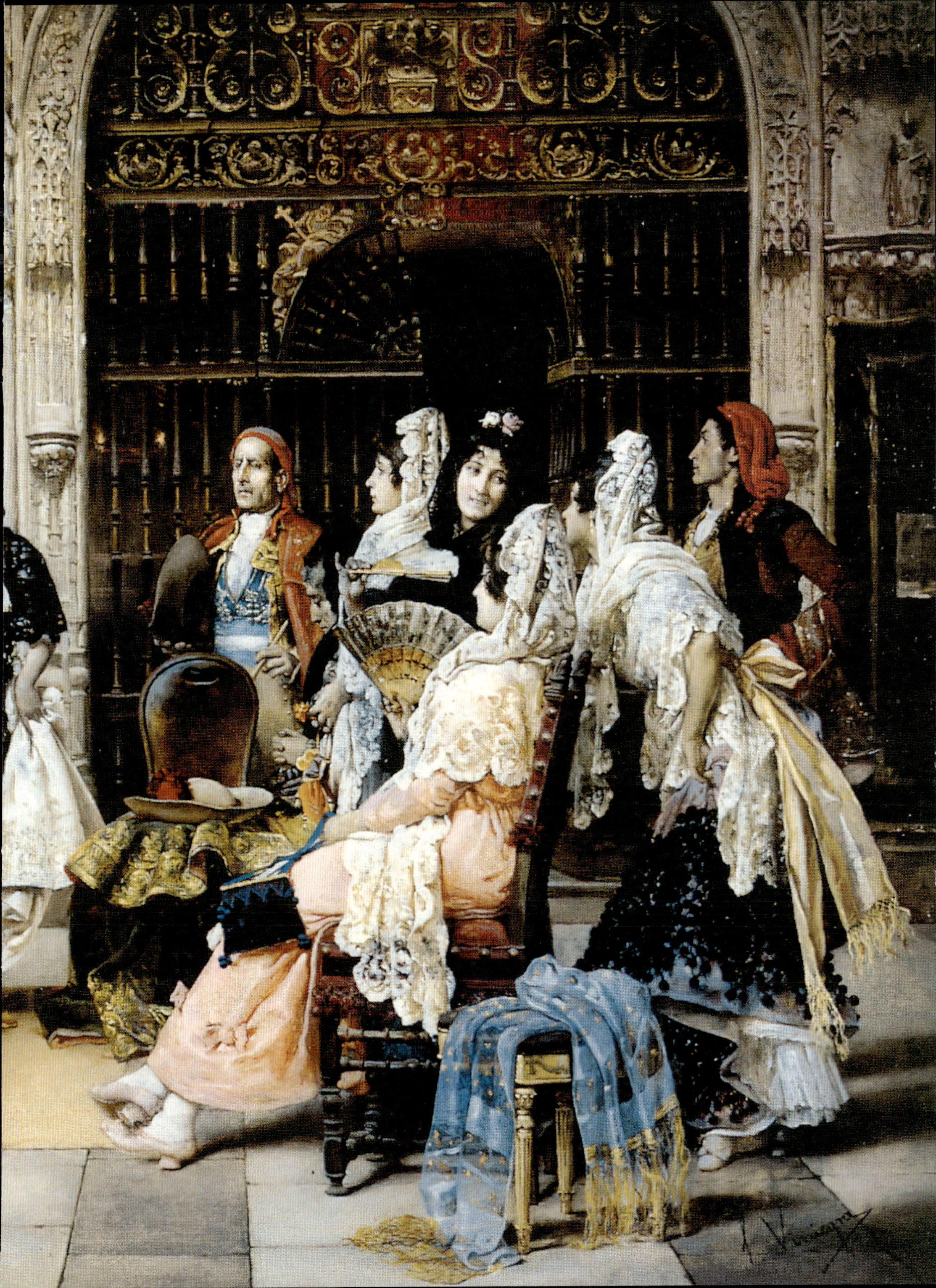

The Seville April Fair

The *Feria de Abril*, or April Fair, which is held two weeks after the conclusion of Holy Week each year, is one of the most famous festivals in the world. A beloved tradition anticipated by visitors and locals alike, it serves as an excellent opportunity for Sevillians to celebrate what makes their culture unique—in the grand, joyous manner with which most things in Seville are done.

Considering its scale and vibrant spirit, the April Fair had curiously banal origins. In 1846, Narciso Bonaplata and José María de Ybarra, two members of the Sevillian city council, wrote a proposal requesting the creation of an annual agrarian and livestock fair, to take place in the spring on the outskirts of the city. Queen Isabella II supported the project, which has transformed through the years into the spectacle it is today: a weeklong event brimming with color, flavor, music, and dance.

At first, the fair was held at the Prado de San Sebastian, a field beside the Royal Tobacco Factory—a beautiful eighteenth-century building commissioned by the government to

Sevillian woman dancing in a *caseta* during the April Fair.
Right: Etching of a scene at a bullfight, one of the many highlights of the fair.

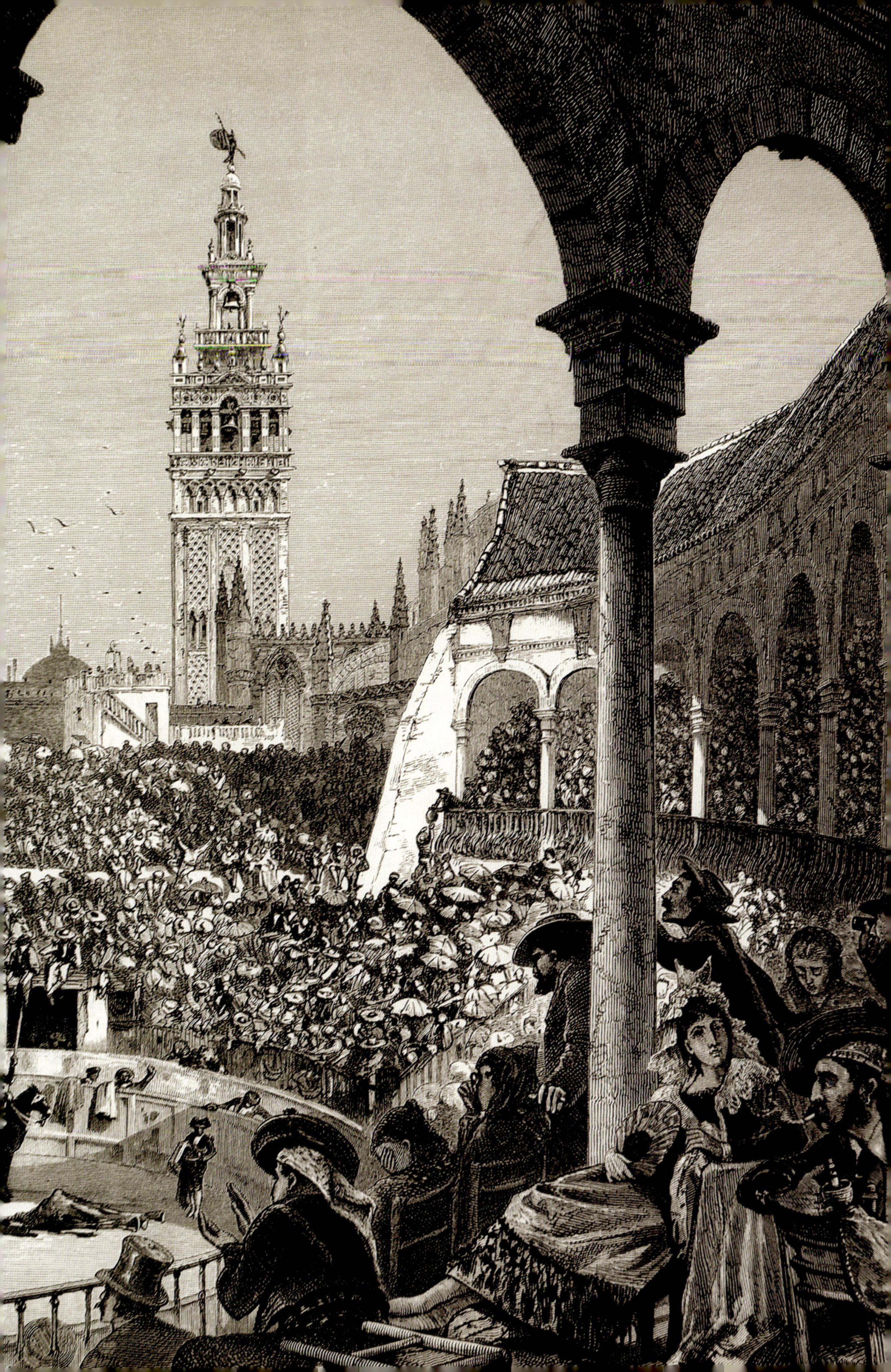

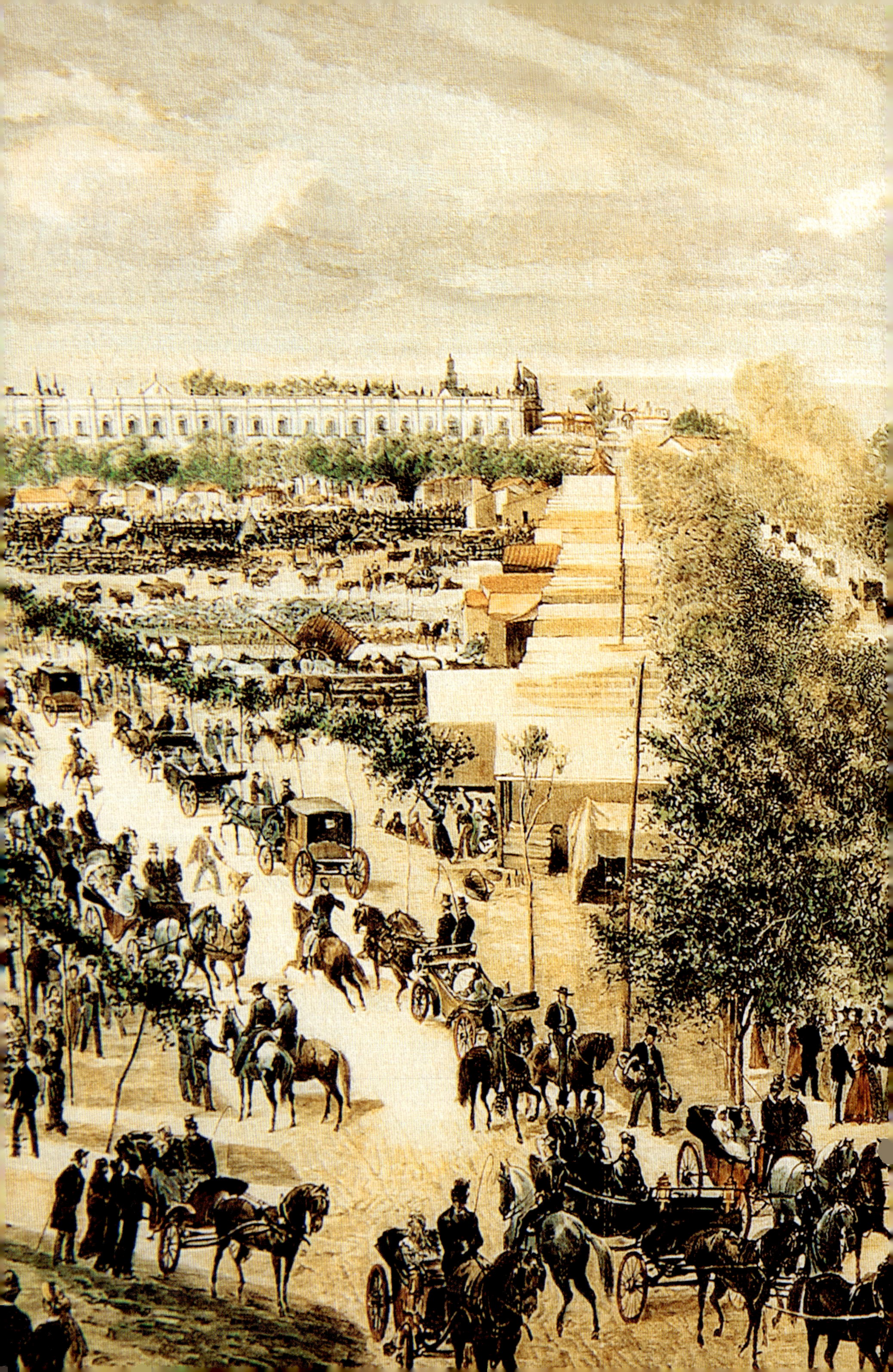

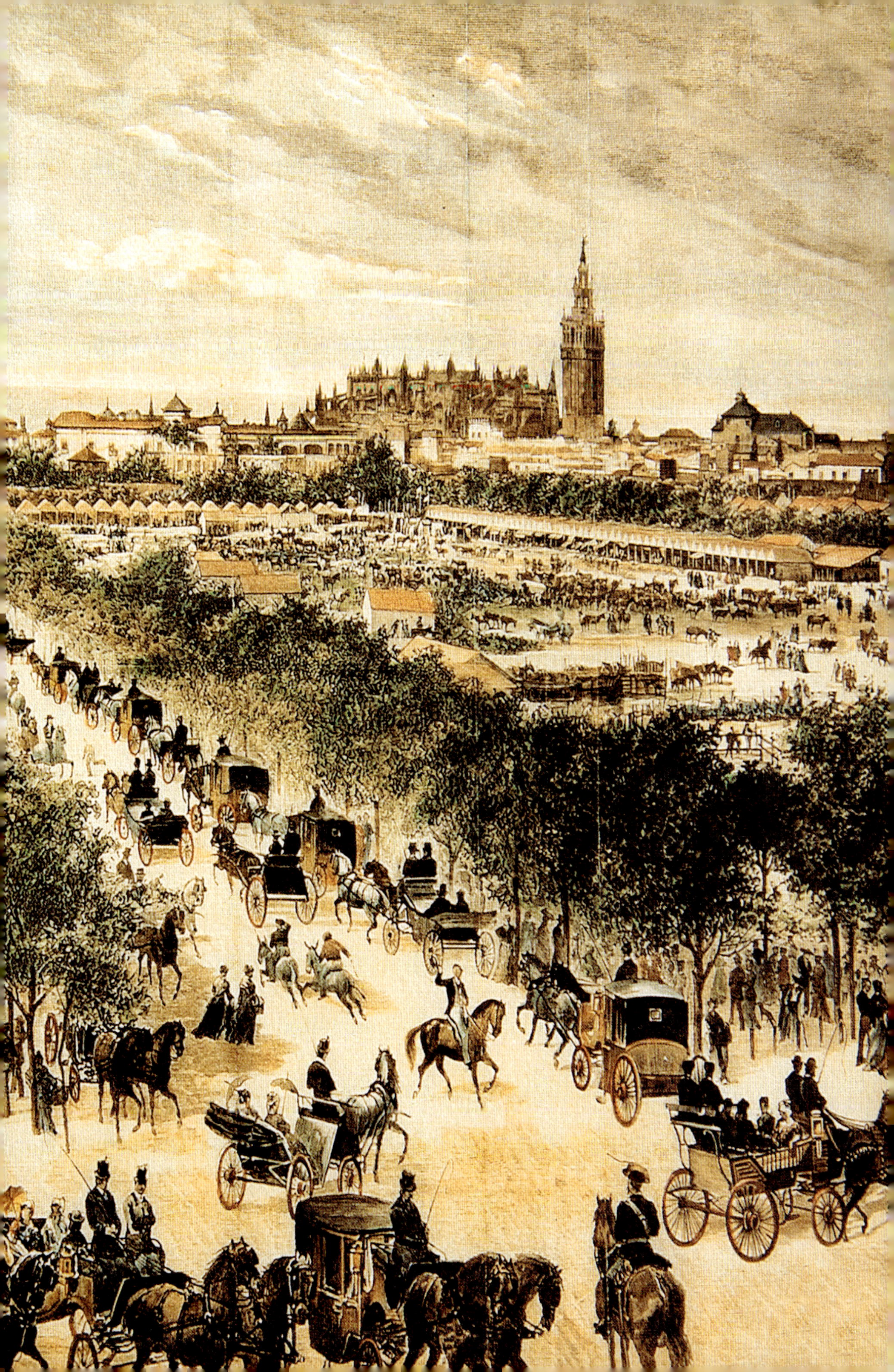

Cayetana (*front*) and Jacqueline Kennedy Onassis in traditional dress, riding at the April Fair, 1966.
Previous pages: The Seville Fair, by Enero Riudaverts, 1881.

consolidate tobacco manufacturing (and the setting of Bizet's *Carmen*). The rich landowners built stands out of wood and cloth where tradesmen and their guests could conduct business. Little by little, the decoration of the stalls became a competition. People brought their servants, luxurious carriages, and Arabian steeds to show off their wealth to passersby.

By the 1920s, the Seville Fair had progressed beyond its commercial beginnings, and today the event sees the streets of Seville filled with revelry. More than a thousand brightly colored tents, known as *casetas*, pack the massive fairground near the river and the Los Remedios neighborhood, echoing the grandeur of the stands of the old tradesmen. Around two million visitors come from all over the world to experience the fete, attracted by the formidable eruption of sights and sounds, and the legendary party atmosphere. The city seems to explode in color during the fair; indeed, this is the only time of year when the women of Seville (and many of the men) dress in traditional flamenco-inspired costumes, called *trajes de gitana,* which unfailingly flatter them. In the mornings, one can appreciate the parades of horses pulling carriages, and the elegant jockeys and *amazonas*—women who ride sidesaddle in modest traditional skirts, wearing stiff, wide-brimmed hats—astride the most beautiful of Andalusian horses.

Above, middle: Princess Grace of Monaco, Prince Rainier, and Jacqueline Kennedy Onassis at the April Fair.
Right: The Harness Exhibition. *Following pages:* Dress code for the Seville Fair.

Daily bullfights provide additional entertainment and excitement, as does the amusement park, called La Calle del Infierno ("Hell's Street"), set up especially for the fair. Visitors can enjoy a breathtaking view of the festivities from atop the giant Ferris wheel, or take a ride on the roller coaster. Vendors selling cotton candy, hot dogs, and *churros con chocolate,* that delicious Spanish staple, dot the fairgrounds, providing much-needed sustenance in the midst of this weeklong party.

Although the April Fair has evolved over the century-plus since its inception, its heart has remained the same. Sevillians, then and today, prepare their *casetas* as if they are extensions of their own living rooms and graciously welcome guests with their renowned Sevillian hospitality, offering tapas and wine. In the evenings, the revelry continues through the night, with the whole city out in the streets enjoying the lights, the music, and the vibrant spirit of this cherished insitution.

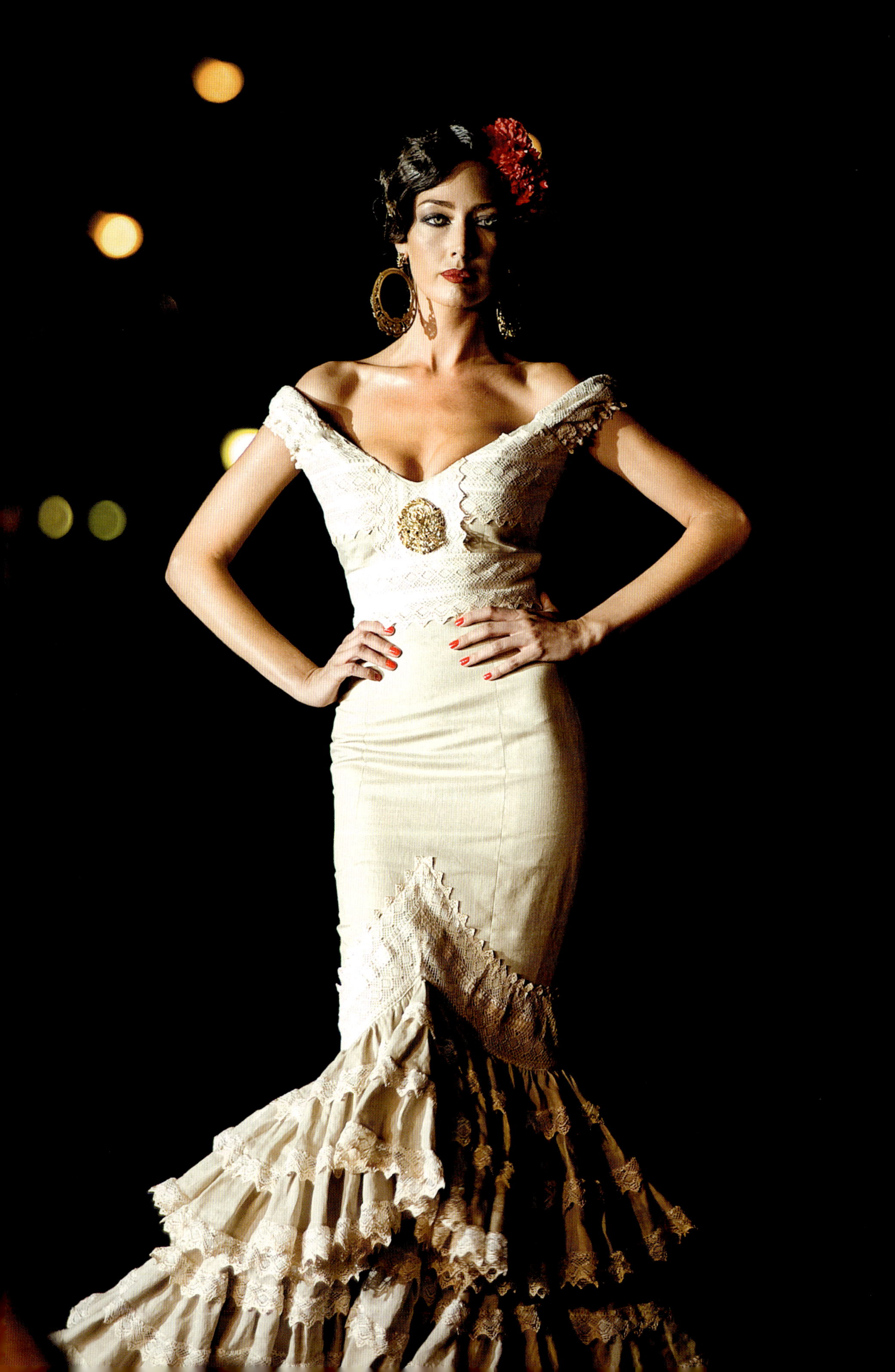

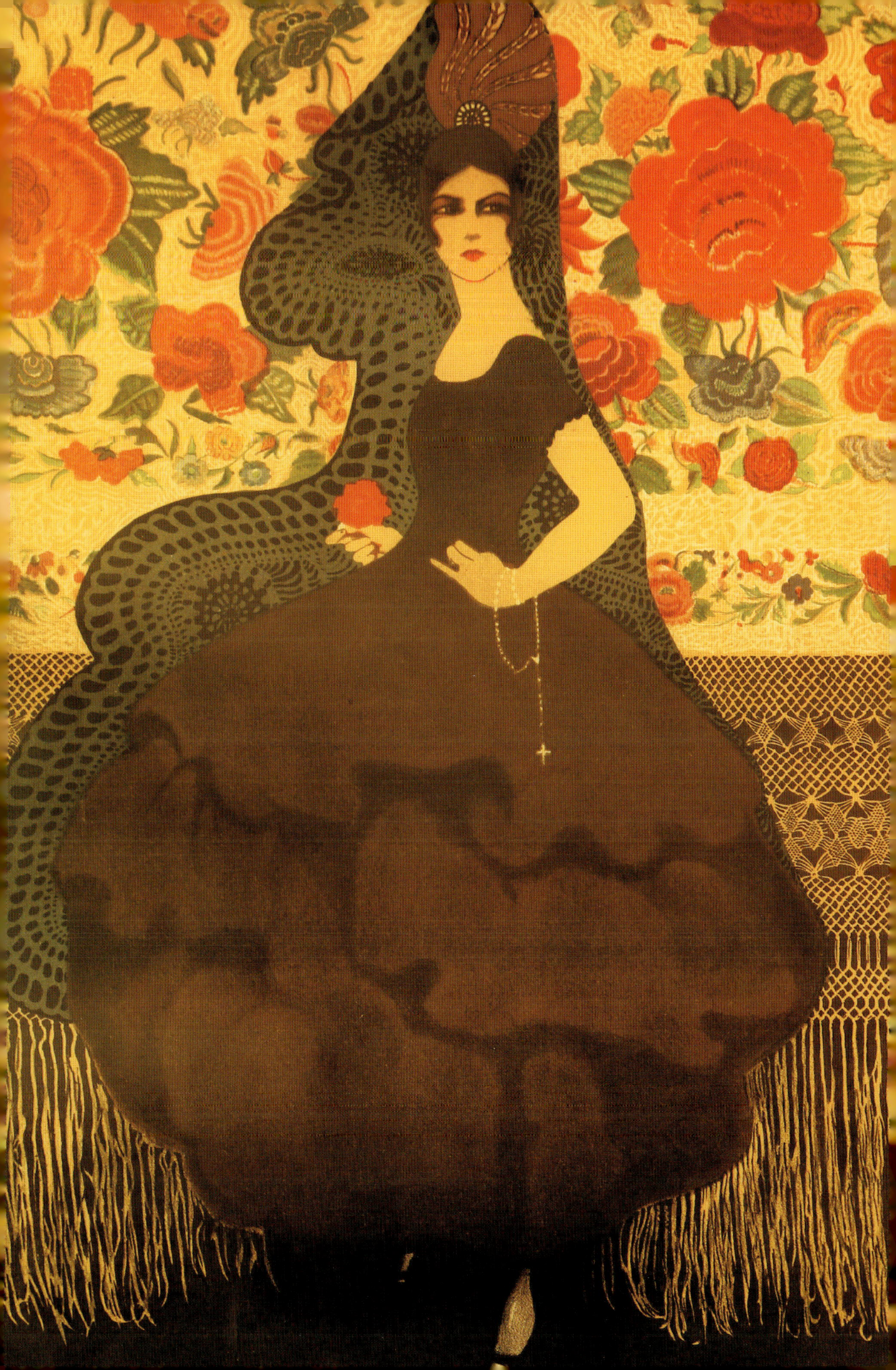

> *The air was as soft as that of Seville in April, and so fragrant that it was delicious to breathe it.*

CHRISTOPHER COLUMBUS,
THE LIFE OF CHRISTOPHER COLUMBUS –
FROM HIS OWN LETTERS AND JOURNALS

Sevillanas at the April Fair. *Following pages:* Manuela Barrios dancing; Flamenco artist Manuel Molina singing. *Pages 96–97:* Young women dressed in traditional mantillas on Holy Thursday; horsemen greeting each other during the April Fair.

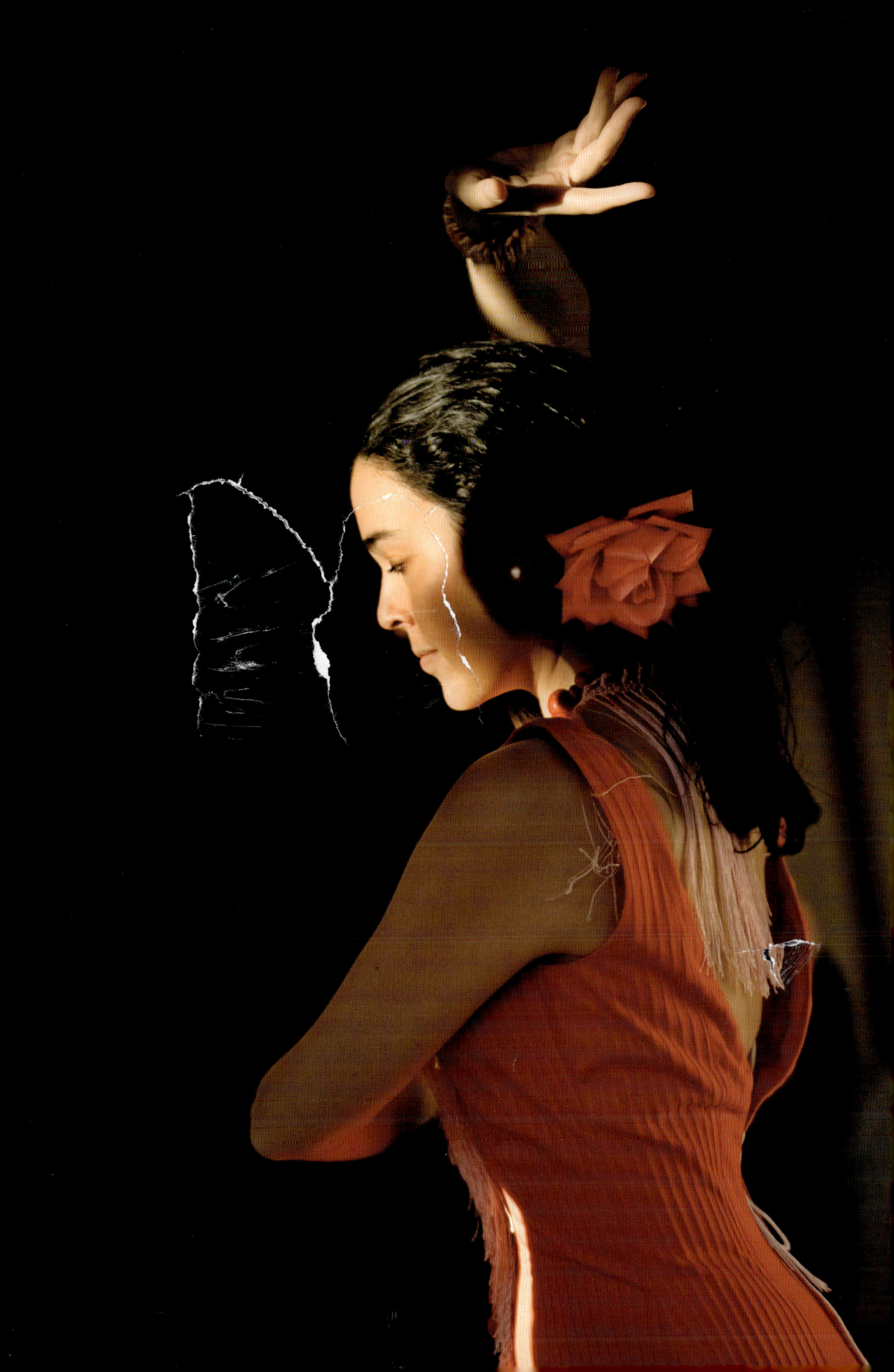

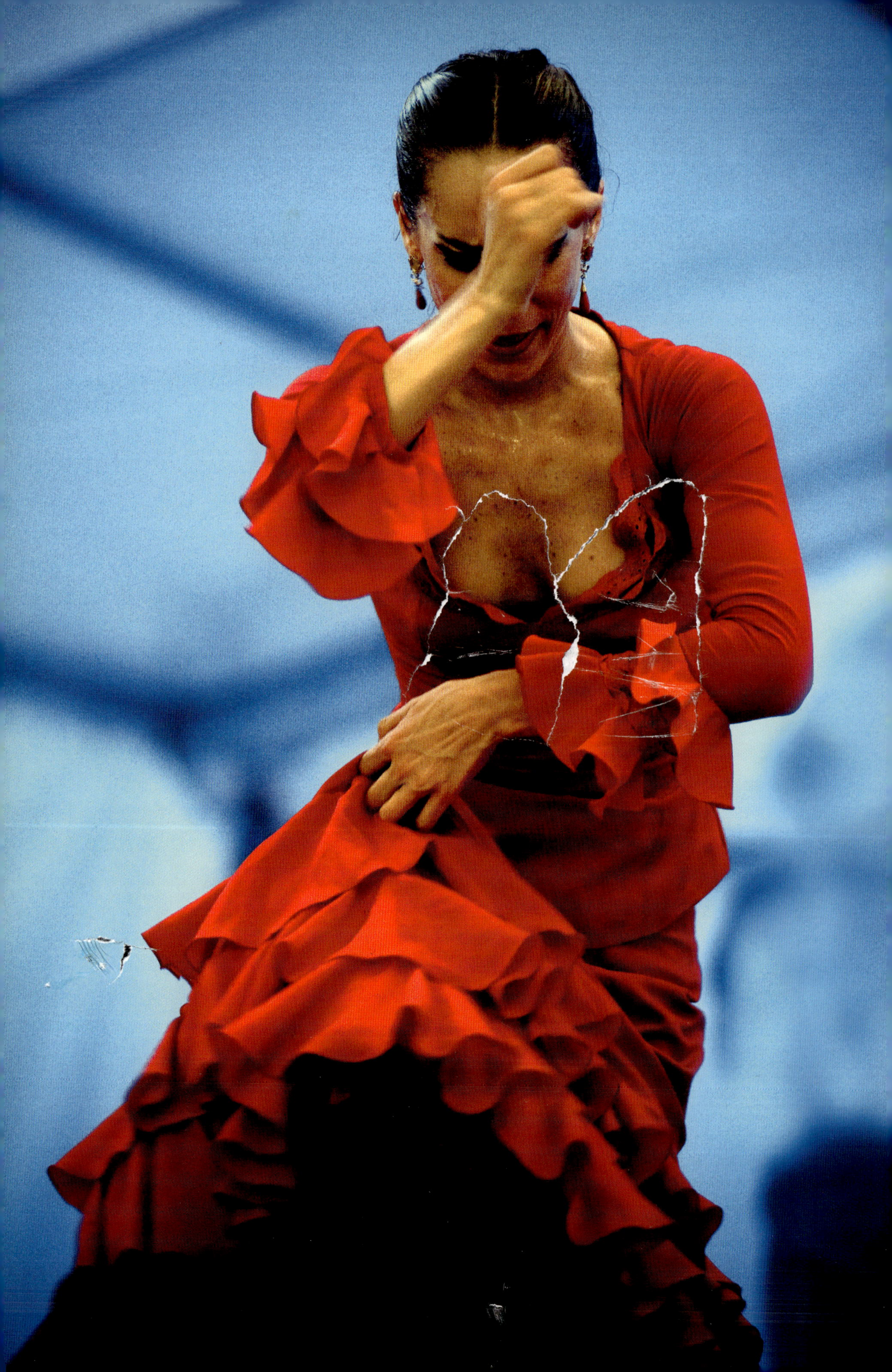

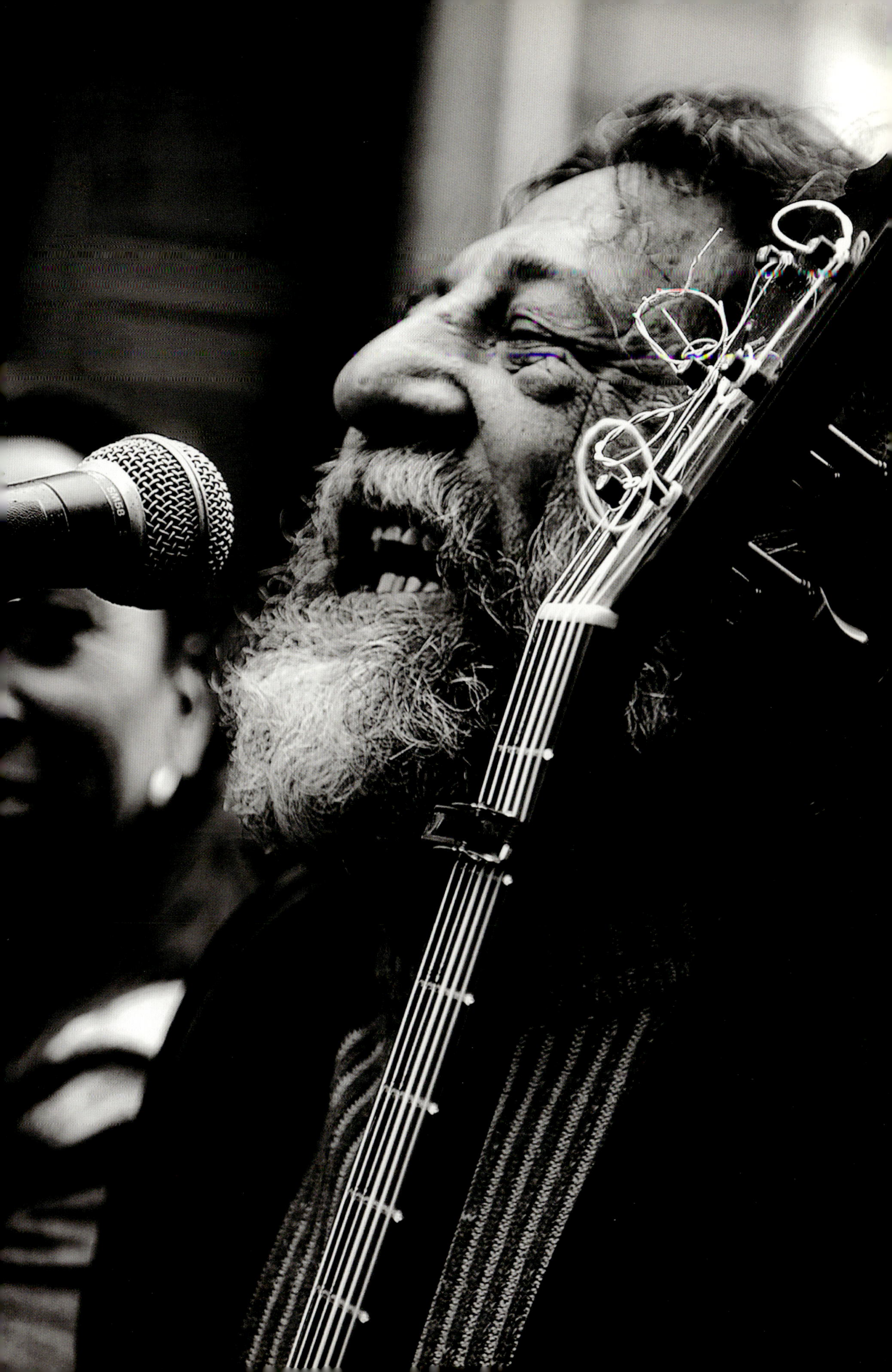

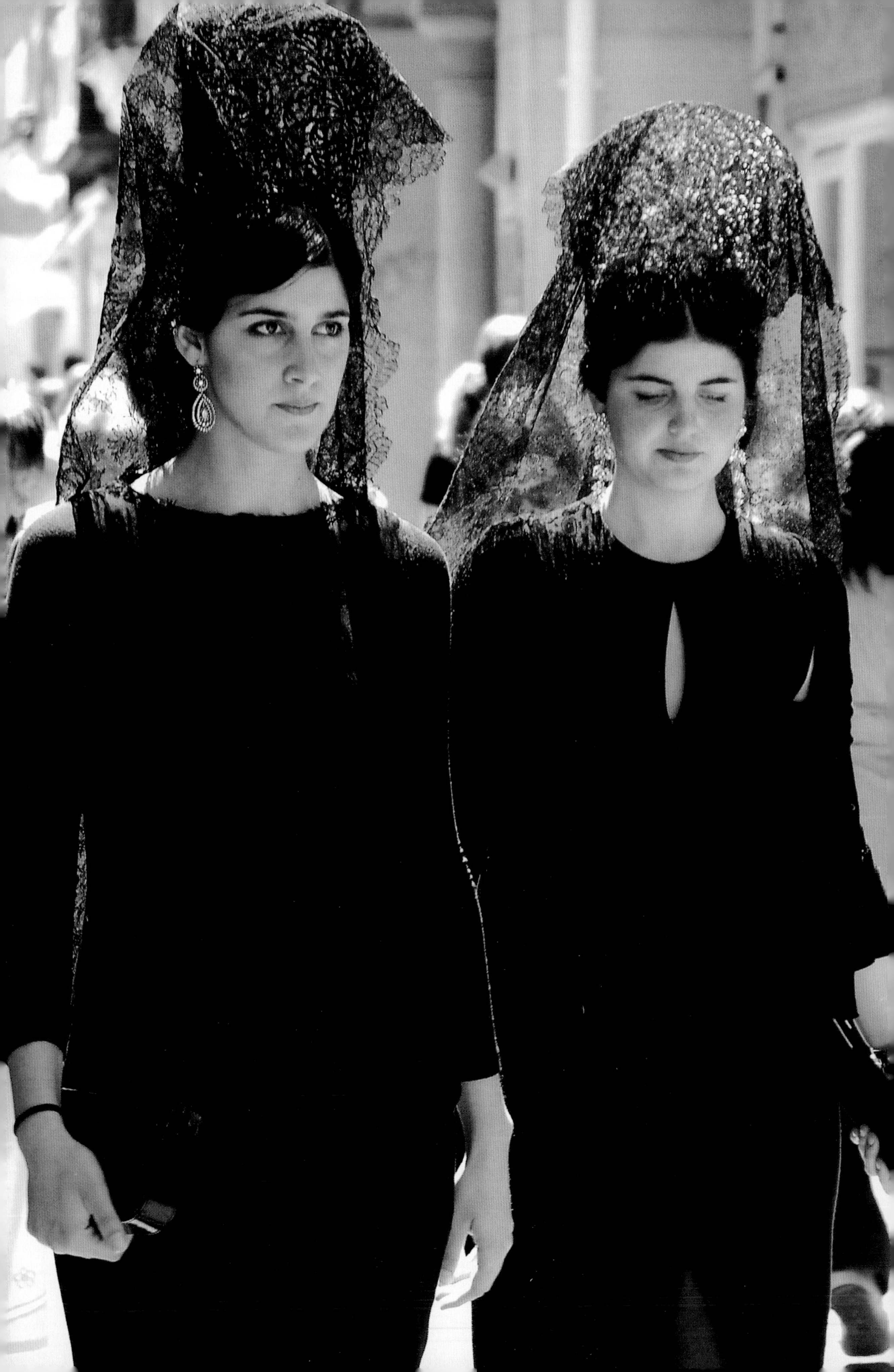

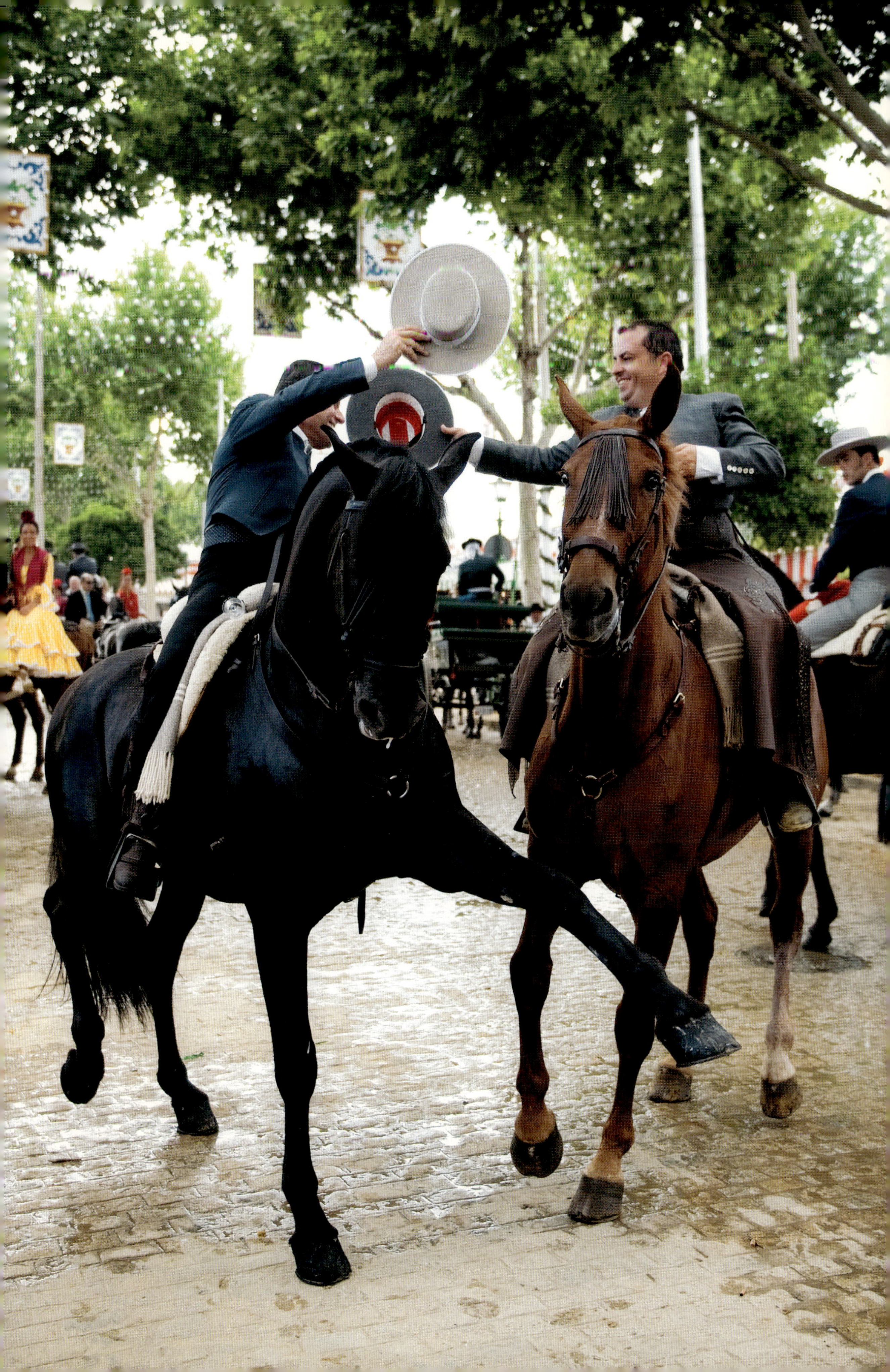

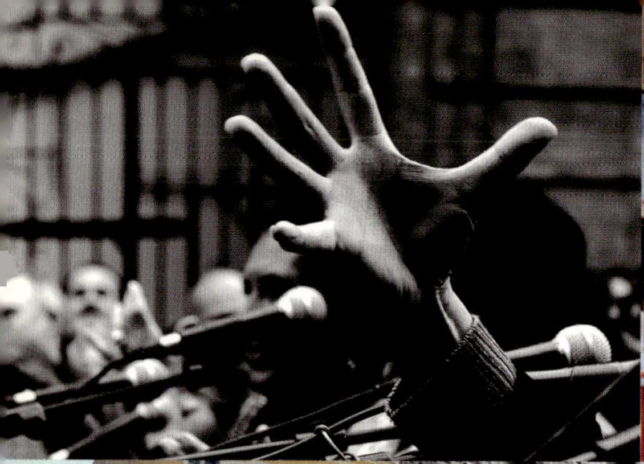
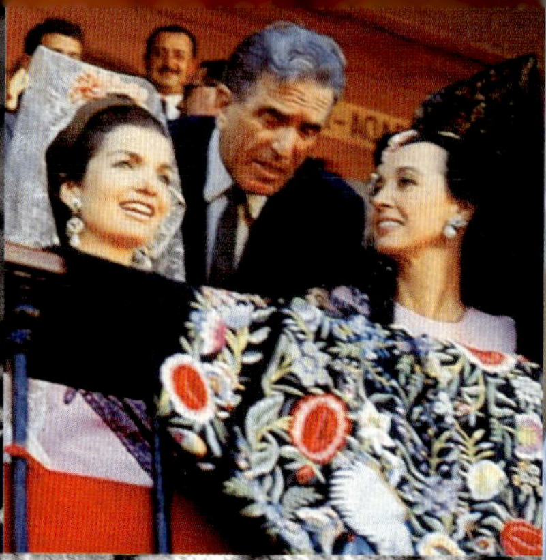
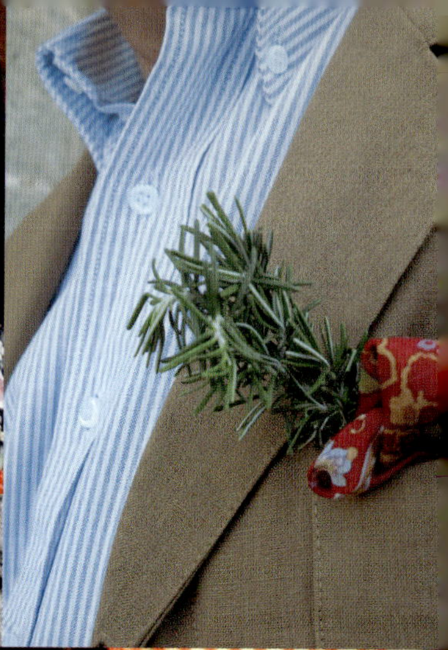
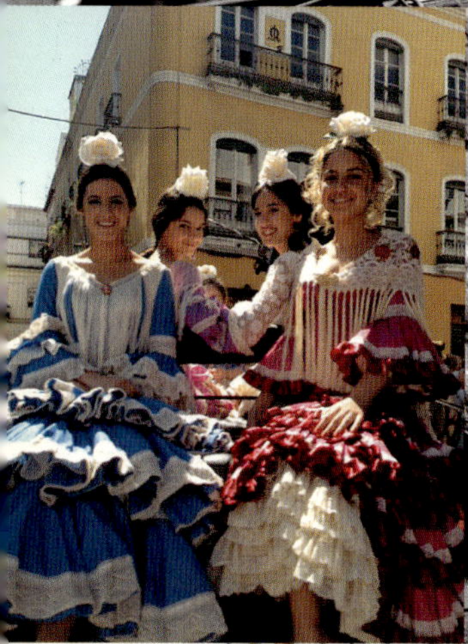
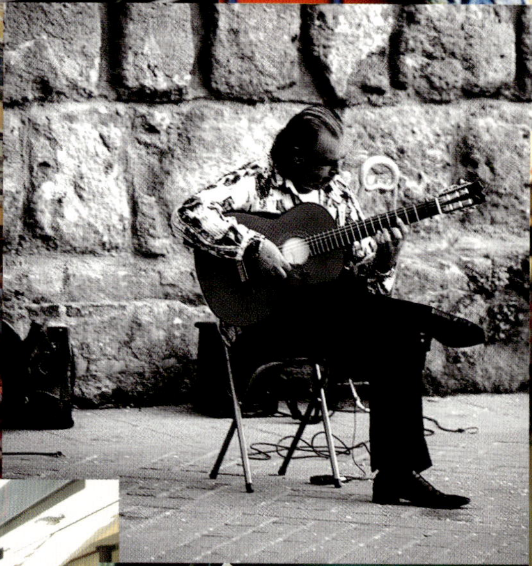
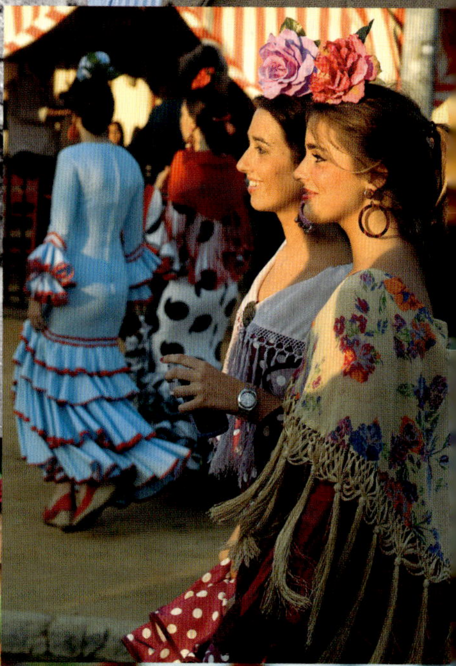
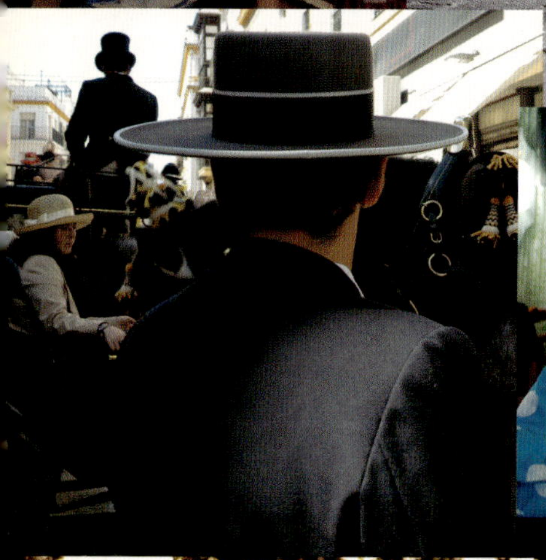
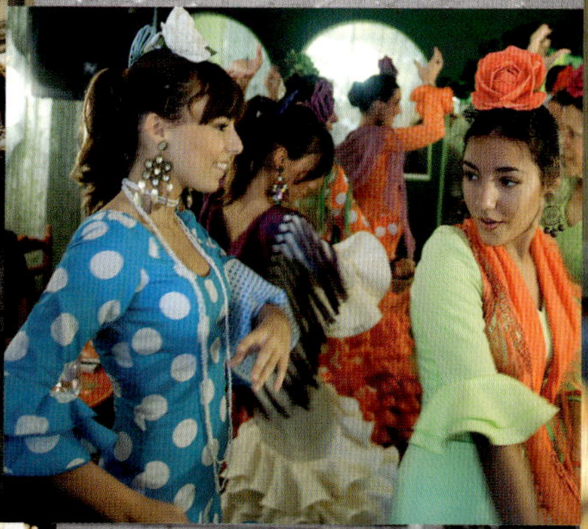
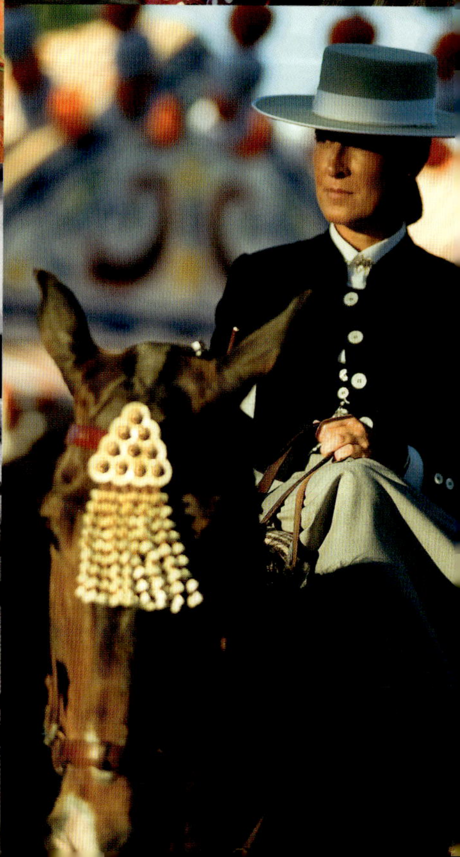
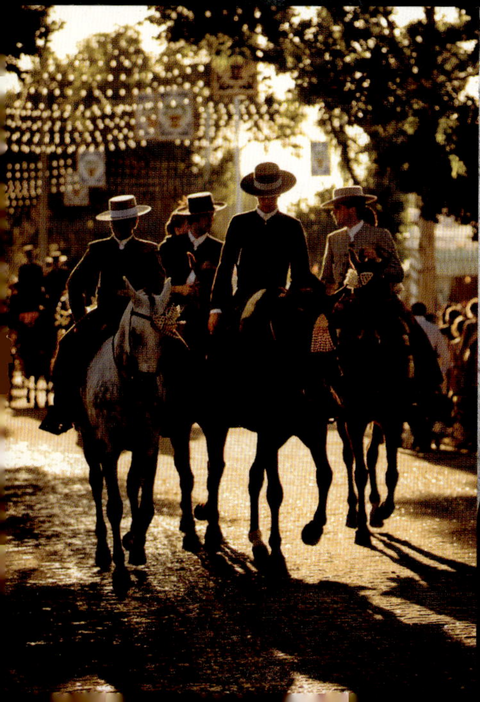
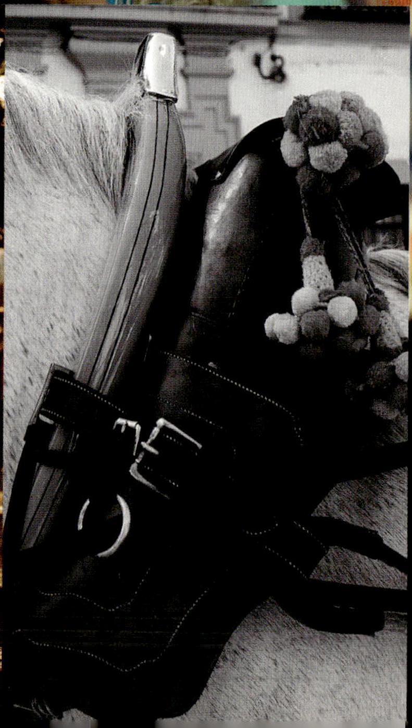

Opposite, clockwise from top: Singing at the April Fair; Jacqueline Kennedy Onassis in a traditional mantilla at the Maestranza; April Fair accessory; Esther and Rocío, relatives of the author, dancing Sevillianas; *Amazona* riding during the April Fair; detail of a saddle; a group of horsemen ride out at sunset; a rider in traditional dress at the Harness Exhibition; girls in traditional dress at the annual Harness Exhibition outside the Maestranza; guitarist Carlos del Río performs near the outer wall of the Alcázar; two young women in gypsy dresses during the April Fair. *This page, clockwise from top left:* Painting of set decoration for the opera *Carmen*; the Harness Exhibition outside the Maestranza; a horseman and a woman in gypsy dress; flamenco guitarist Pedro Sierra; learning to dance flamenco at the Cristina Heeren Flamenco Foundation; Ferris wheel at the April Fair's Calle del Infierno; riding on horseback during the April Fair; Sevillian girl in gypsy dress.

The Seville Cathedral

"One of the great landmarks in Seville."
—Conde Nast Traveler

Few buildings in Seville cast such an imposing—and impressive—shadow as the Seville Cathedral. At approximately 150 yards long by 100 yards wide, it is the second-largest Catholic church in Europe, after Saint Peter's Basilica in Rome. Along with the Alcázar and the Archivo de Indias, the building was declared a UNESCO World Heritage Site in 1987.

Like many other buildings in Seville, the cathedral represents an amalgamation of the many cultures that have called the city home over the centuries. After the forces of King Ferdinand III reclaimed control of Seville from the Almohads in 1248, the Great Mosque of Ixbilia was consecrated for use as a church. But it would be another 150 years before construction of the current cathedral began.

It is said that the canons who decided to build the cathedral wanted to create something so exceptional that future generations would think them mad—or, at least, visionary engineers who knew no limits. Given the cathedral's monumentality, with heights that were unheard of at the time, it's easy to imagine that this feat of engineering was the source of much admiration to all who saw it.

In 1506, after a century of work, the construction was finally completed. A harmonious and unprecedented mix of Gothic, Renaissance, and Baroque styles, it still retains a few vestiges of its Moorish past, namely the Patio de los Naranjos (the Orange Tree Courtyard), a massive open space in the center of the cathedral filled with orange trees and fountains, an oasis of calm away from the chaos of the city.

The Giralda bell tower, one of Seville's most recognizable and distinctive architectural features, also has Moorish origins. When his forces had reconquered the city, King Ferdinand gave the order that the Great Mosque's minaret tower should be spared; for years, it stood intact alongside the cathedral. In the sixteenth century, following an earthquake that, two hundred years prior, had destroyed the upper portion of the structure, architect Hernán Ruiz added the belfry and the statue, the *Giraldillo*, that crowns it and gives the tower its name; it functions as a weather vane, turning (*girar*) according to the direction of the wind—and named La Giralda.

The Infanta Elena and her father, King Juan Carlos, at her wedding to Don Jaime de Marichalar at the Seville Cathedral on March 18, 1995. *Following pages:* The beautiful exterior of the cathedral.

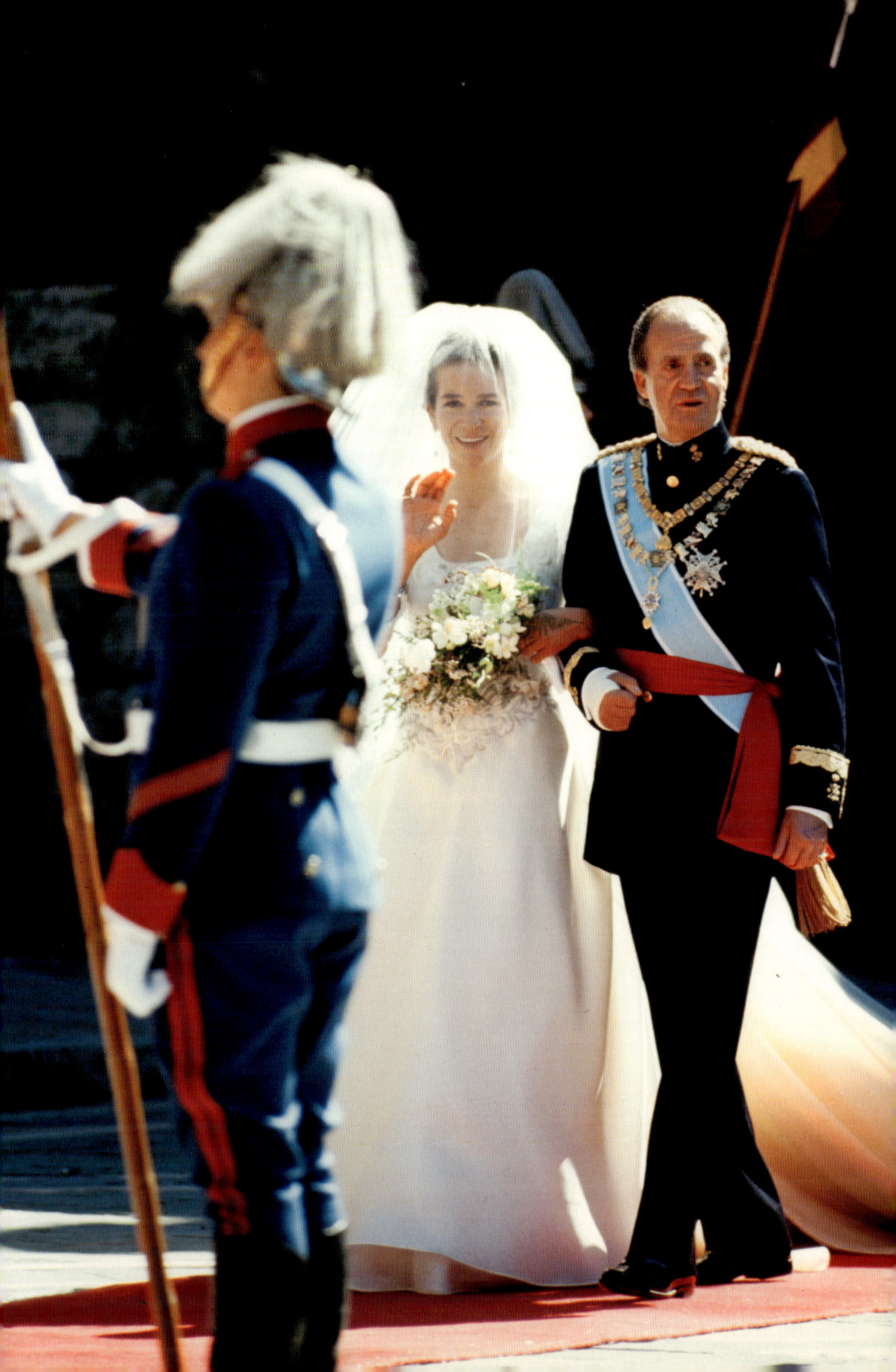

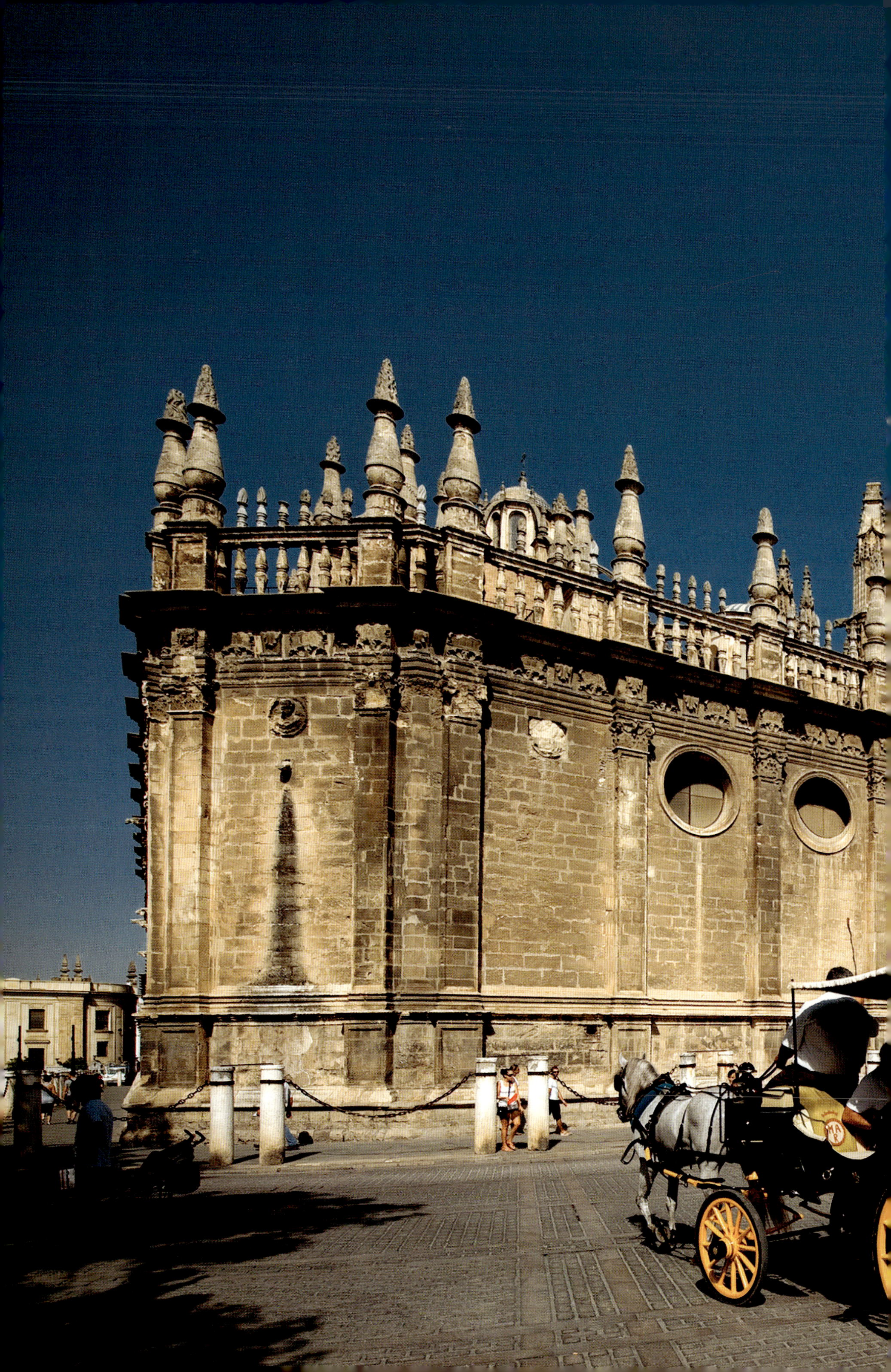

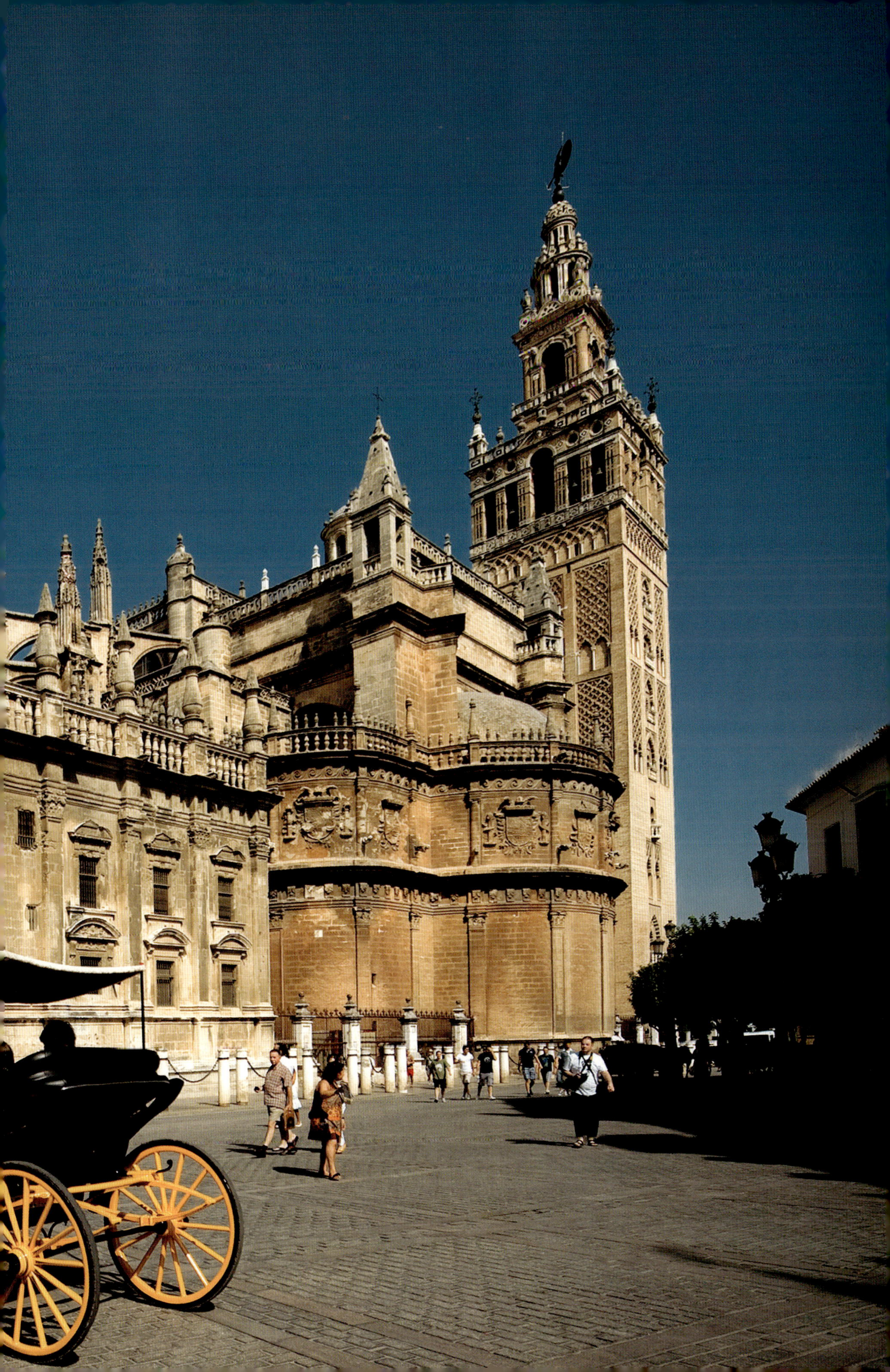

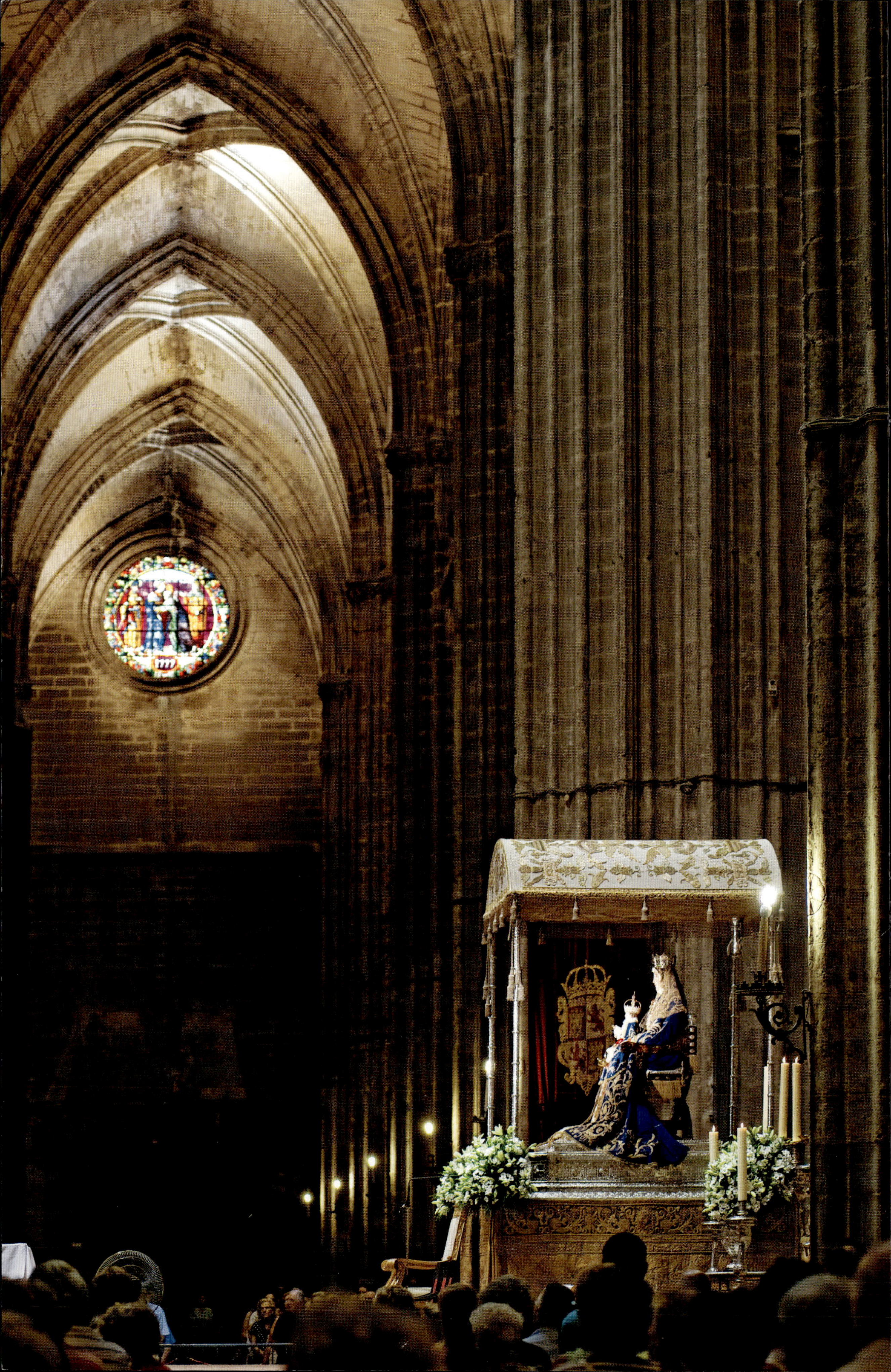

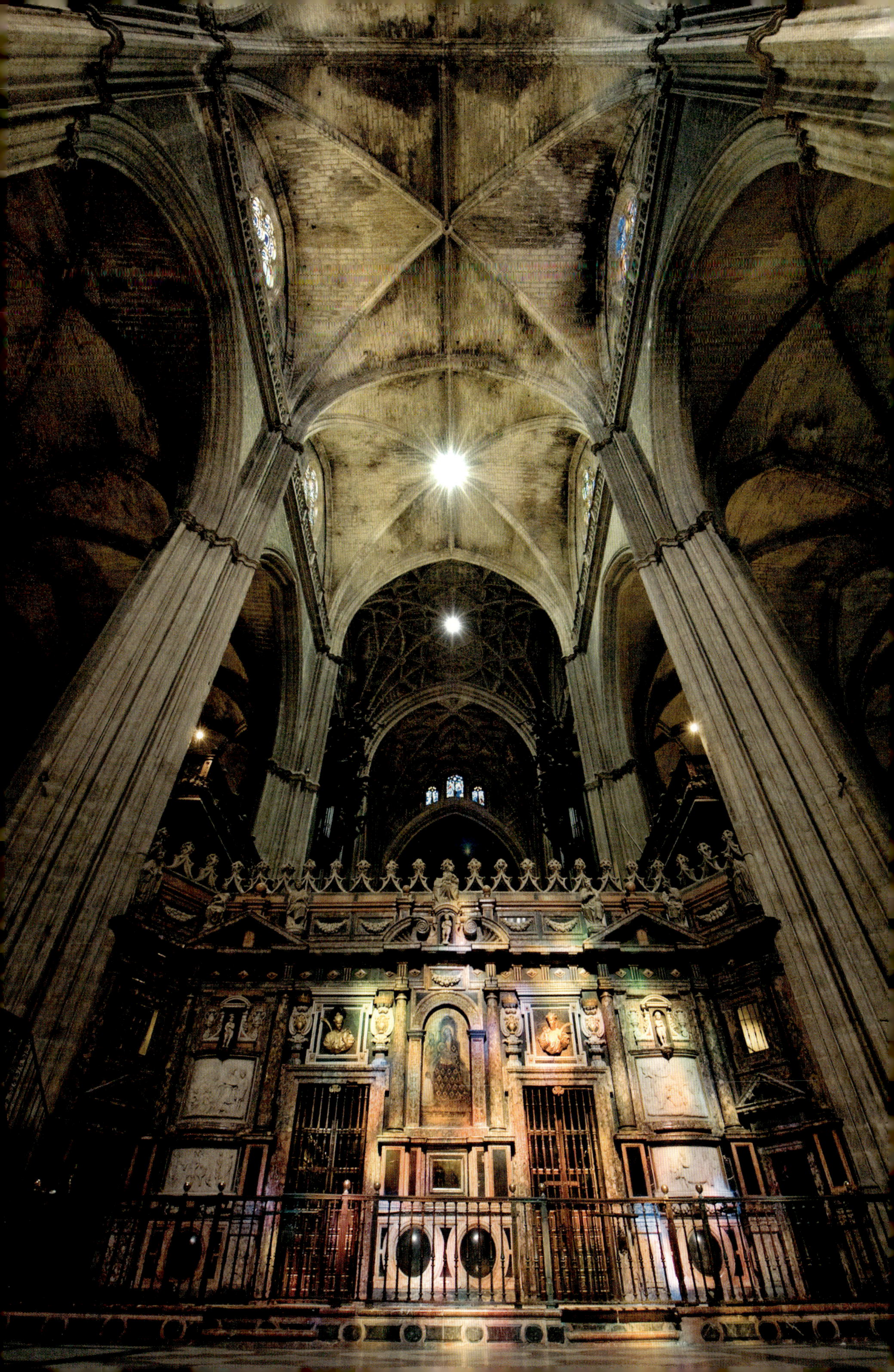

Inside, the cathedral is one of the finest examples of Gothic architecture in Spain. The vaults of the central nave, which rises 46 yards high, feature intricate, gilded, carved motifs; the altar stands in front of a stunning carved retablo depicting scenes from the life of Jesus, as well as a towering pipe organ. The dome, which collapsed in 1511 and again in 1888, allows just the right amount of light into the nave. Numerous chapels and other structures add to the immense size of the cathedral, as well as the huge volume of art contained within.

Since its completion, the cathedral has been an important part of the religious and cultural life in Seville. Of course, it functions as the primary site where Sevillians, and visitors, observe major religious events. Christopher Columbus is buried here, along with King Ferdinand III, King Alfonso X, and other royals. More recently, it has also served as the setting of several high-profile weddings, such as that of Infanta Elena, the daughter of King Juan Carlos, to Don Jaime de Marichalar in 1995, and the 1998 wedding of Eugenia Martínez de Irujo, Duchess of Montoro and daughter of the Duchess of Alba, to the bullfighter Francisco Rivera, son of the legendary bullfighter Paquirri. The cathedral's grand scale provides a fitting backdrop for spectacles that capture the collective imagination of all of Spain.

The young performers of Seise emerge from the cathedral to dance in the Corpus Christi festivities.
Previous pages: The Virgin of the Kings, preparing to emerge from the cathedral for her procession; view of the retrochoir of the cathedral.

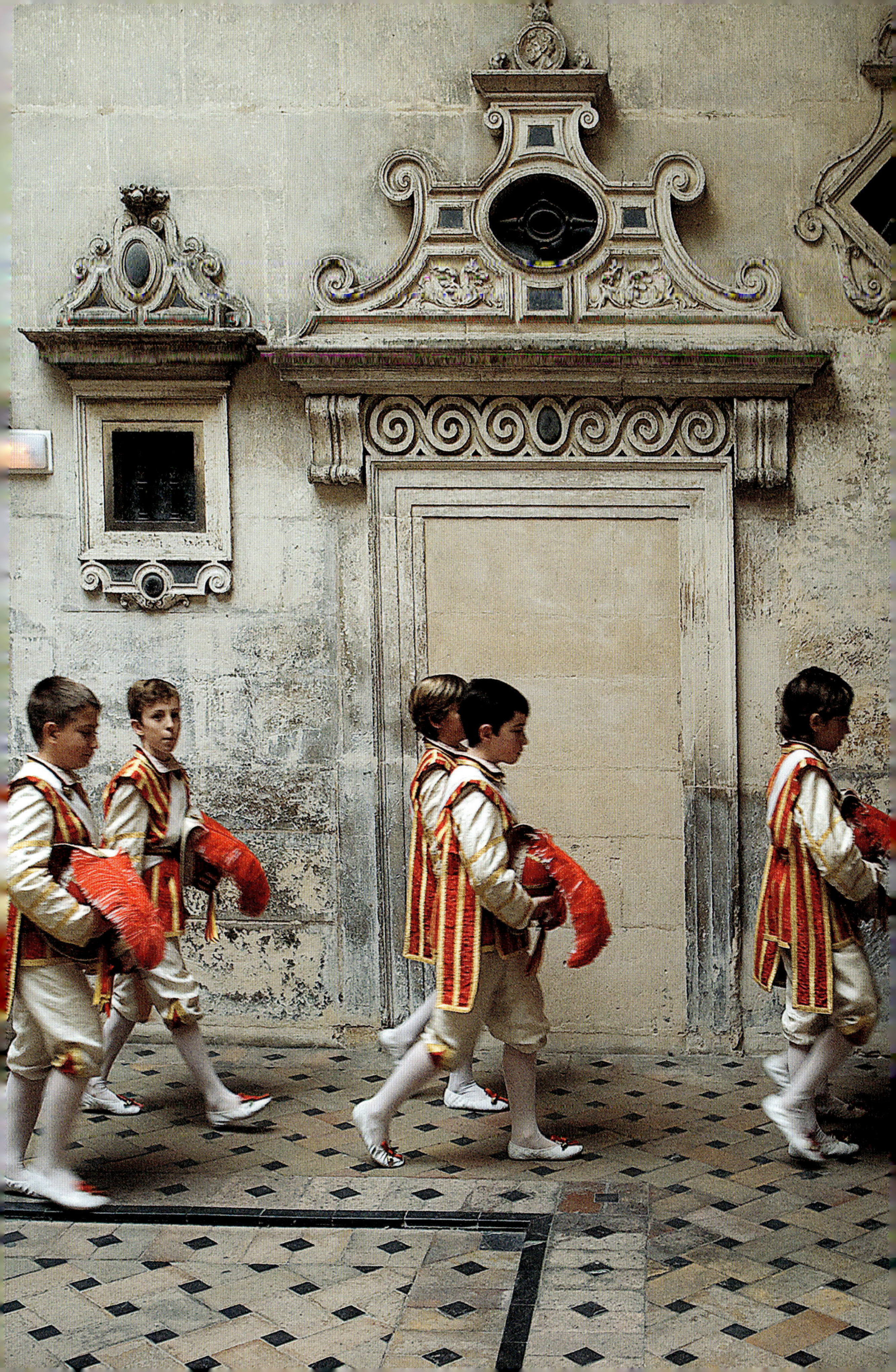

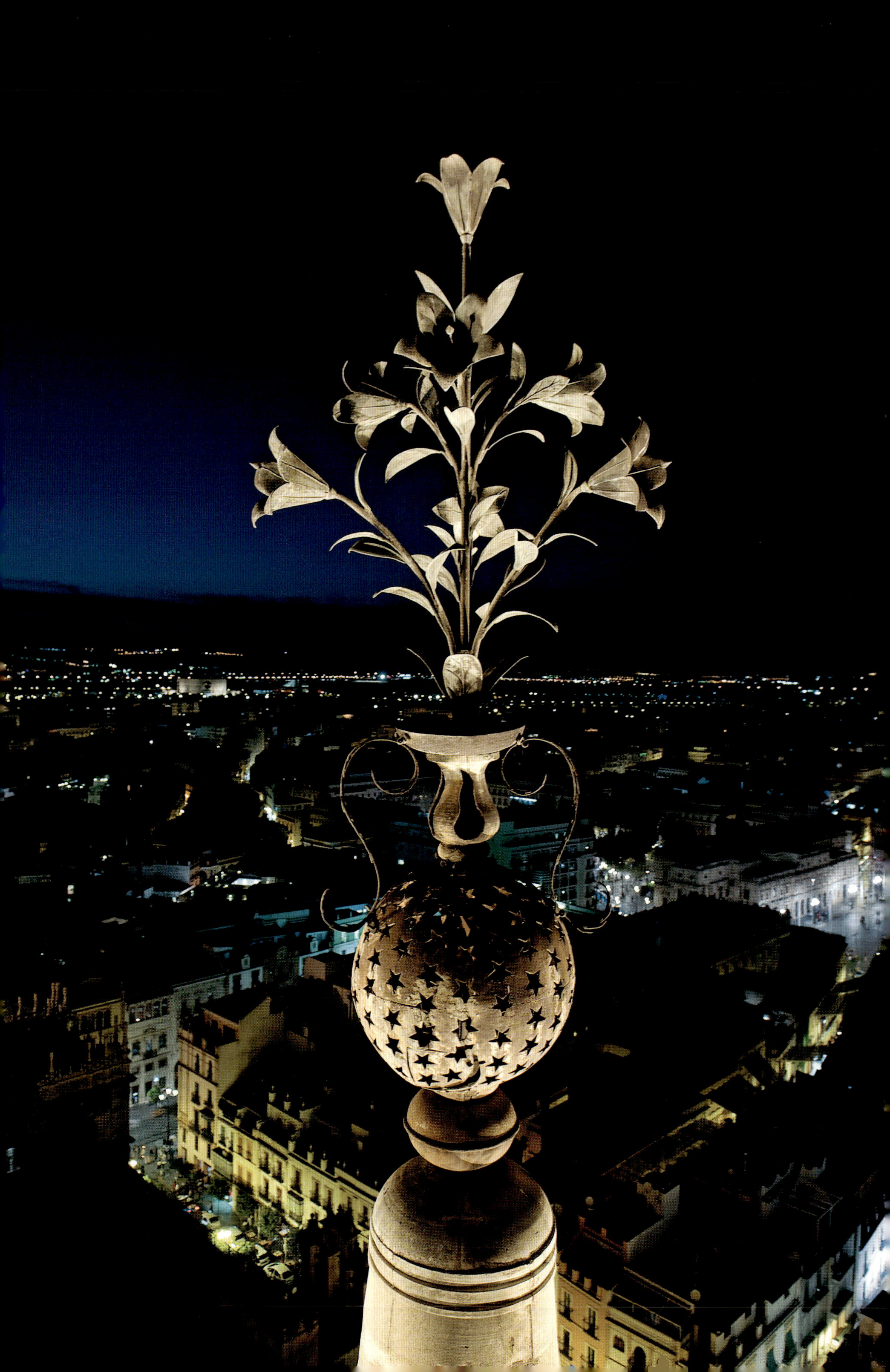

Clockwise from opposite: The Giralda's lily sculpture, with the city of Seville in the background; the cathedral's many chapels and spires create a multidimensional rooftop; the cathedral's roof at sundown; view of the chapel of the Virgen de los Reyes; detail of the *Giraldillo;* sun clock in the cathedral's Patio de los Naranjos; interior of the cathedral; the crucifixion seen from the clerestory; the San Miguel Portal of the cathedral, with statues by Lorenzo Mercadante de Bretaña.

> *The immense cathedral with its five naves is the largest Gothic edifice in Europe. The elliptical space of the Cabildo, created by Hernán Ruiz, is one of the most beautiful architectural works of the Renaissance.*
> UNESCO, DIVISION OF CULTURAL HERITAGE

Spiral staircase leading to the cathedral's roof.

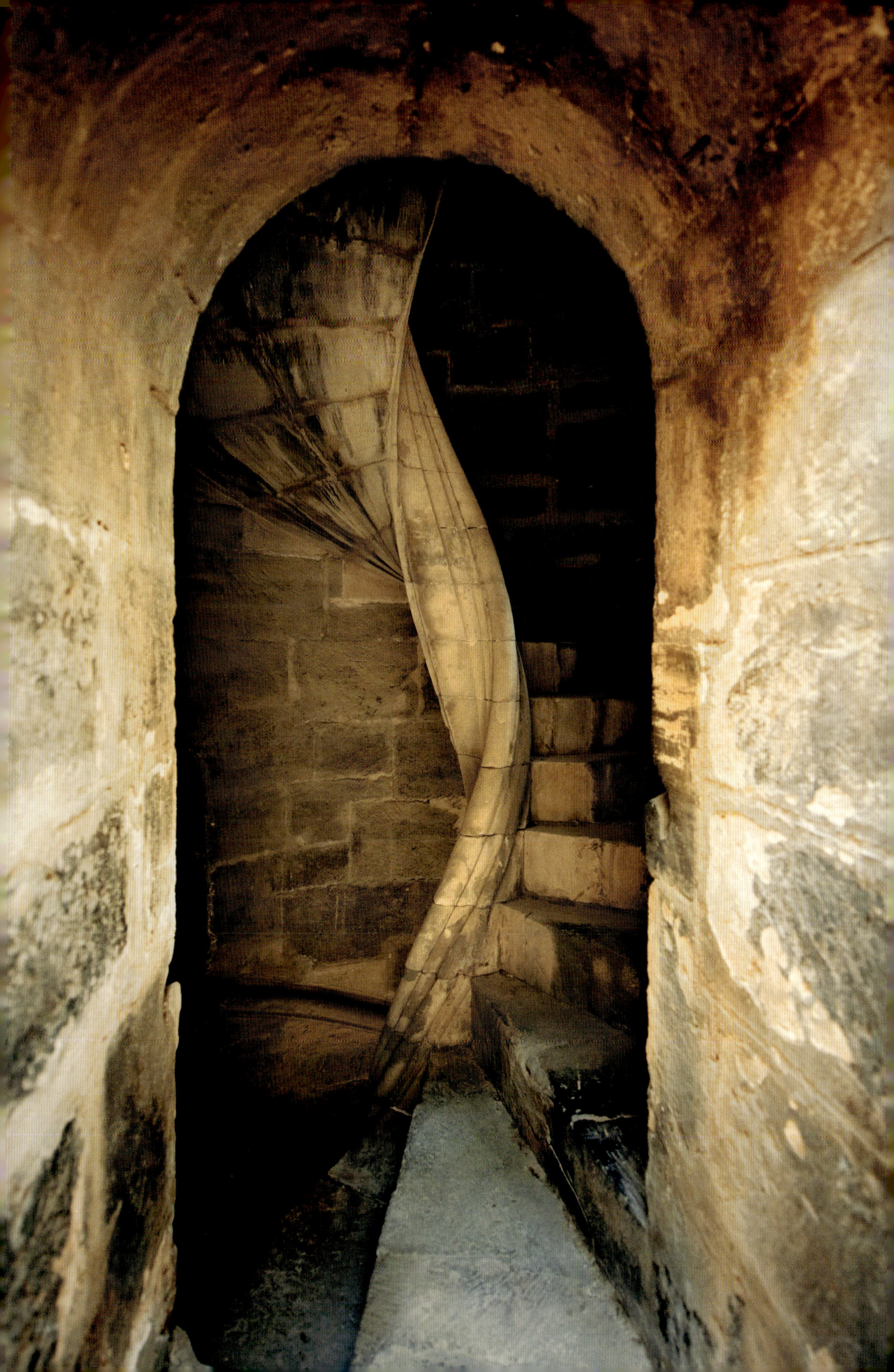

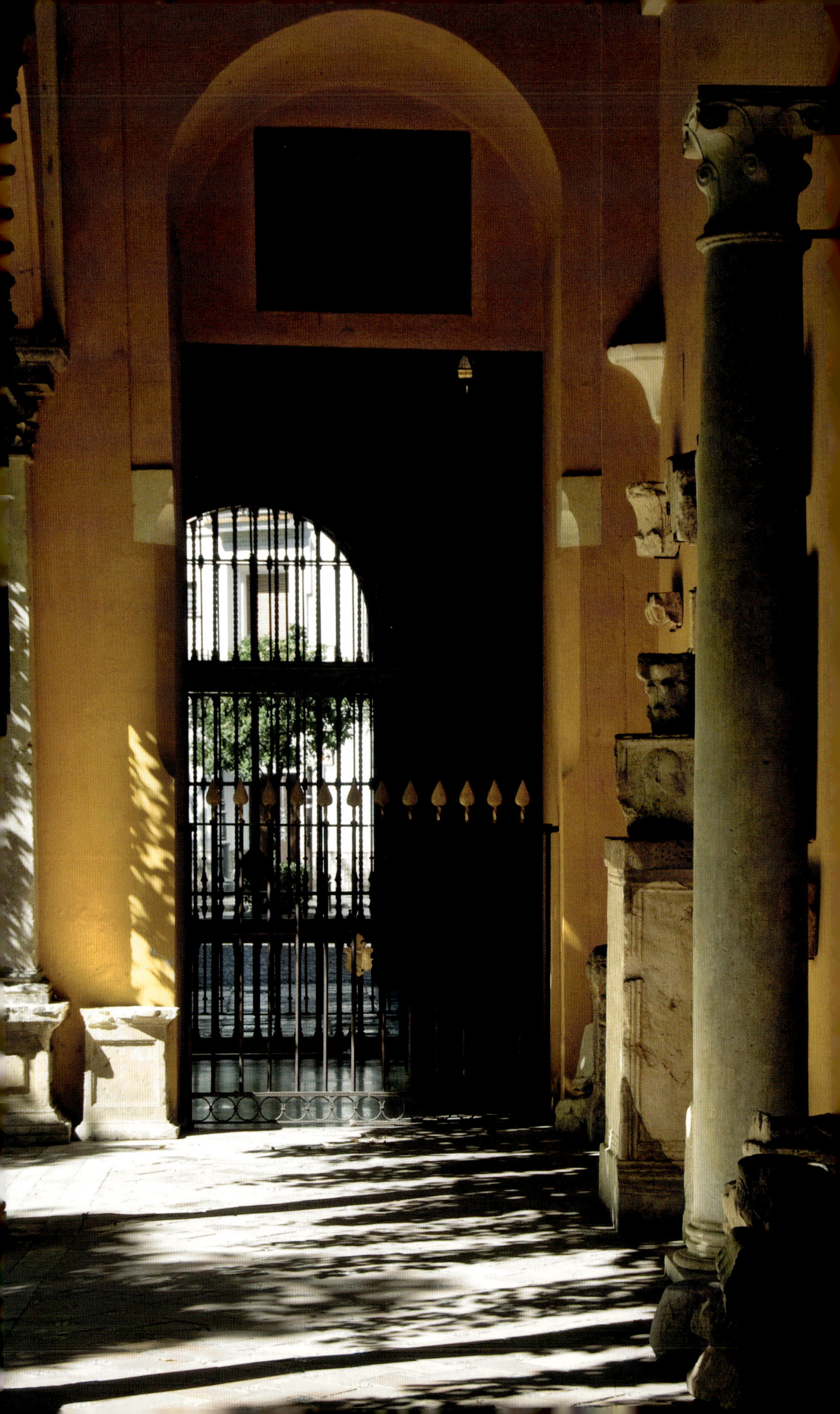

La Casa de Pilatos

One of Seville's most beautiful Renaissance-era structures, the Casa de Pilatos is an immaculately preserved expression of the region's architectural heritage.

In the fifteenth century, construction began on this complex of gardens and palaces, but it wasn't until the year 1520, when Don Fadrique Enríquez de Rivera, the first Marquis of Tarifa, returned from a trip through Europe and the Holy Land fascinated by the Renaissance that enriched Italian cities, that he decided to remodel the entire compound in a mix of Renaissance Italian and Mudéjar Spanish styles. The resulting design influenced the aesthetic path of much of Andalusia's architecture, particularly in Seville, for centuries.

The estate's name references Pontius Pilate, the former governor of Jerusalem who sentenced Jesus to be crucified. Some say Enríquez was inspired by a structure he saw on his trip to Jerusalem that is said to have belonged to Pilate. Others believe the complex was named for Pilate because, while in Jerusalem, Enríquez discovered that the distance between Pilate's house and Calvary, where Jesus had been crucified, was equal to the distance between his Seville house and the Cruz del Campo shrine on the outskirts of town. This discovery led Enríquez to initiate the Via Crucis processions that would come to characterize Holy Week in Seville.

The Casa de Pilatos is a monumental compound of great beauty, with a plethora of courtyards and gardens. In addition, the house invites artists to help restore its magnificent Renaissance paintings and ancient Roman sculptures—one dating back to the first century A.D., and others even earlier. The most magnificent part of the house is the main patio, with its stunning marble fountain and lavishly tiled walls, surrounded by the many grand balconies and the Moorish arcade that run around the interior of the structure.

Historic and majestic, the Casa de Pilatos has also been the setting for several films, from *Lawrence of Arabia* to Ridley Scott's *Kingdom of Heaven* and *1492: Conquest of Paradise*.

Today, even though the house serves as the private residence of the Dukes of Medinaceli, parts of this Andalusian treasure are open to visitors, who can explore its exquisite grounds.

A Roman bust in the Casa de Pilatos. *Left:* Courtyard in the Casa de Pilatos. *Following pages:* Fresco on a wall of the Casa de Pilatos showing the palace complex. *Pages 116–117:* Roman statue; bas-relief of the goddess Minerva's shield, with the head of Medusa.

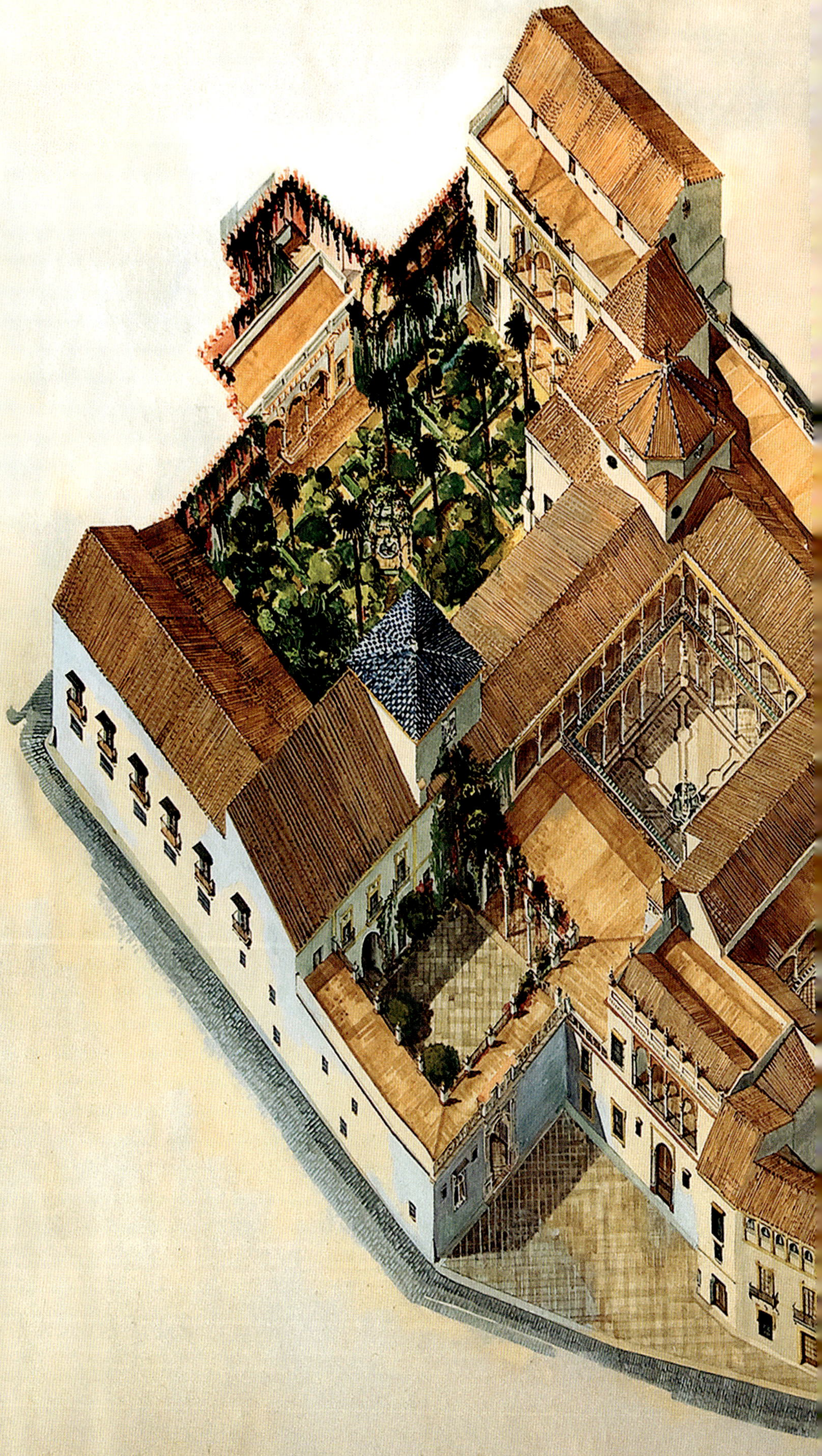

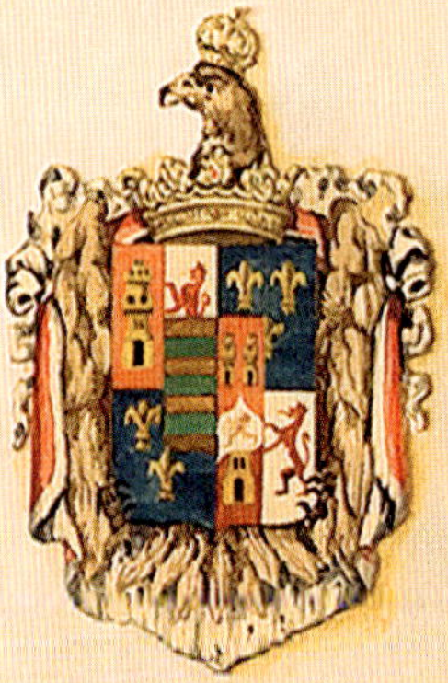

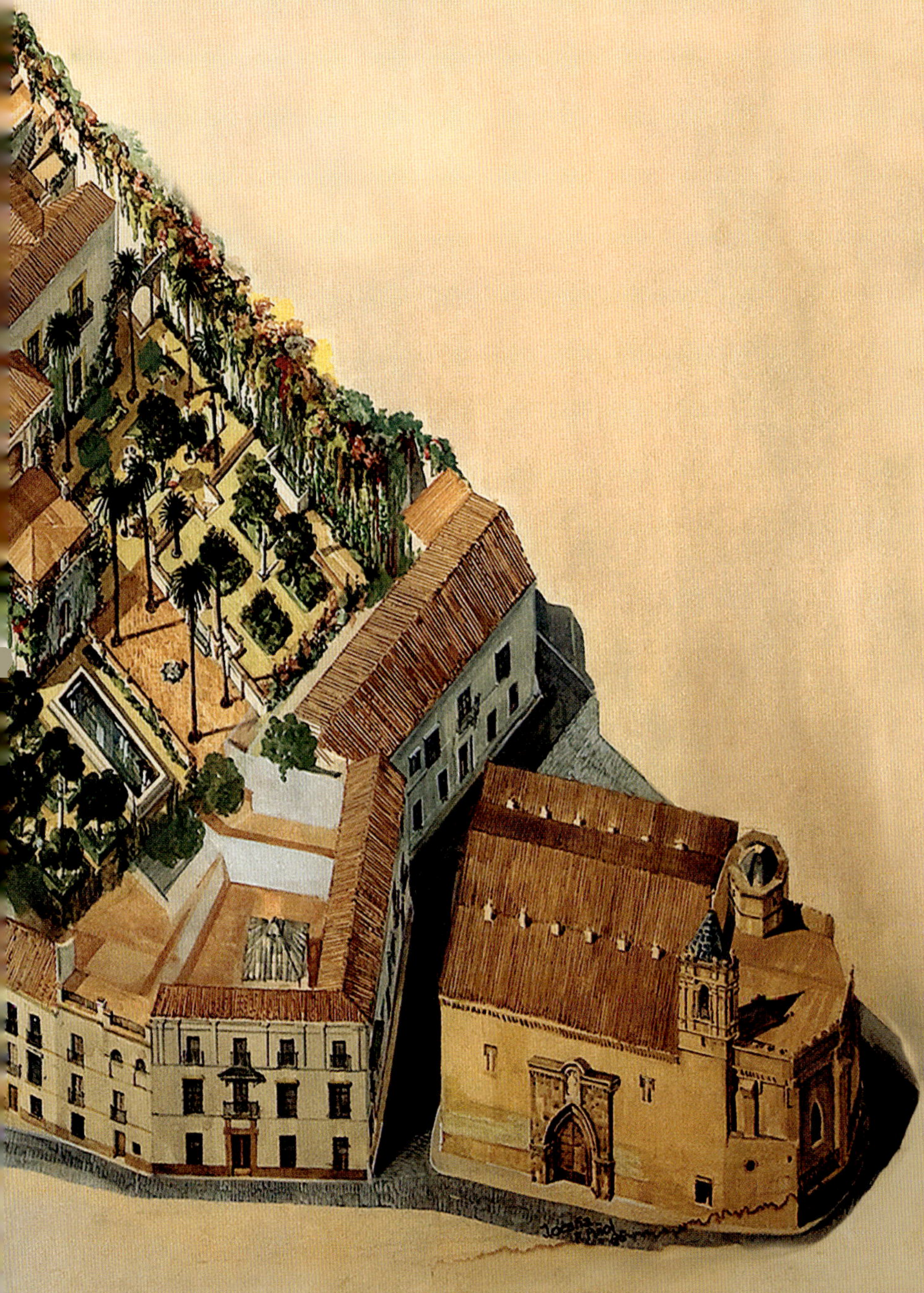

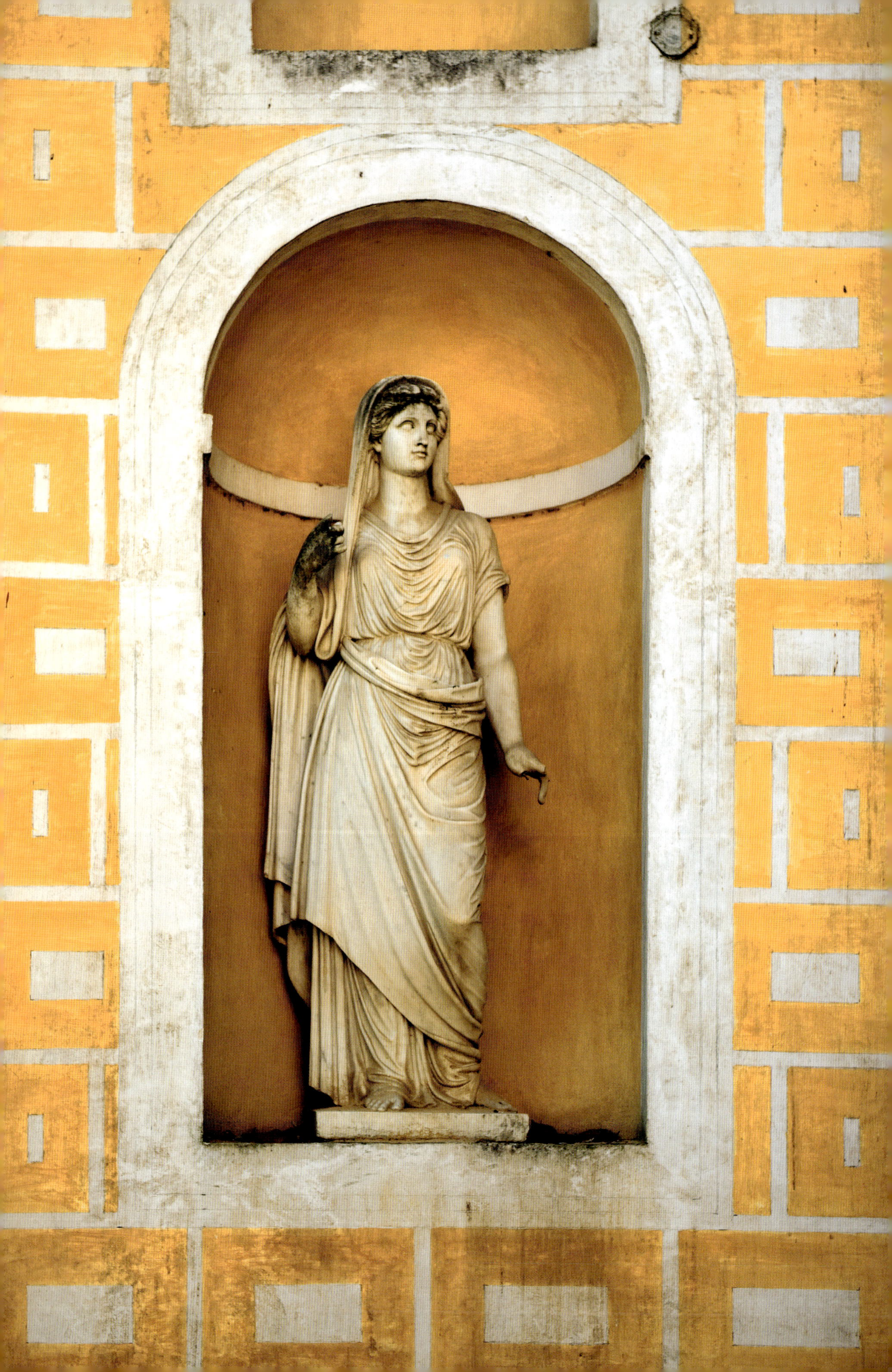

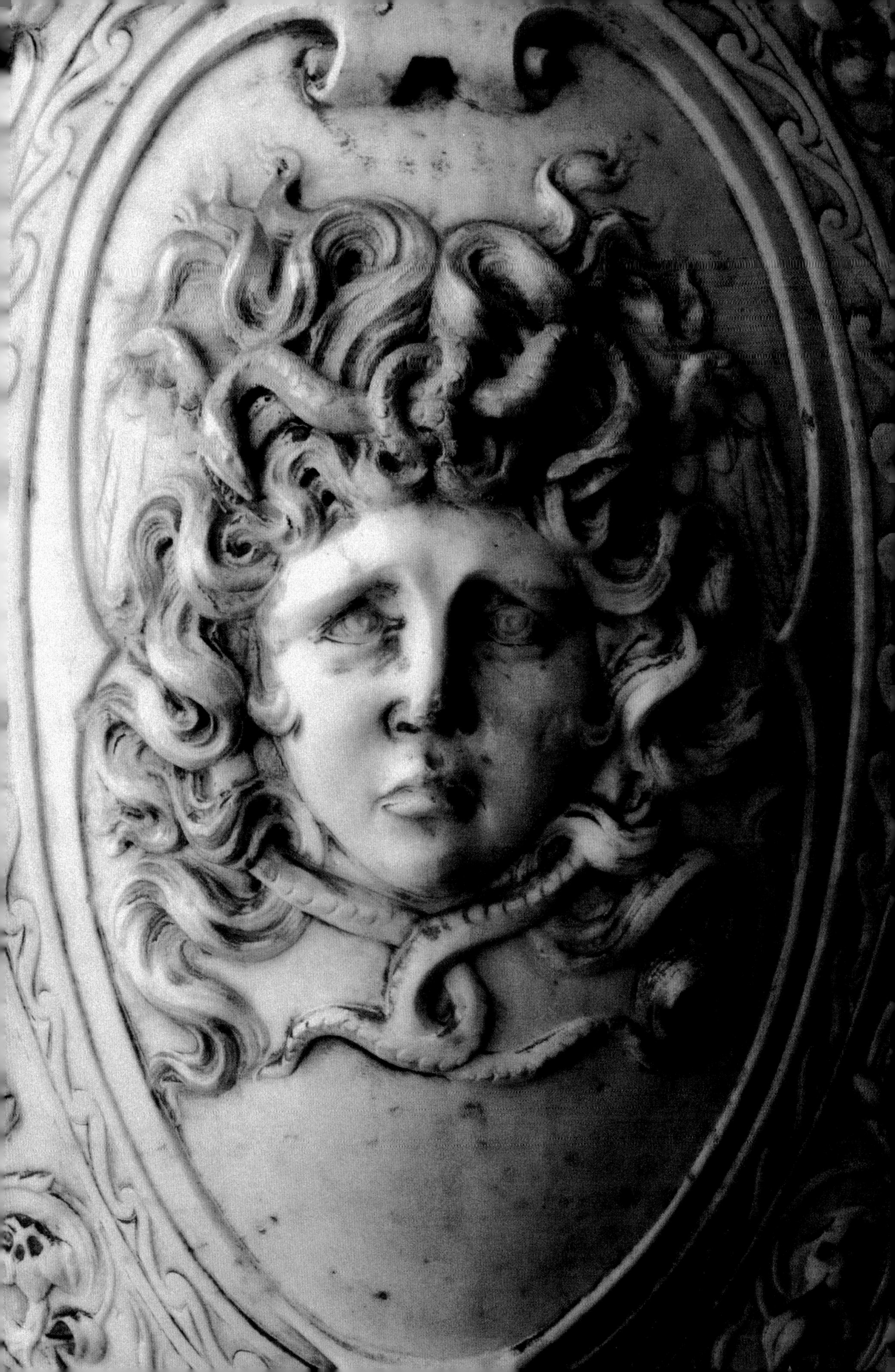

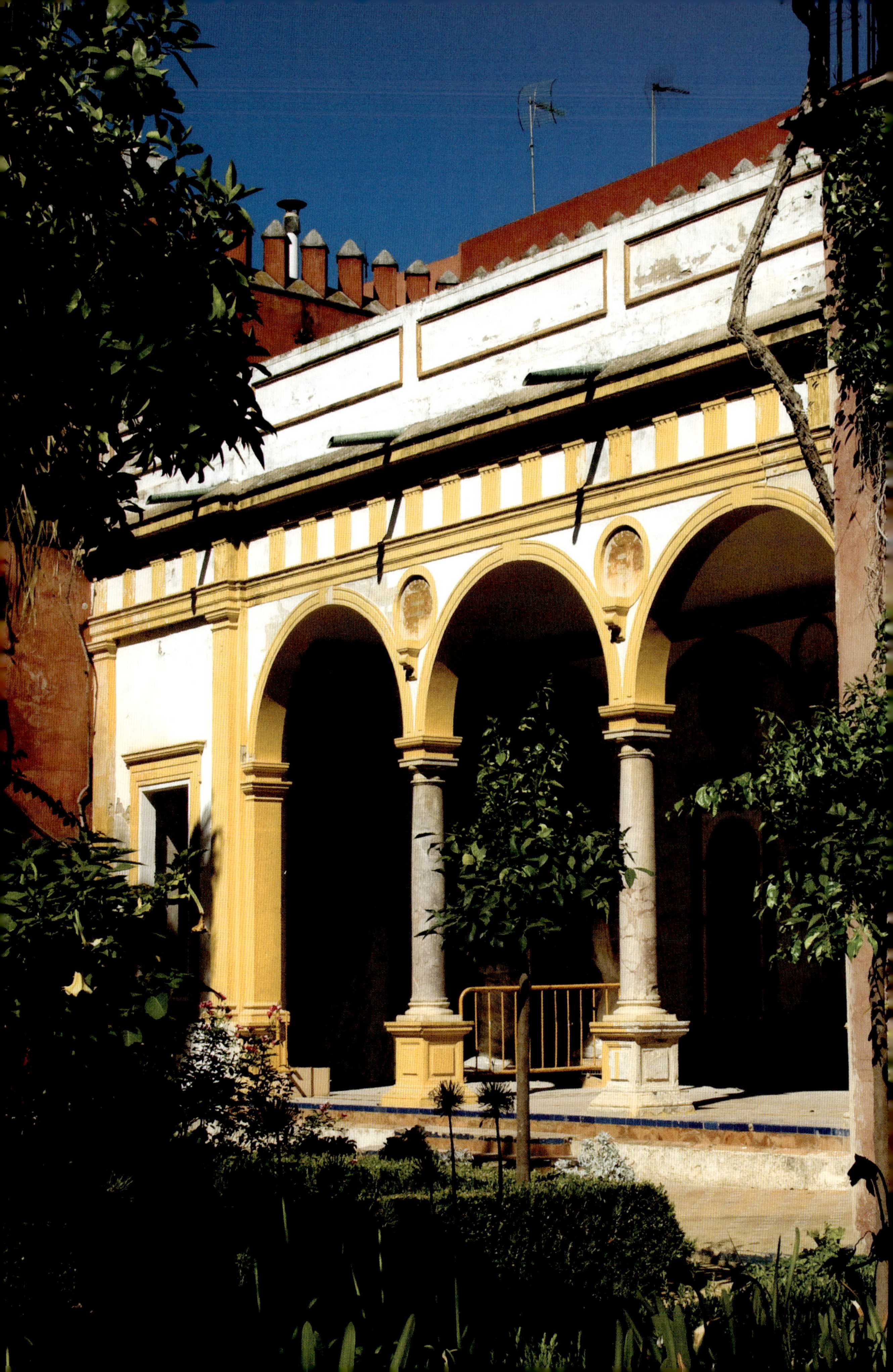

Clockwise from opposite: Loggia in one of the gardens in the Casa de Pilatos; a room containing Roman art; grotesque-style doorway; one of several tranquil gardens within Casa de Pilatos; a tile outside the Casa de Pilatos marks the first Station of the Cross and the beginning of the Vía Crucis during Holy Week; wedding reception in a courtyard; Roman statue in one of the courtyards; one of the beautiful rooms in the Casa de Pilatos.

PRIMERA ✠ ESTACION

AQVI SE CONTEMPLA QVANDO
XPT.° NRO. SR. LO SENTENCIA-
RON A MVERTE DE CRVZ. SE
RESTAVRA ESTE VIA CRVCIS EL
8 DE MARZO DEL AÑO MCMLVII
POR LOS EXCMOS. SRS. DVQVES
DE MEDINACELI. AMDG.

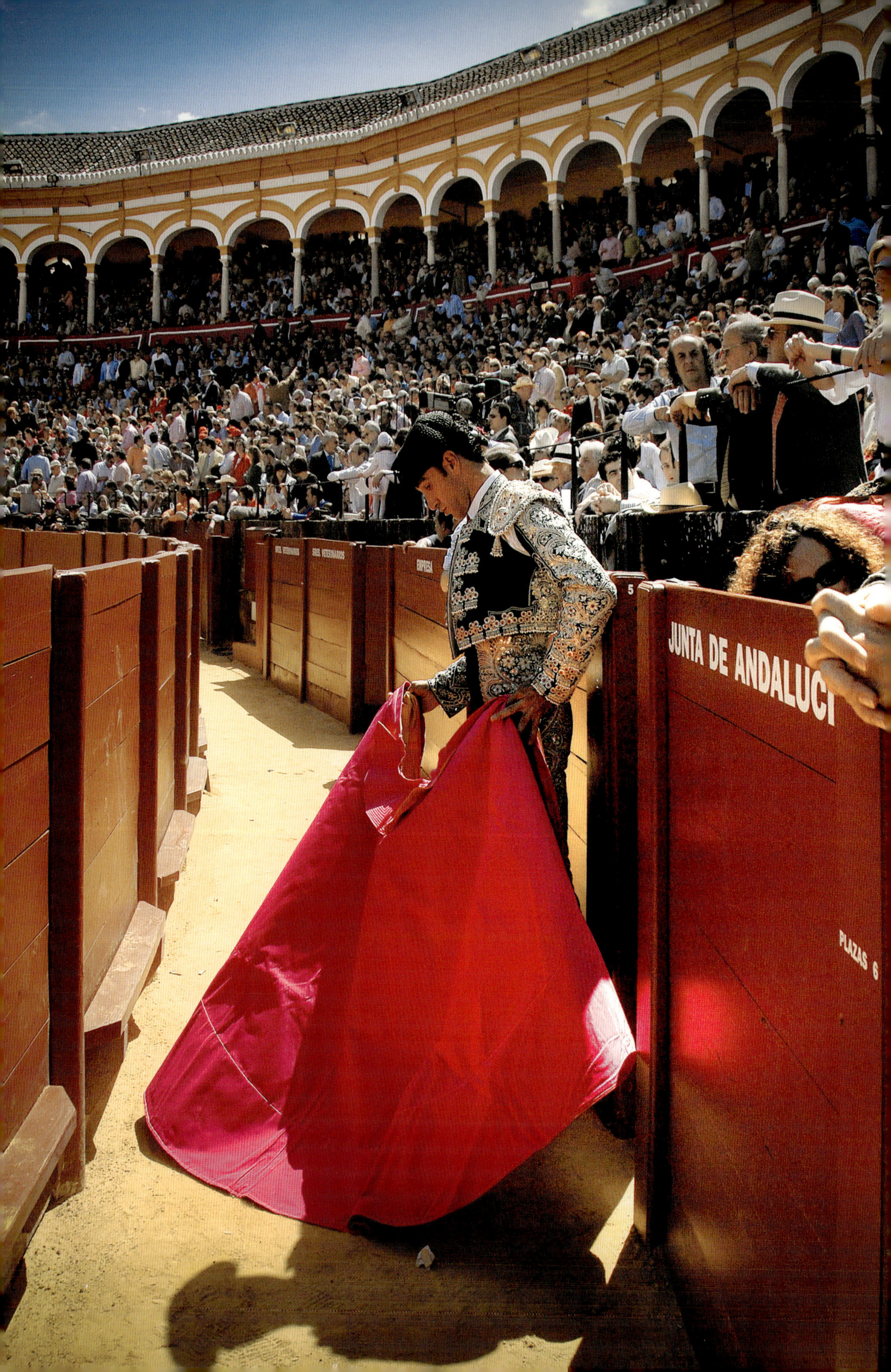
JUNTA DE ANDALUCI
PLAZAS 6

The Princes of Seville

The princes of Seville are not actors, athletes, or politicians. They are the matadors.

A tradition that has been a key part of Spanish heritage for millennia, bullfighting is a mysterious (and, today, controversial) sport that is closely tied to the Spanish soul, and especially to Seville, home of some of the world's most famous matadors as well as Spain's oldest bullring, the Plaza de Toros at the Real Maestranza de Caballería de Sevilla. The Spanish bullfighting season starts on Easter Sunday and continues through mid-October. Some of the world's most anticipated bullfights (corridas) take place during the April Fair, and people come from far and wide to see this unique spectacle in action.

The origins of Spanish bullfighting can be traced as far back as the Bronze Age: The Minoans believed in the mystical power of the bull, worshipping it and making it a central part of their religion, with animal sacrifices and rituals that involved grabbing a bull's horns and vaulting over it. By the eleventh century A.D., records note instances of noblemen on horseback fighting bulls with lances or javelins before audiences, as a form of entertainment. Today, these bullfighters have more in common with modern-day picadors, horsemen who assist the matador by poking the bulls near their shoulders and neck to weaken them.

It was in the first half of the eighteenth century that the basis of modern bullfighting was established in Spain, in which the horse-borne matador was replaced by one on foot. The rise of livestock breeding around that time led to the practice of selecting and mating bulls specifically for the corridas.

Originally, the bullfights were held in an open, public area. However, once the sport became more popular, it was necessary to build arenas (*plazas de toros*) to hold the events. These stadiums were circular in shape, so everyone in the audience would have a view of what was happening.

It was in the second half of the eighteenth century that the first bullfighting regulations were written, establishing the techniques and strict rules that define the art of bullfighting. All of the participants enter the bullring at the start of the fight, introducing themselves to the audience. The group includes two men who lead the players into the ring, three *matadores*, their flaggers, and the *picadores* on horseback. The *presidente* is the referee who calls all the shots and indicates when the bulls can be brought into the ring. Over the course of one corrida, each matador generally ends up

Matador preparing for a fight in the Maestranza's callejón before entering the bullring.
Following pages: The Prince's Gate at the Maestranza.

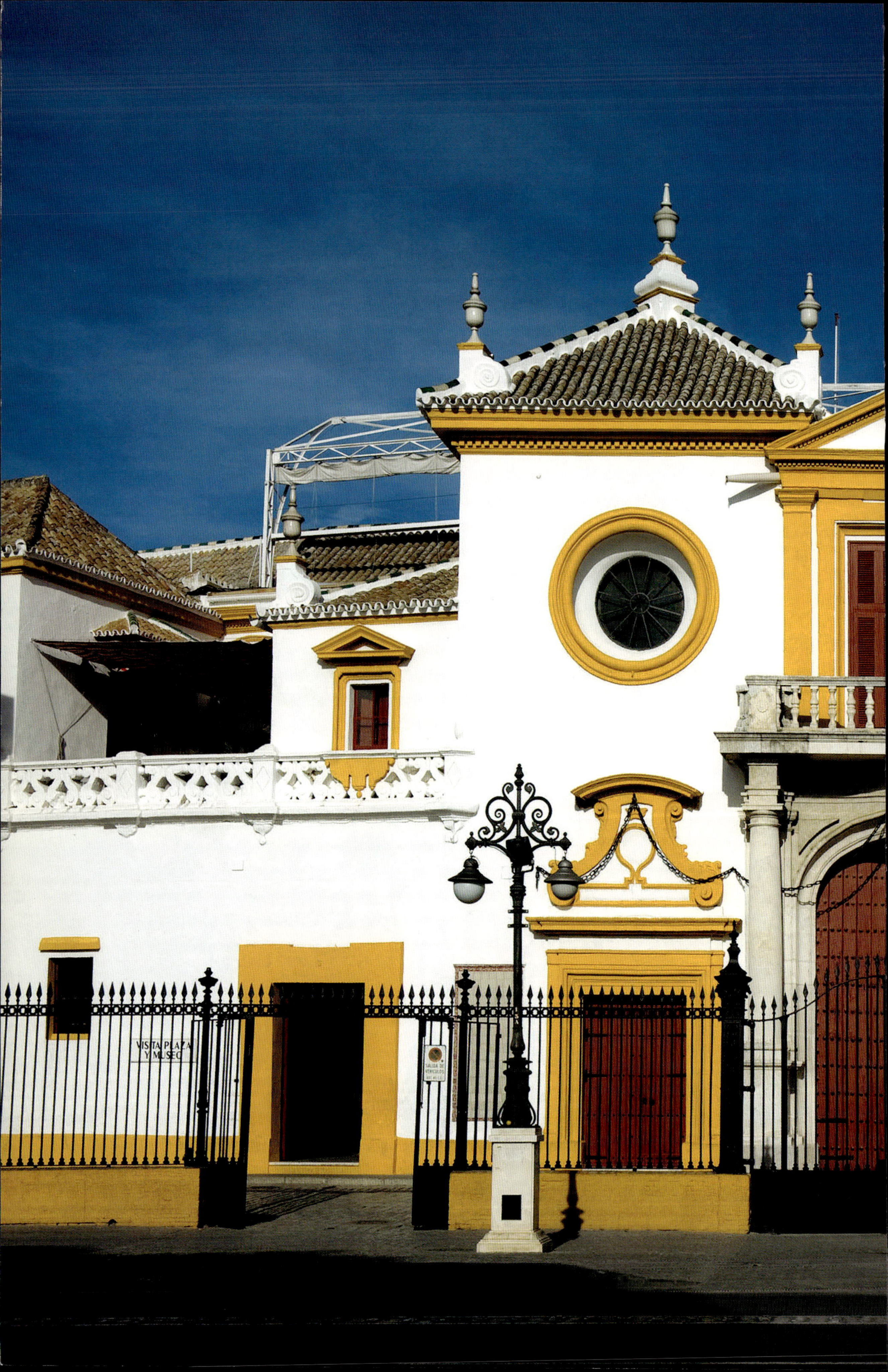

Nº 2

GRADAS SOMBRA-A y 2
PALCOS del 16 AL 36

RETIRADA GRUA

Nº 4

SOMBRA
BARRERAS
TENDIDOS 2-4-6
SILLON DE TENDIDO DEL 2 AL 166

Nº 6

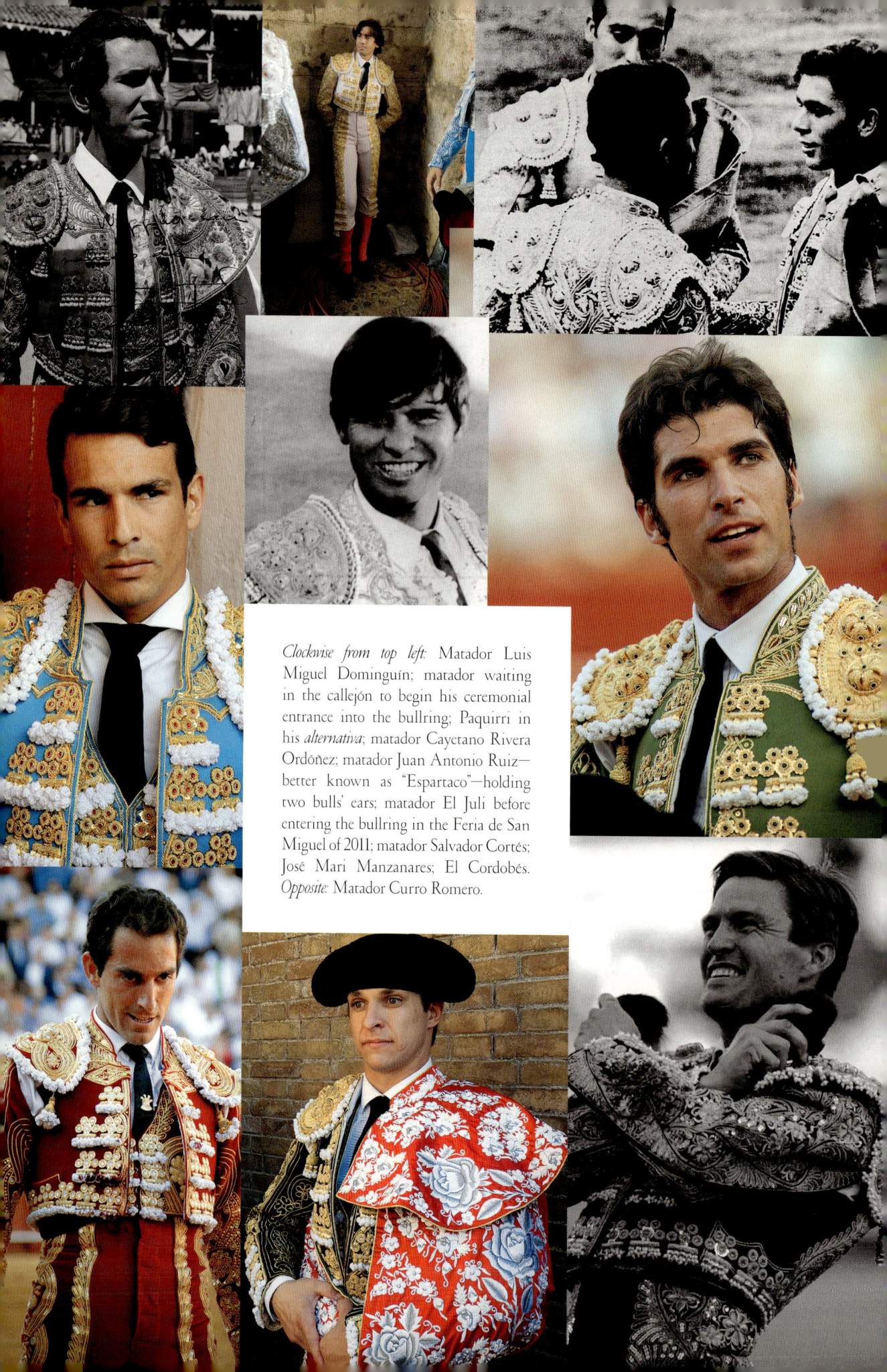

Clockwise from top left: Matador Luis Miguel Dominguín; matador waiting in the callejón to begin his ceremonial entrance into the bullring; Paquirri in his *alternativa*; matador Cayetano Rivera Ordóñez; matador Juan Antonio Ruiz— better known as "Espartaco"—holding two bulls' ears; matador El Juli before entering the bullring in the Feria de San Miguel of 2011; matador Salvador Cortés; José Mari Manzanares; El Cordobés. *Opposite:* Matador Curro Romero.

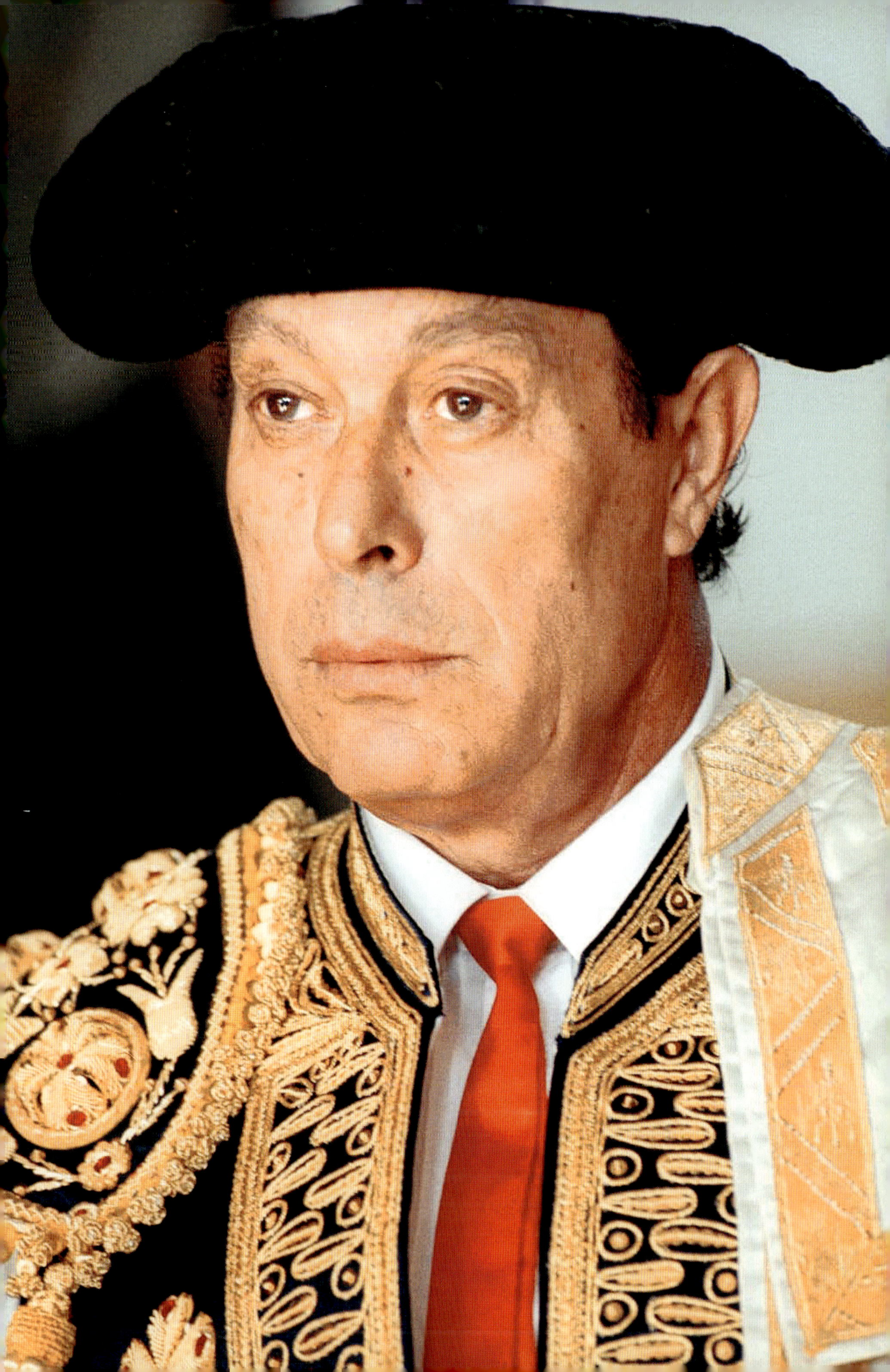

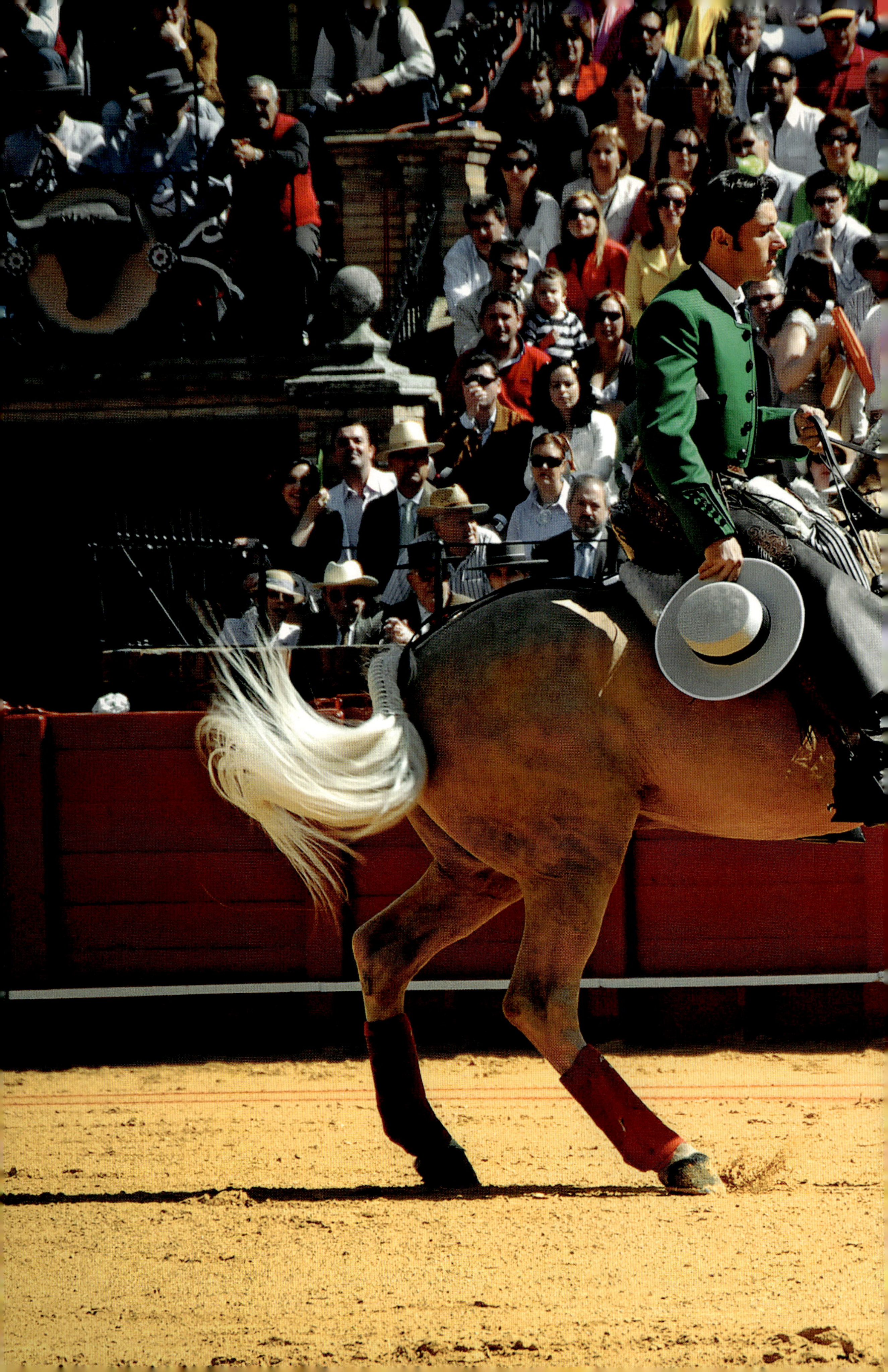

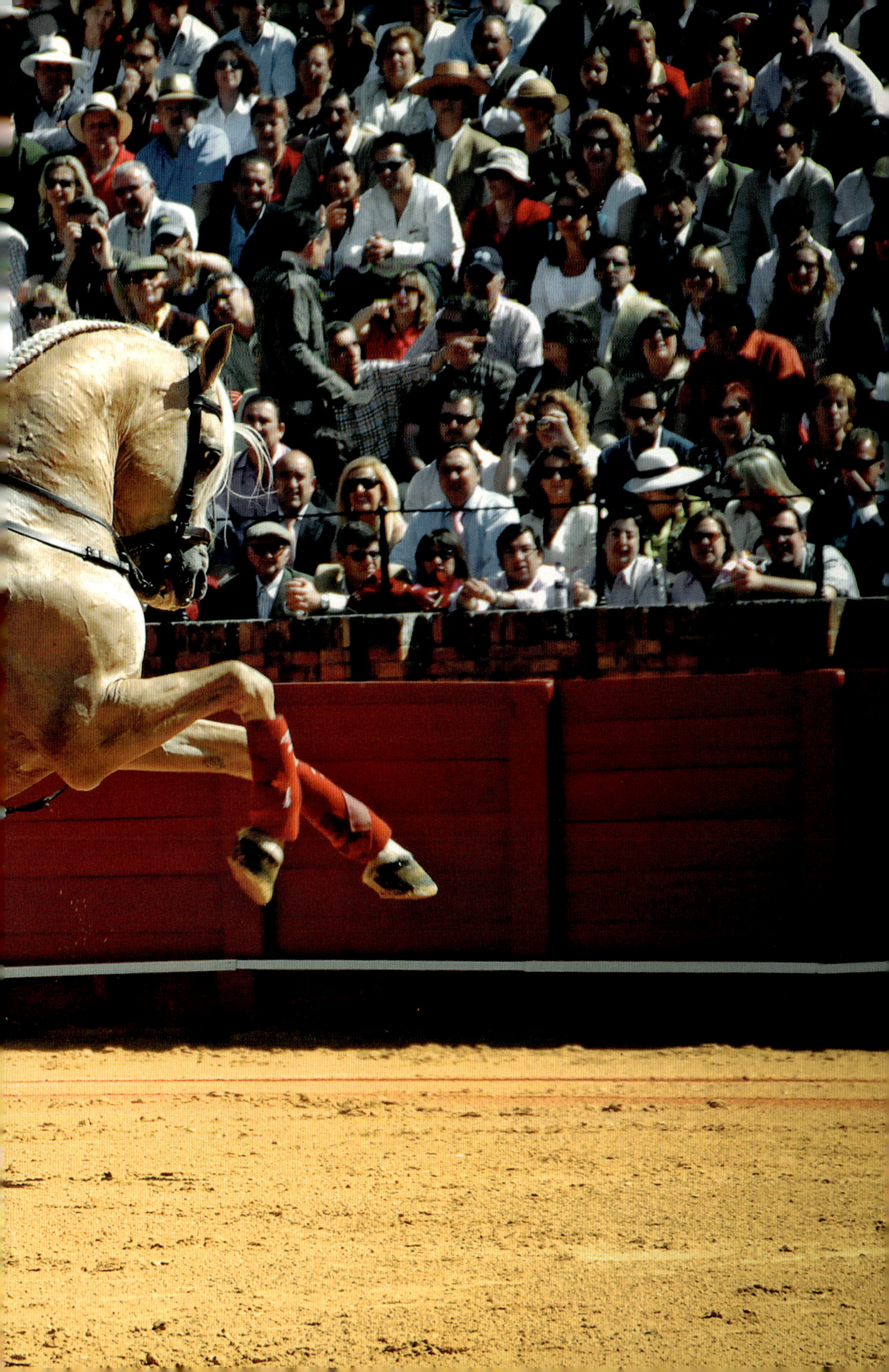

fighting two bulls. The bullfights are divided into three acts, and the matador claims his victory at the end of the third act.

In Spain, toreros truly are treated like princes, revered by the public for their talent and charisma in the ring. Some of the most famous include the legendary Belmonte, Joselito, and Manolete, as well as Curro Romero, Espartaco, Morante de la Puebla, José Tomás, Juan José Padilla, the late Francisco Rivera Pérez (known as Paquirri)—who was killed during a fight in 1984—and his two sons, Francisco Rivera Ordóñez and Cayetano Rivera Ordóñez. Most recently, thirty-one-year-old José María Manzanares, the latest generation of a family of celebrated *toreros* who made his debut in the ring at the age of nineteen, has become a bona fide celebrity in Spain.

Although bullfighting remains popular today, there is a considerable amount of controversy surrounding the tradition. Some feel the practice is an art form essential to Spanish culture, but others believe it to be an archaic and cruel ritual. In fact, following legislation on animal cruelty, bullfighting has been banned in many parts of Spain, most notably in Catalonia in 2012. Regardless, it represents an important and significant part of Seville's history.

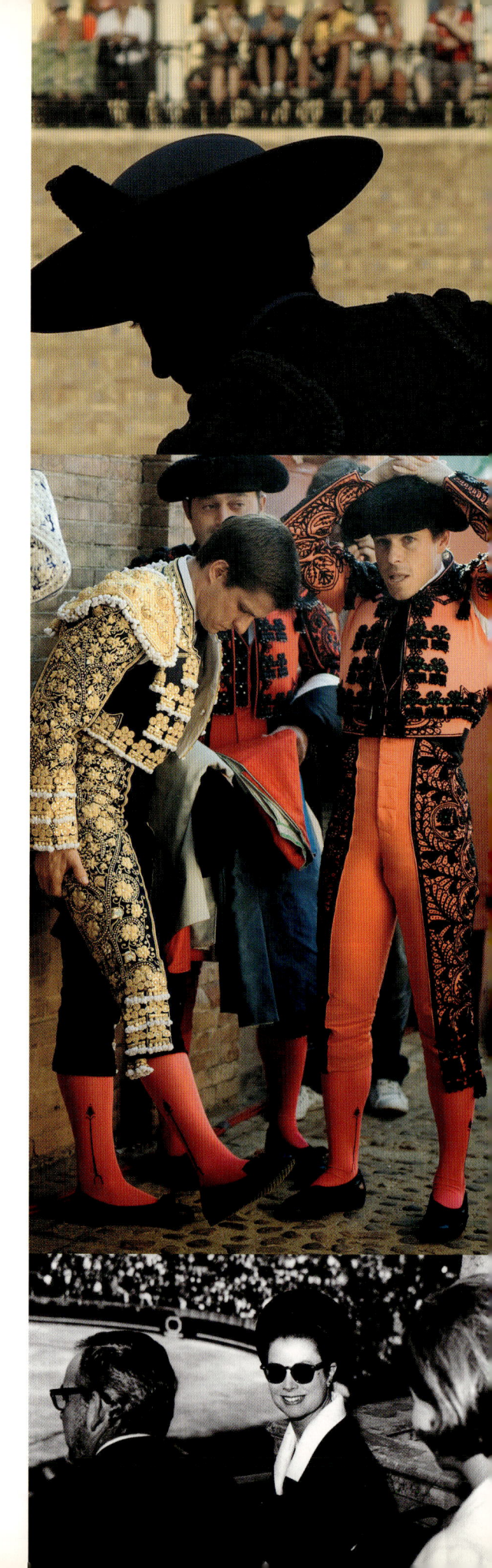

Previous pages: Matador Diego Ventura on horseback.

Clockwise from opposite, top left: Silhouette of a picador; bullfighters preparing the *paseíllo* that start the *corrida*; Ava Gardner watches a bullfight during the April Fair, 1964; Ernest Hemingway at a bullfight in Seville, 1964; beckoning the bull, matador Manzanares; Grace Kelly, El Juli with an assistant entering the bullring in the Feria de San Miguel of 2011.

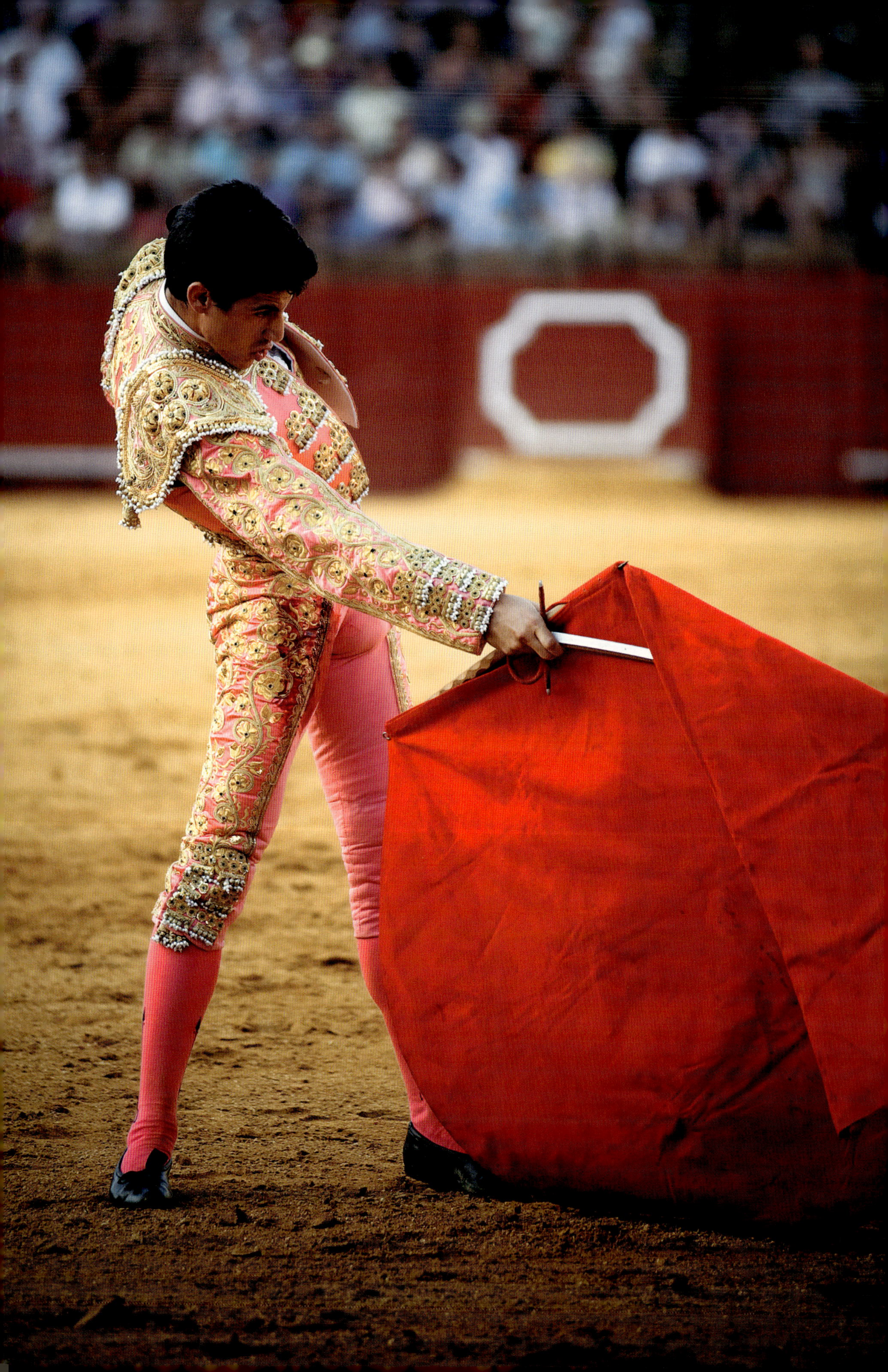

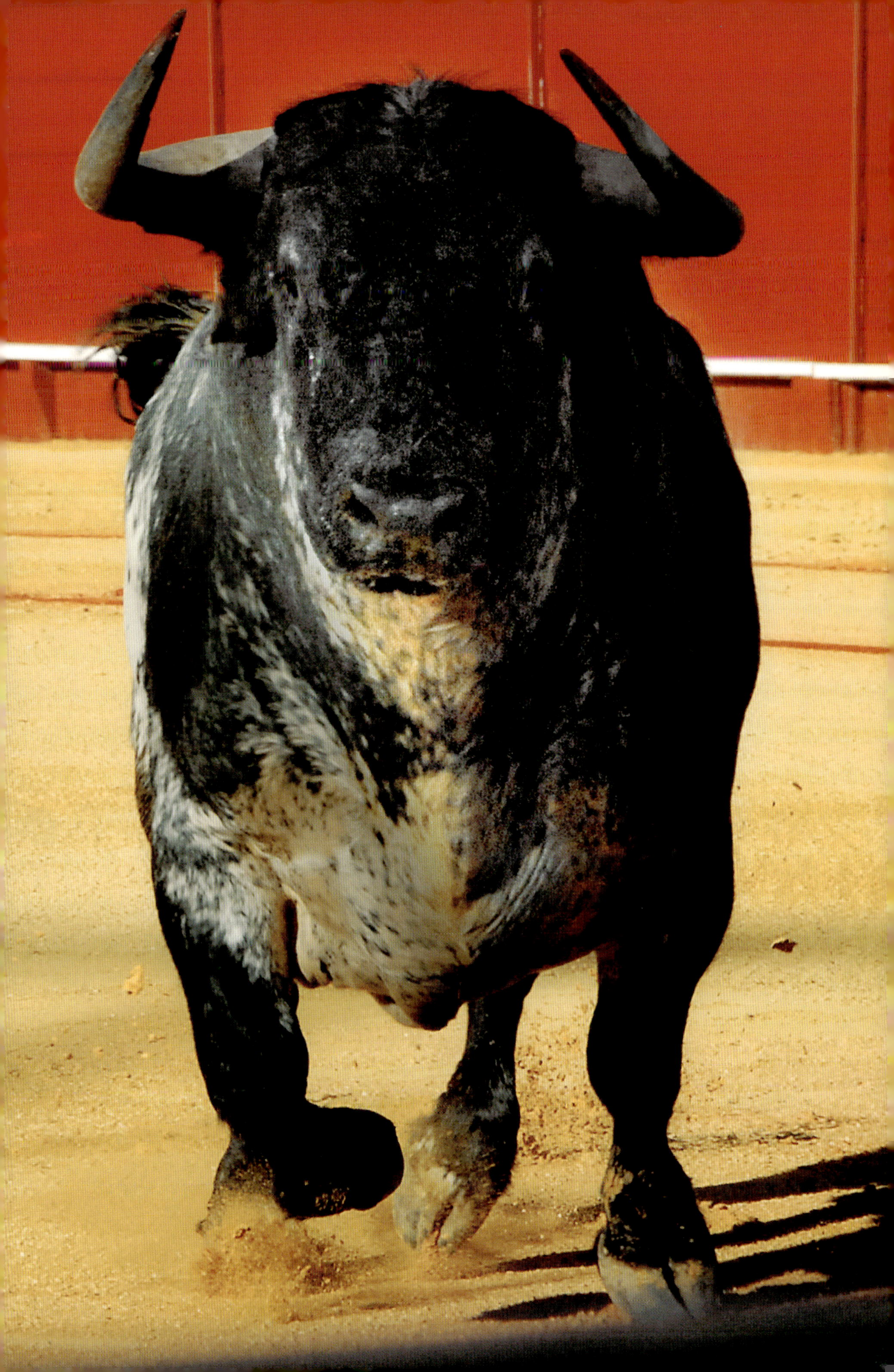

> *The history of bullfighting is so tied to Spain's history that without knowing about the former, it is impossible to understand the latter.*
> JOSÉ ORTEGA Y GASSET

Matador Morante de la Puebla. *Previous pages:* During the third and final act of the bullfight, the matador uses a traditional red cape and a sword to lure the bull and to claim his victory.

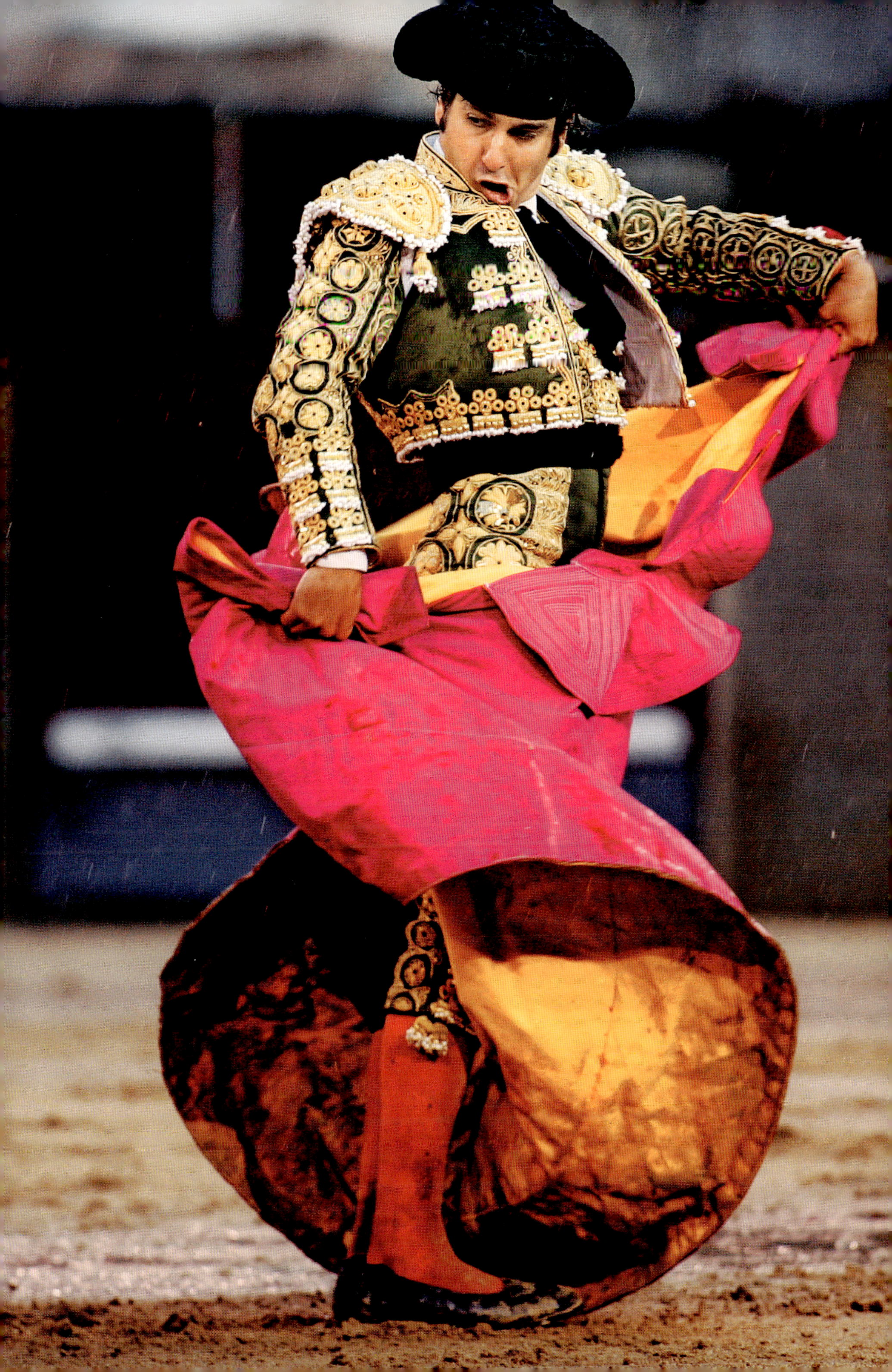

Flamenco

"The Gypsy epitomizes the loftiest, the most profound, the most aristocratic characteristics of my country; he is the most representative of its way of living, the keeper of the flame, the blood, and the alphabet of a truth both Andalusian and universal."
—Federico Garcia Lorca

Flamenco is the true heart of Seville. It is the language that Seville speaks, the voice with which it sings, and inspiring to all, regardless of ethnicity or religion. In fact, in November 2010, UNESCO declared flamenco to be part of the Intangible Cultural Heritage of Humanity.

This musical form became popular in the eighteenth century. A mix of Moorish, Judeo-Sephardic, gypsy, and native Andalusian musical styles, flamenco is an art that encompasses both song and dance to express the soul and spirit of the region.

Flamenco is most often associated with and credited to the gypsy culture; throughout the twentieth century and today, flamenco has been synonymous with Andalusian gypsies. Gypsies, members of the Romani ethnic group, are wanderers who live in every corner of the world. Yet only in Andalusia do they add their voices, their costumes, and their melodies to the rhythms left behind by the Moors, allowing for this truly unique mixture, this melding of cultures through music, to take place.

Like many of Spain's unique art forms, the central idea behind flamenco is the *duende*, which roughly translates as the "soul," the spirit of evocation, that connects emotion and expression in performance and elicits a visceral, physical response from the audience. Perhaps not surprisingly, then, most of those who are considered truly skilled in the art of flamenco are in their forties and fifties; younger people rarely have the maturity required to truly comprehend and convey the *duende* of the form.

Singing (*cante*), guitar playing (*toque*), and dance (*baile*) are the main facets of flamenco. The singing is very unique and complex. Flamenco singers are called *cantaores* and *cantaoras*, and their voices seem to break and tear, reaching extraordinary levels of expression.

Likewise, the toque is a very particular way of playing the guitar, with distinctive strumming patterns, postures, and tones. Originally, the guitar simply accompanied the singer, but it has become

Flamenco lessons at the Cristina Heeren Flamenco Foundation. *Following pages:* Dancing Sevillanas during the April Fair. *Pages 138–139:* Francisco Bernier, director of the International Guitar Festival of Seville; flamenco *cantaora* at the Lope de Vega theater festival.

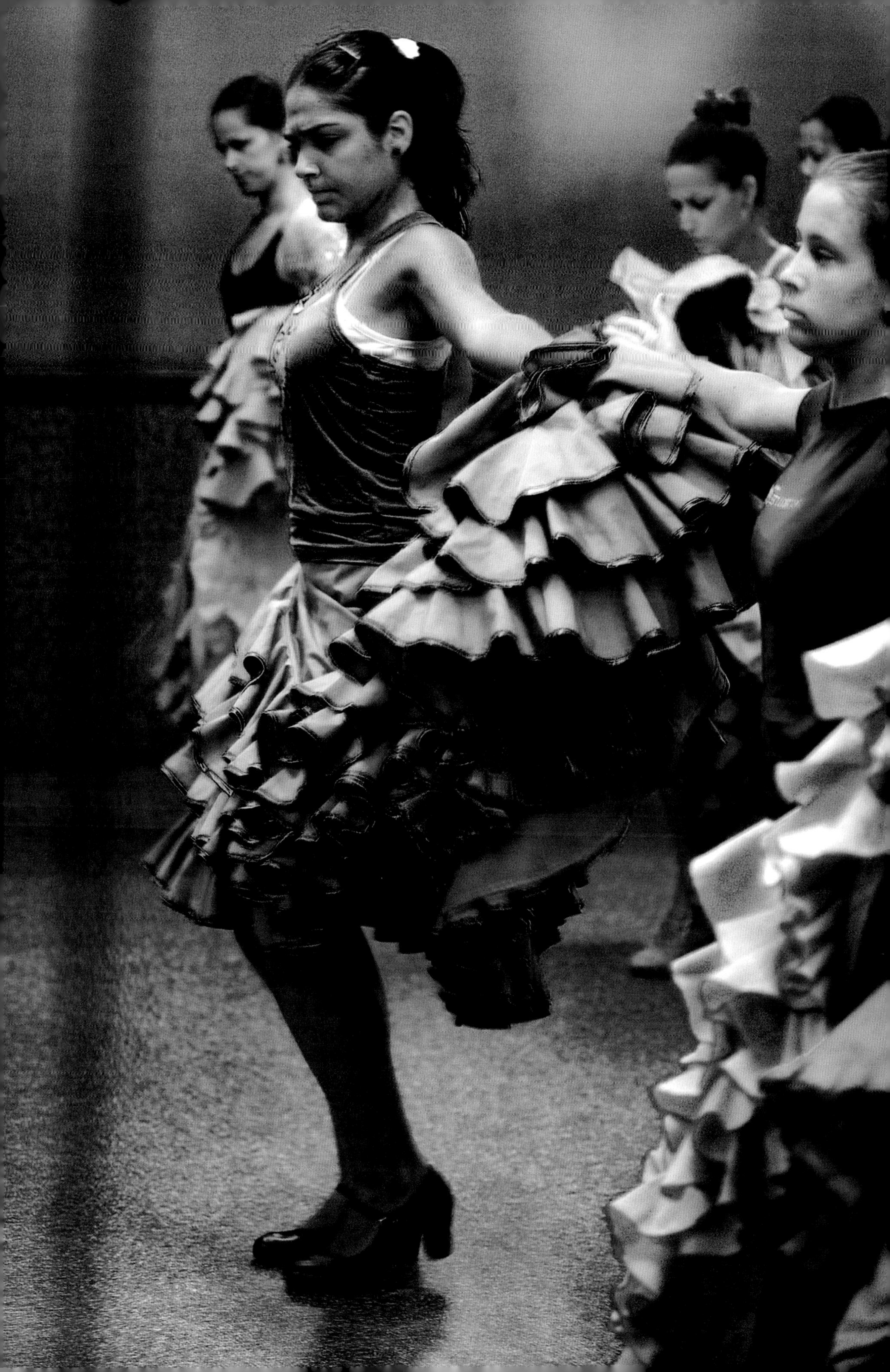

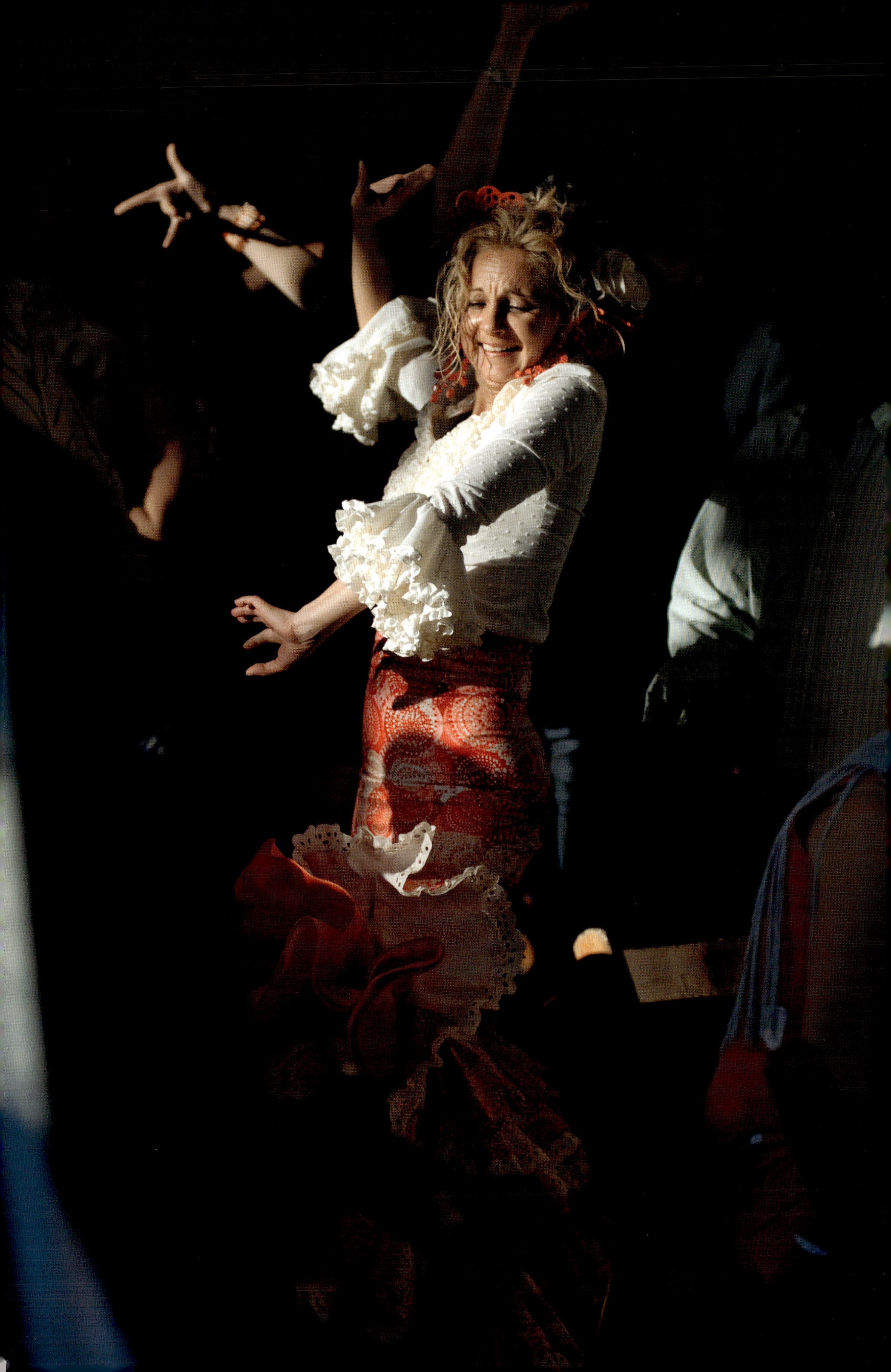

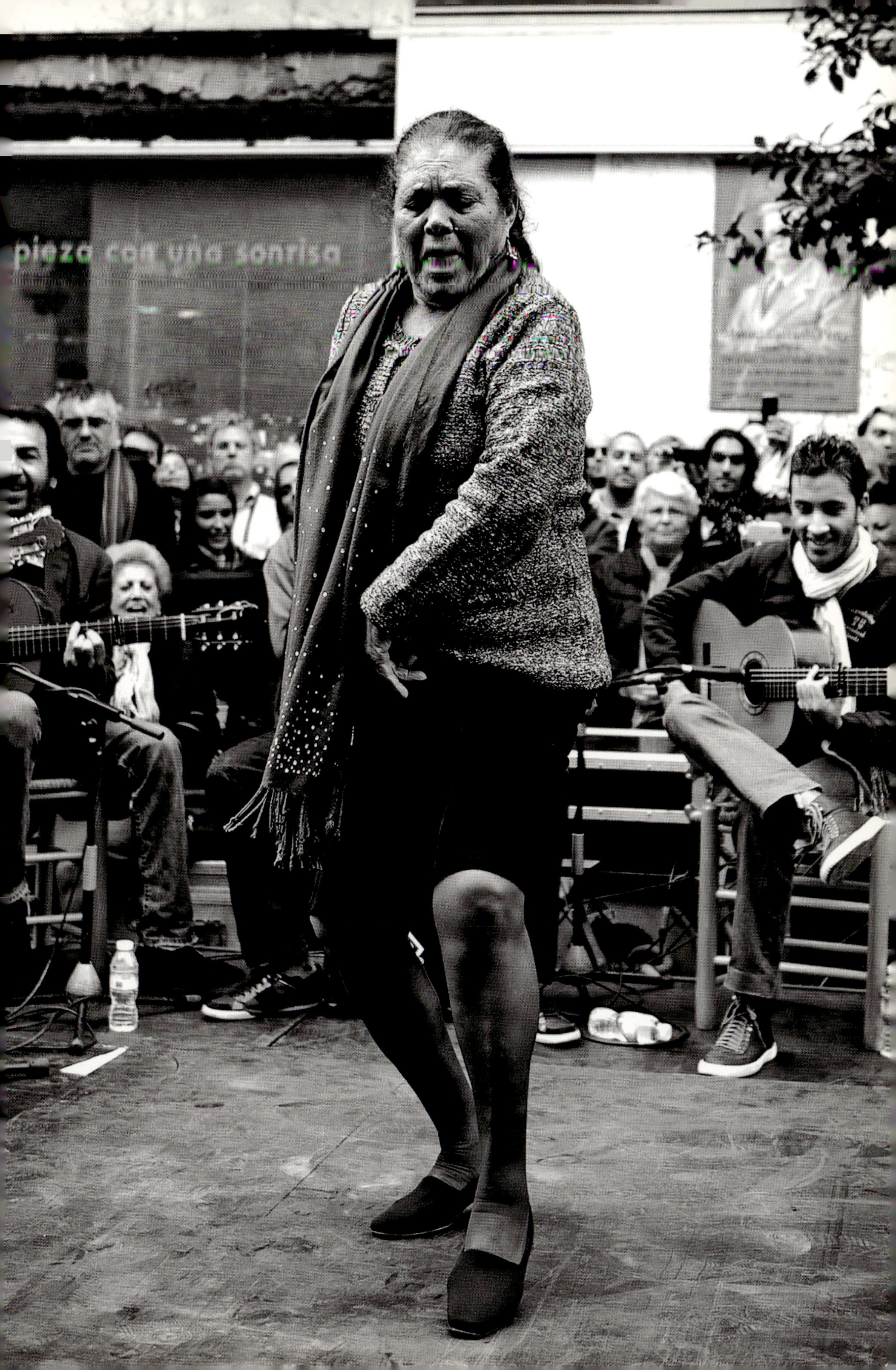
pizza con una sonrisa

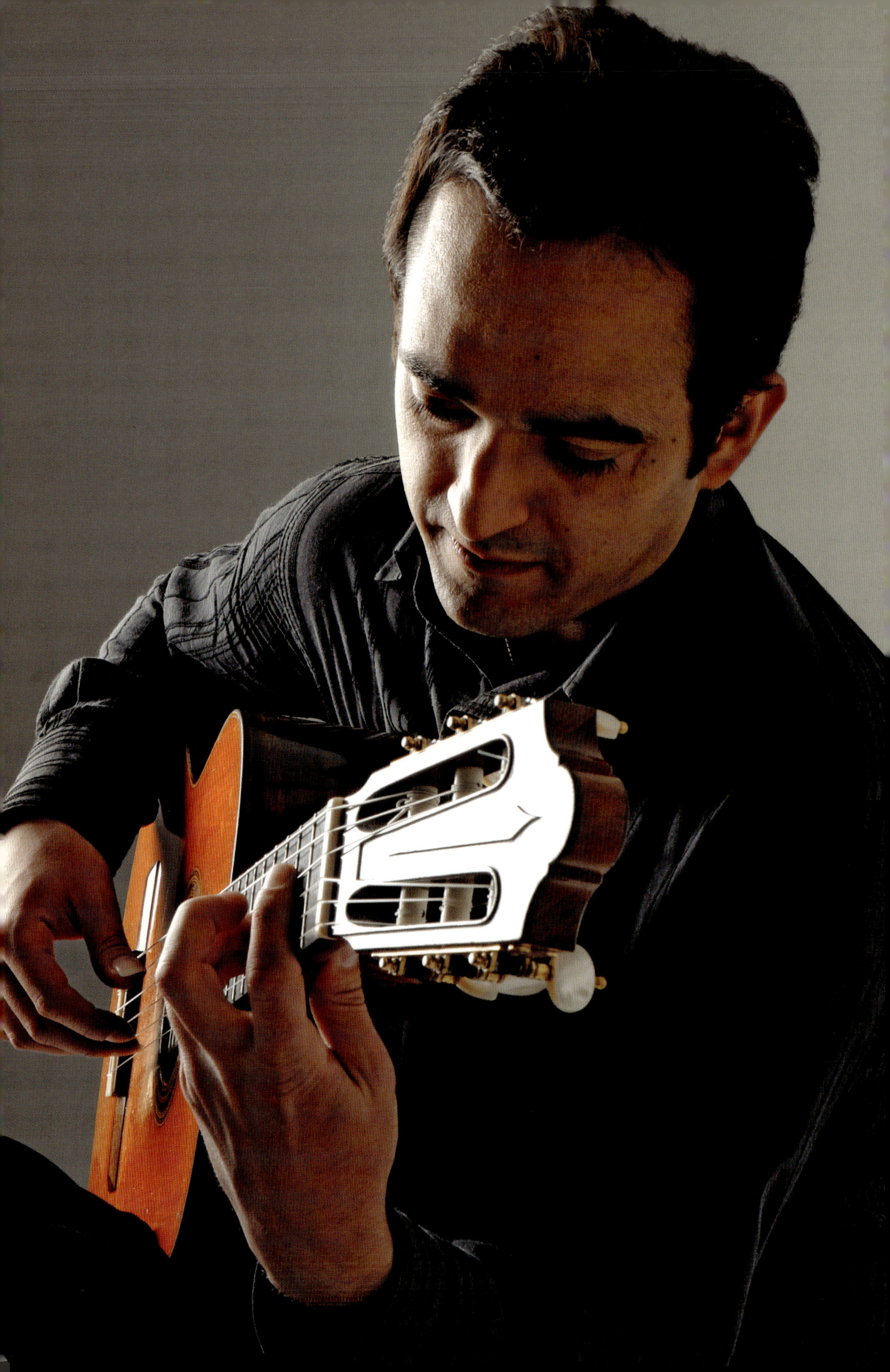

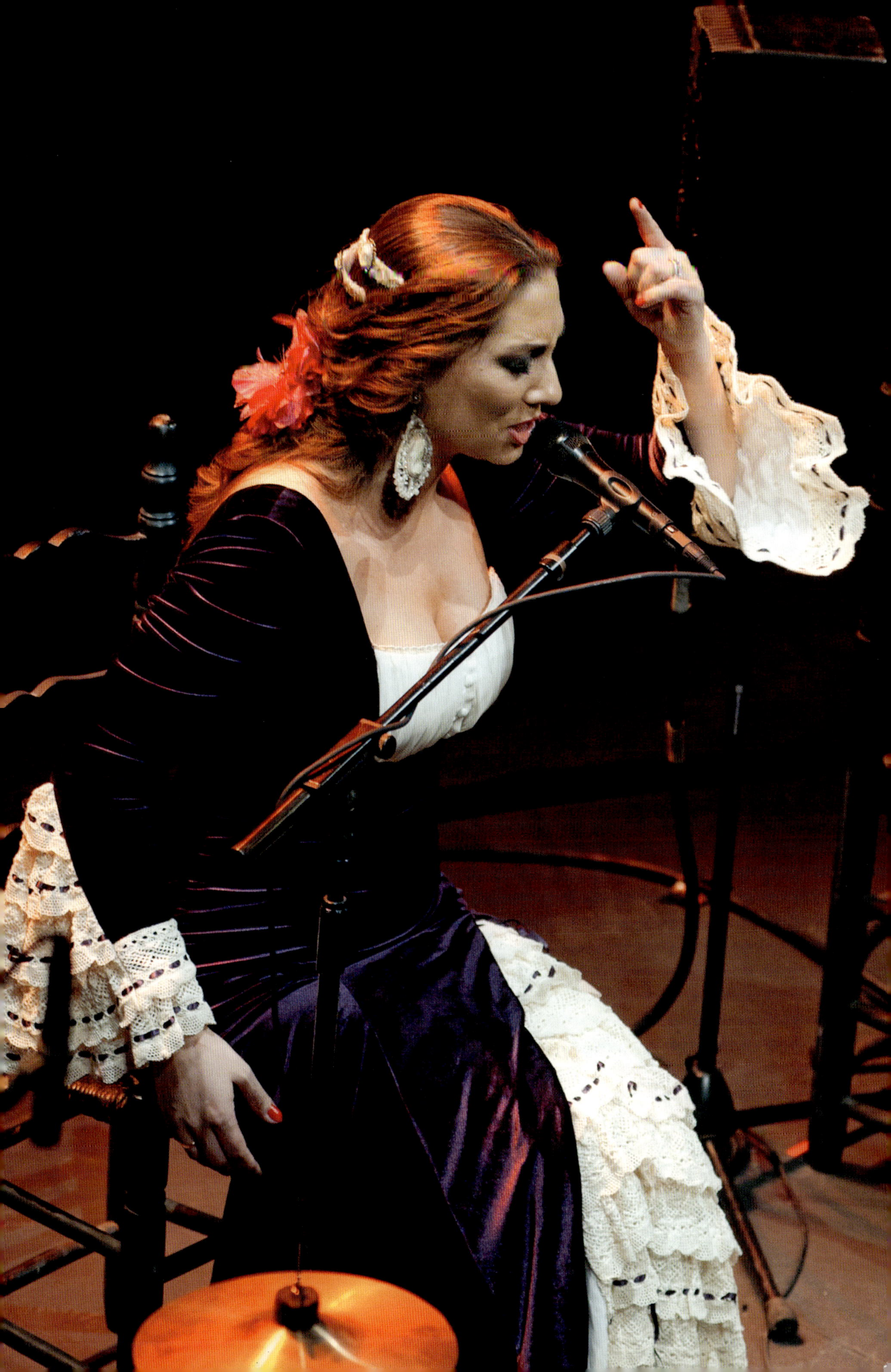

a genre in its own right. Popular solo *tocaores* include the legendary Manitas de Plata, the renowned Paco de Lucía, who single-handedly raised the caliber of the toque to a true art, Manolo Sanlúcar, and Vicente Amigo.

Flamenco dance is extremely passionate and, at the same time, perfectly measured and governed by exacting rules. The dancers (*bailaores* and *bailaoras*) move their arms in an expressive manner, gliding them elegantly through the air while their feet tap precisely to complex syncopated rhythms (known as *palos*) at dizzying speeds, making flamenco *baile* a particularly entertaining art form. The ruffles and colors of the *trajes de flamenca*, the traditional flamenco style of dress, as well as the use of props like castanets, shawls, and fans, add to the spectacle and the traditional spirit of a flamenco performance.

During the April Fair and other city festivals, almost every Sevillano—man, woman, or child, old and young—performs Sevillanas, a specific flamenco dance set enchantingly to four sung verses, where the choreography corresponds with each verse. To watch the Duchess of Alba perform a Sevillana, who danced so artfully at the April Fair, is truly a special experience.

The neighborhood of Triana is home to what is widely considered the best flamenco in the world. It's here amid tapas, wines from Jerez, song, and dance at the neighborhood's many *tablaos*—performance halls specifically for flamenco—that the essence of the flamenco spirit lives.

Manuela Barrios, flamenco dancer. *Following pages:* Dancing in the streets: flamenco dancer La Montoya (*second from left*) and singer Alba Molina (*third from left*), 2011.

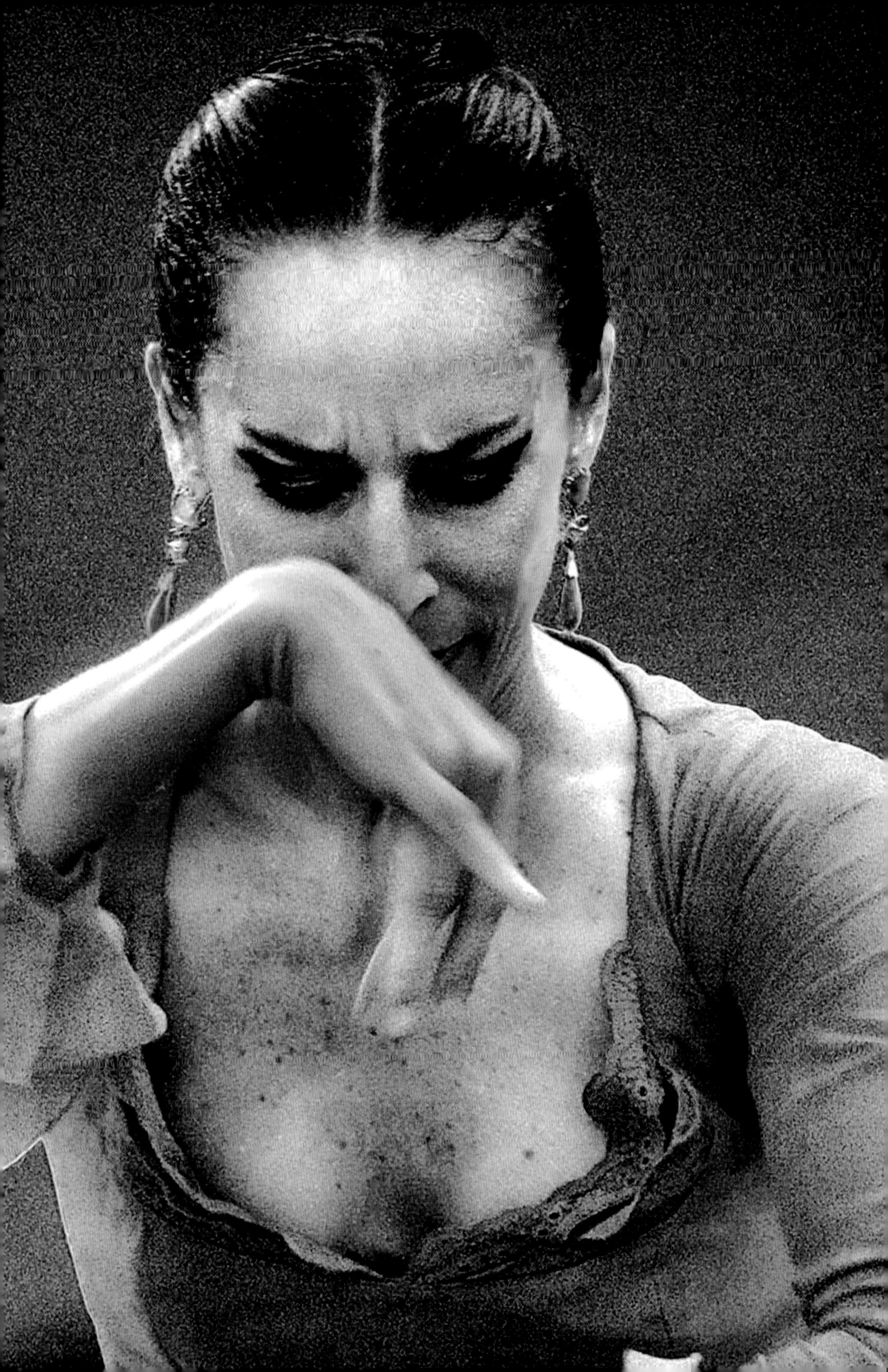

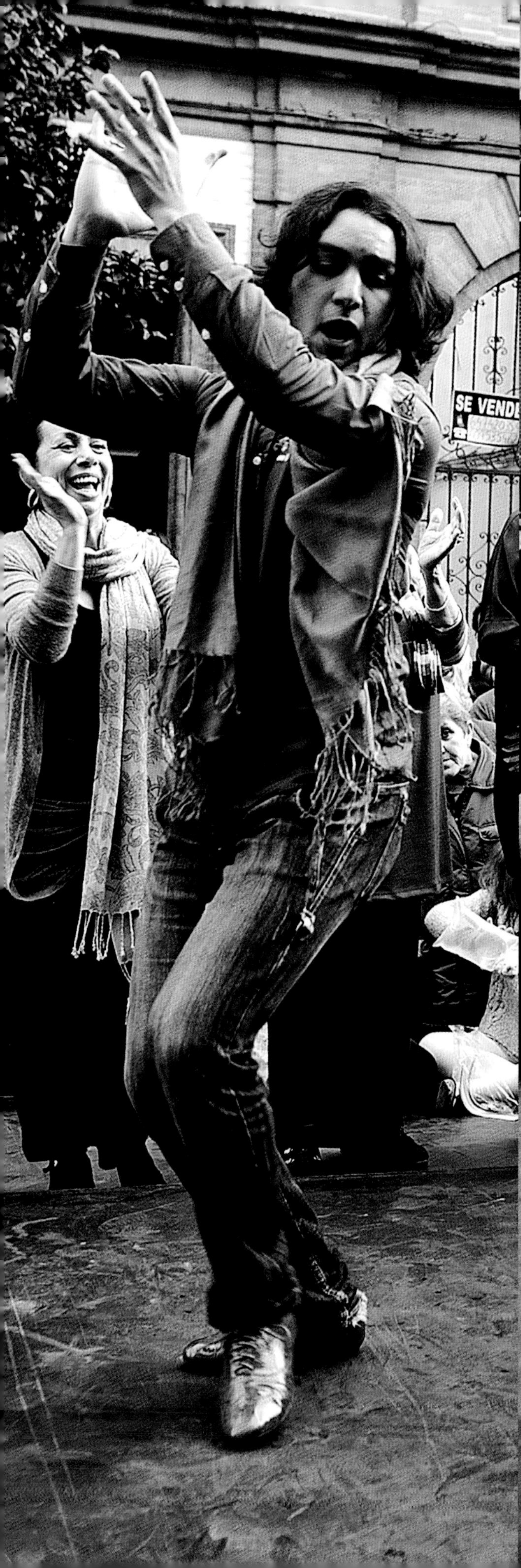
SE VENDE
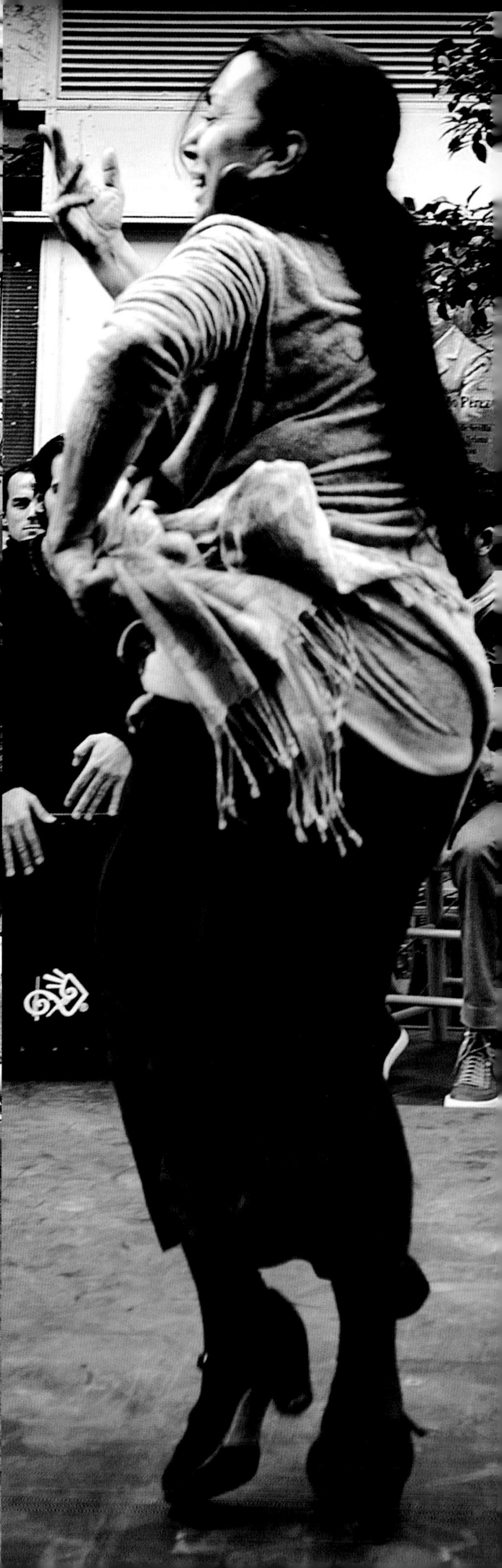

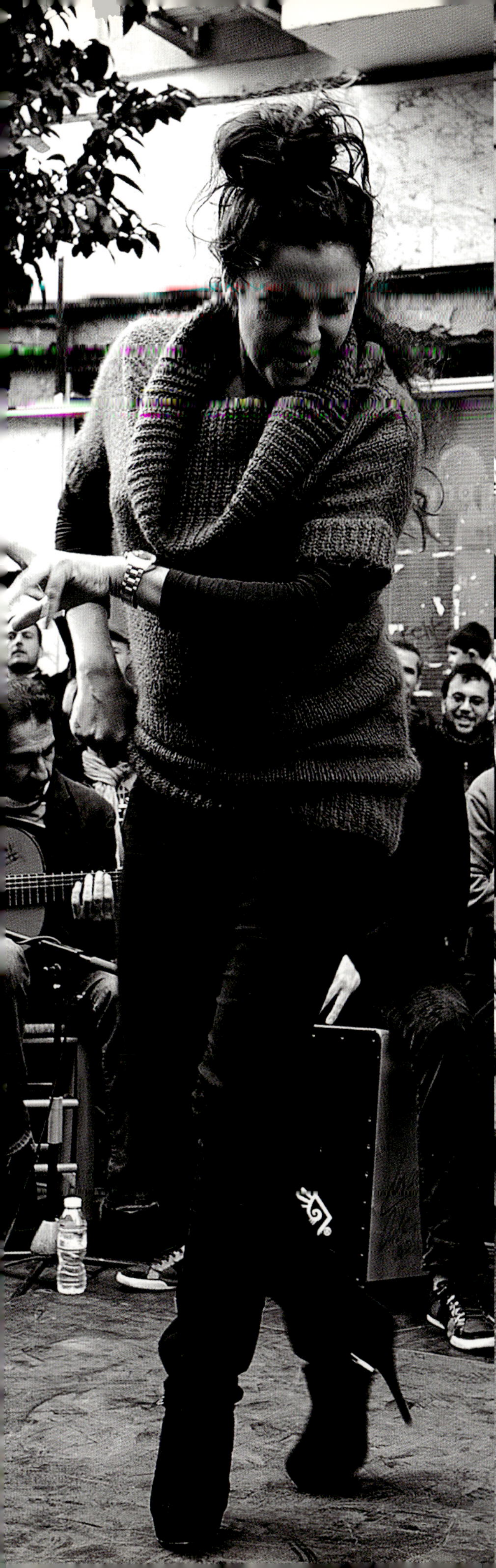

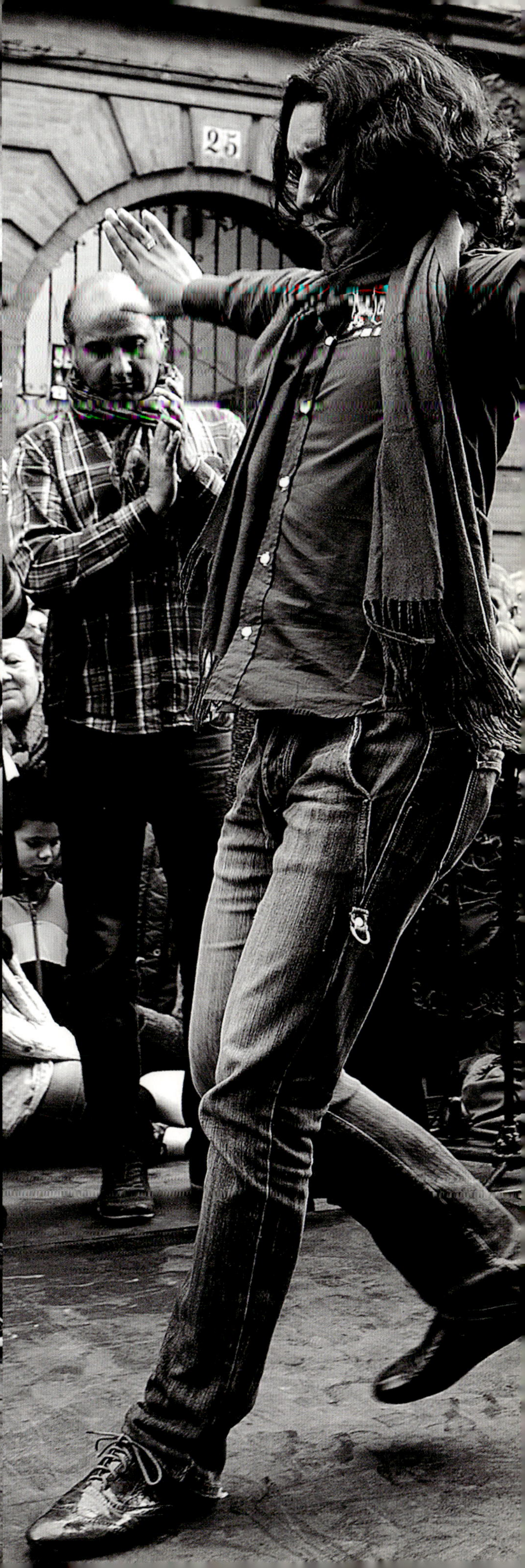
25

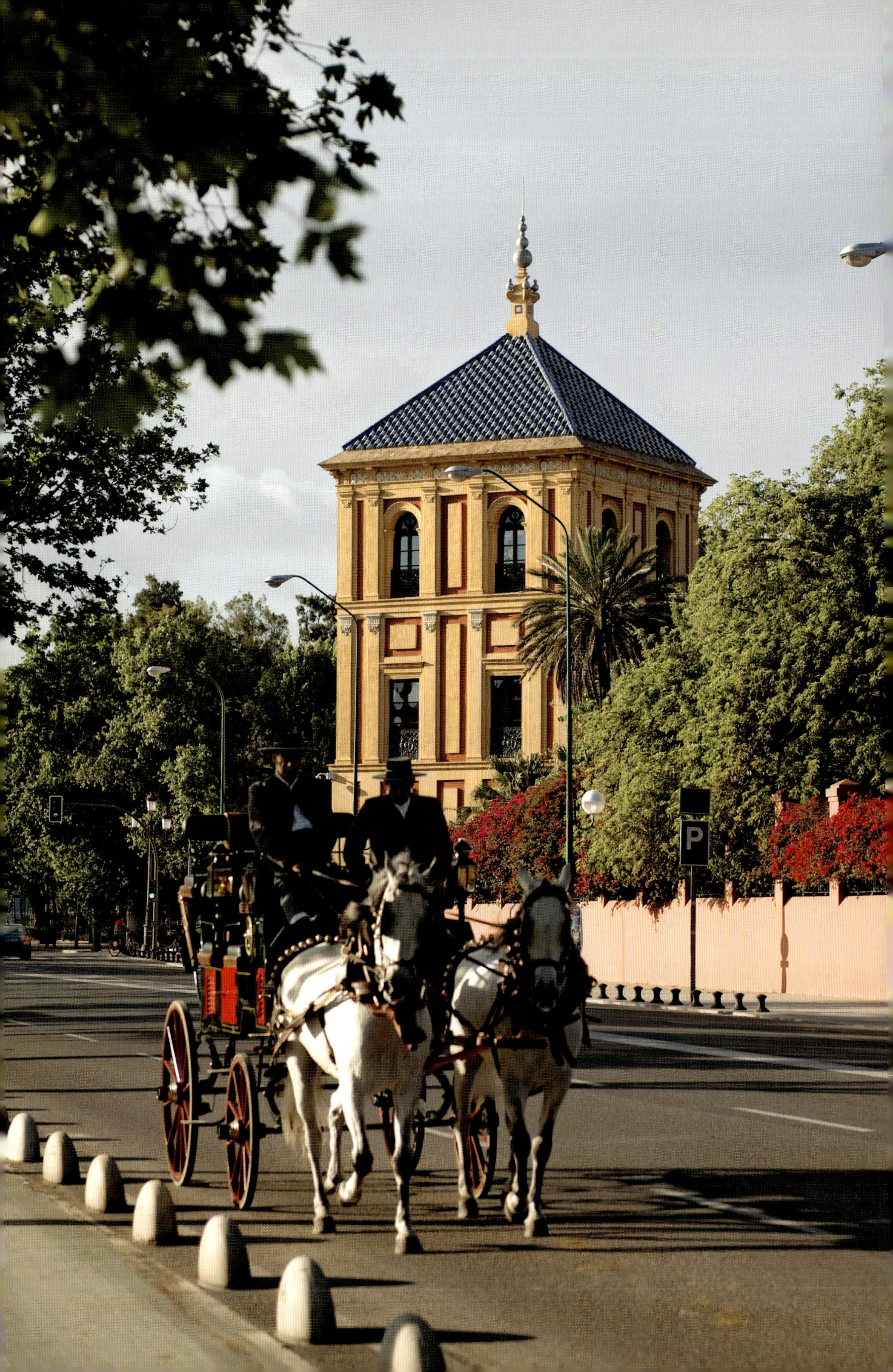
P

Exceptional Neighborhoods and Buildings

"People in Seville are very happy, the lifestyle here is very relaxed, you can walk everywhere; it's very easy."
—Paz Vega

The historic center of Seville is among the largest in Europe. It's not just a single neighborhood but rather many neighborhoods, each of them special, full of history, and brimming with legendary stories.

The most visited, and possibly the loveliest, area is Santa Cruz. Together with San Bartolomé, Santa Cruz was the old Jewish quarter, one of the most important Jewish neighborhoods in all of Spain. It is a veritable labyrinth of narrow and quiet alleyways, tucked away near the Alcázar and the Catalina de Ribera park. The abundance of green space helps to keep the district cool during the Sevillian summer, creating welcome breezes through the shaded streets.

In Santa Cruz, one can find many historic bars, such as the Hospedería del Laurel, mentioned in the play *Don Juan Tenorio*; the mythical Bar Giralda, located in what was an old Moorish bathhouse; and the popular Las Columnas, named for the Roman columns in its facade, where one can have an oloroso sherry or an orange wine while admiring the view of the Giralda bell tower at the end of the street. In addition, Santa Cruz is home to some nightspots whose fame has spread beyond the borders of the city—among them Casa Morales, El Rinconcillo, Álvaro Peregil, and Casa Moreno. Like most Sevillian bars, these places are always lively, and they serve the traditional sherries, beers, and tapas until late into the night.

Triana is another very special and well-known part of Seville. It is actually even older than Seville itself; some kid that Seville is, in fact, a neighborhood of Triana, because the latter has been around longer. This former gypsy quarter sitting on the edge of the Guadalquivir River is home to many riverside bars and restaurants, each providing a different and unique ambience.

Among the highlights of Seville is the beautiful María Luisa Park, also located along the Guadalquivir River, and originally part of the grounds of San Telmo Palace. Legend says that it was

Paseo de las Delicias, with the Palace of San Telmo in the background.
Following pages: A view of the Virgin of the Kings Plaza from the top of the Giralda.

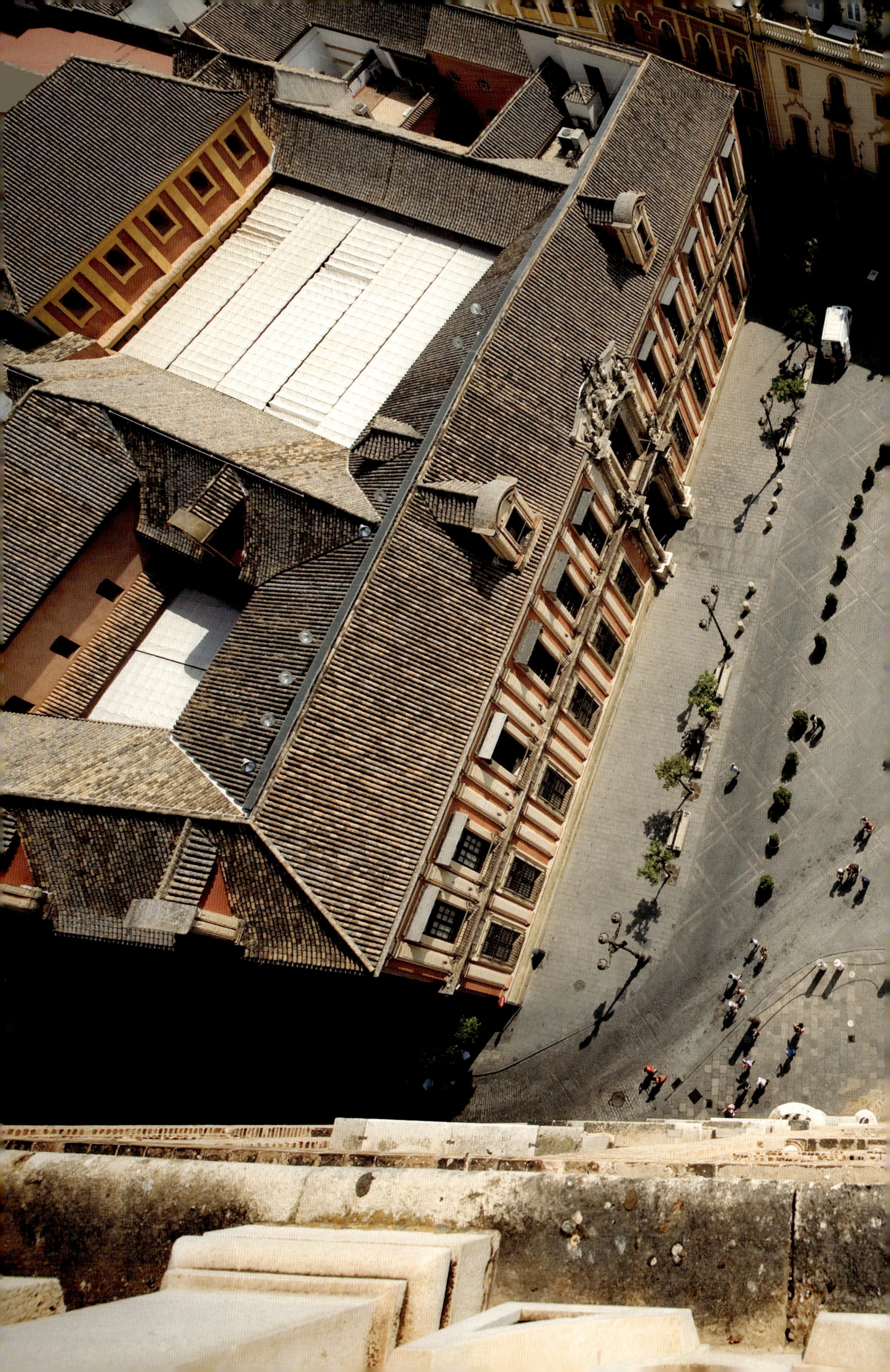

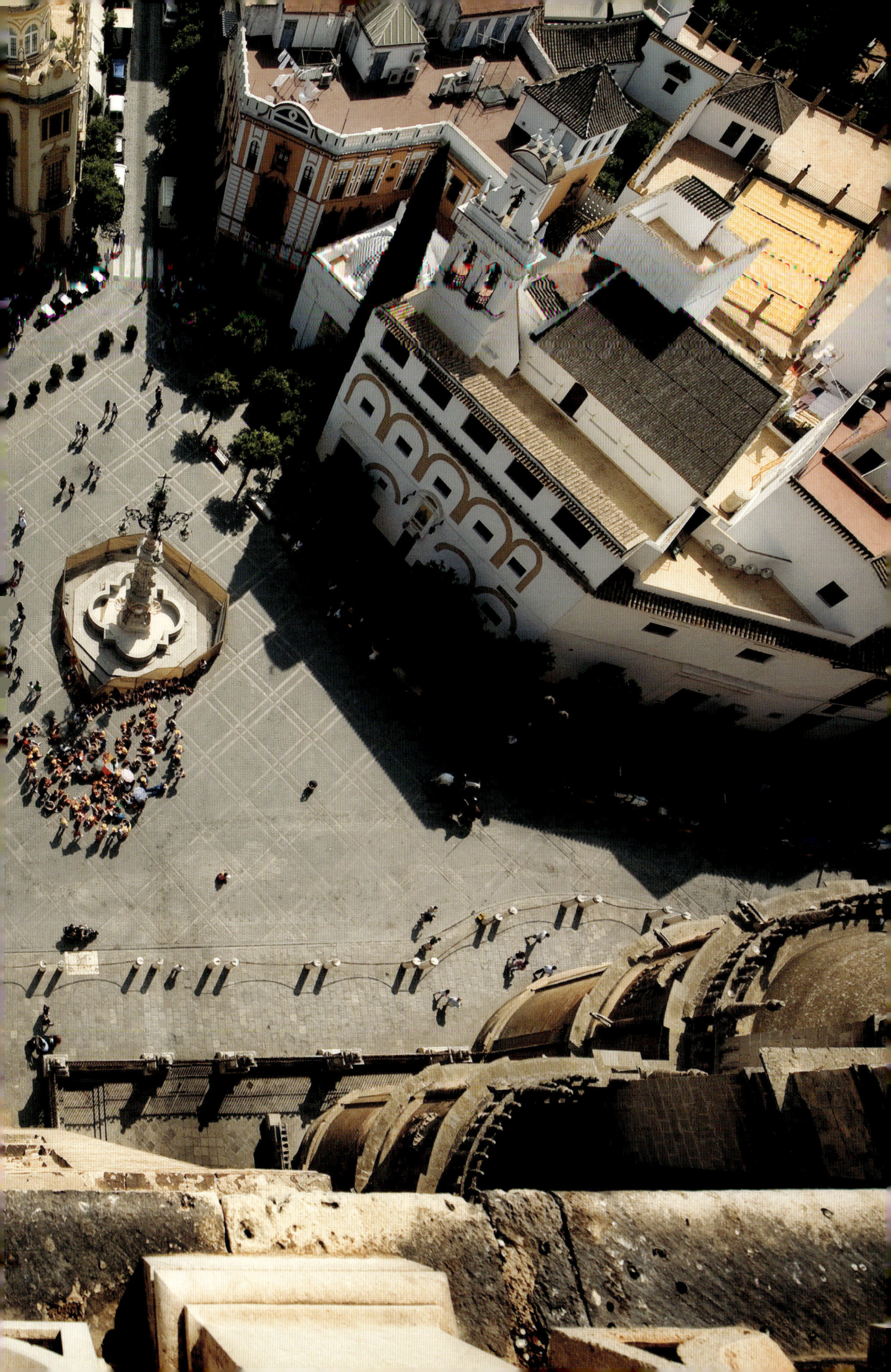

SIERPES

Clockwise from opposite: The steeple of the Baroque-style San José Church; detail of a lamp outside a beautiful Sevillian residence; Bar Giralda, located in what was formerly an Arab bathhouse; common in the city center, venetian blinds made from straw effectively protect the interior of the buildings from the heat; garden of a Sevillian country estate; Callejón del Agua, with peacocks resting on the walls of the Alcázar; Las Columnas bar, where the neighborhood of Santa Cruz begins.

also the old hunting grounds of the Dukes of Montpensier; Infanta Luisa Fernanda, Duchess of Montpensier, donated these stunning gardens to the city in 1893. Other must-visit places include the enormous Plaza de España, located in María Luisa Park and built for the Ibero-American Exposition of 1929, and the famous General Archive of the Indies, which houses all the documents related to Christopher Columbus's discovery of the New World, the later trade along the Guadalquivir River, and the colonies of the Spanish Empire.

Seville is also proud of its famous contemporary buildings, such as the Metropol Parasol complex, a large wooden edifice designed by the German architect Jürgen Mayer-Hermann, erected in 2011, and located in La Encarnación square in the middle of Seville's historic center. It consists of six mushroom-shaped "parasols" suspended above four levels, offering a variety of attractions, including markets and a museum exhibiting antiquties from the Roman and Moorish eras, as well as magnificent, sweeping views of the city center. Other famous structures are the Pelli tower, Seville's only skyscraper; and, of course, the Alamillo Bridge, created by the Spanish architect Santiago Calatrava.

Scattered throughout the historic center of Seville are a large number of palatial homes, such as the Casa de Salinas, the Casa Guardiola, the Palace of the Marquises of Algaba, the Lebrija Palace, and hundreds of other marvelous private residences—in addition to the Palacio de las Dueñas and Casa de Pilatos.

In the area surrounding the city, as well, stand dozens of spectacular estates, including El Esparragal and Hacienda el Vizir, where visitors can enjoy rosy sunsets, Spanish horses running freely through the fields, and the most spectacular silence—all just a few kilometers away from Seville.

View of Seville from the Giralda, with the El Salvador Church and the Alamillo Bridge in the background. *Following pages:* Decor and lifestyle at Hacienda de la Buzona.

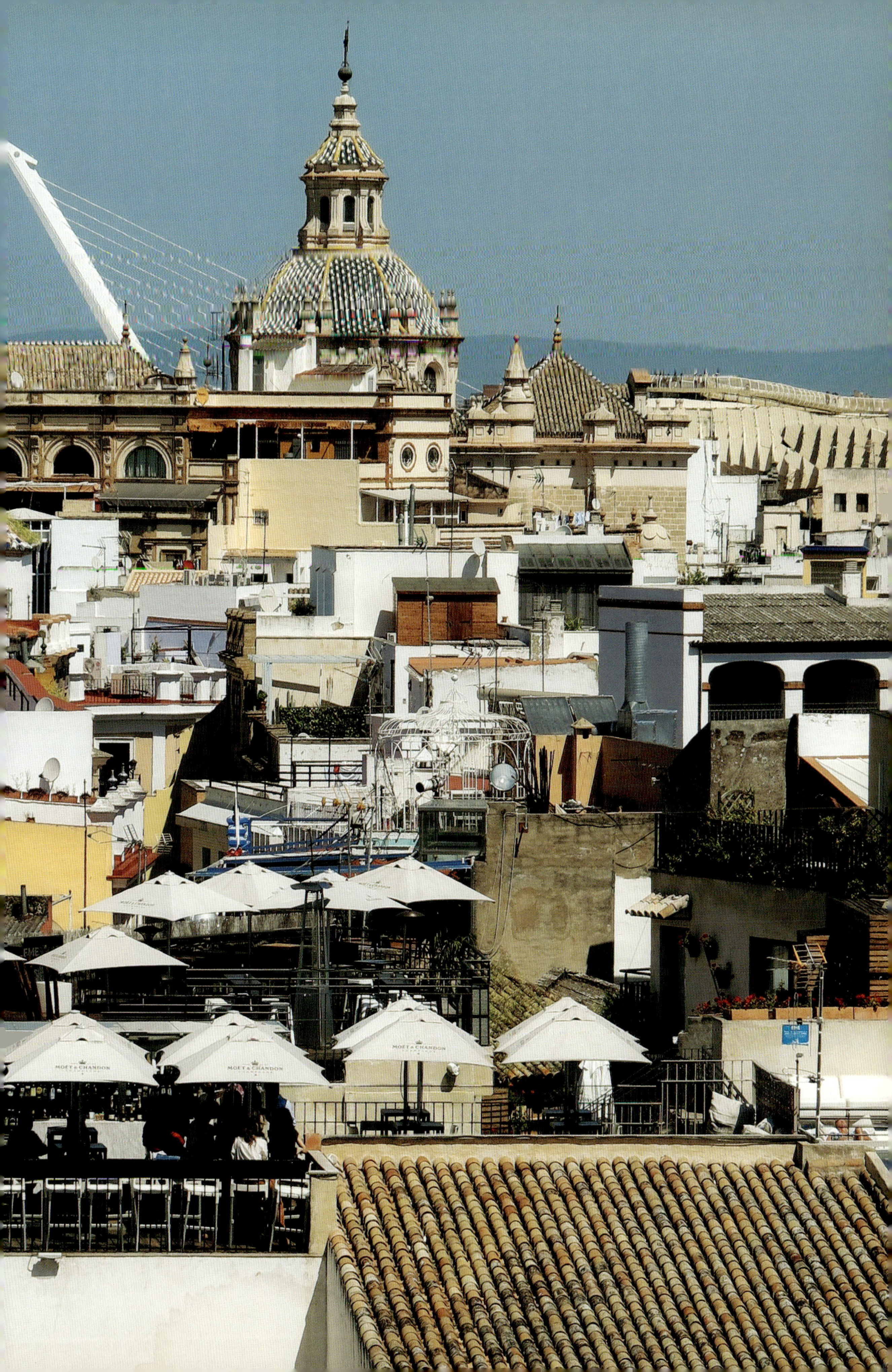
MOËT & CHANDON

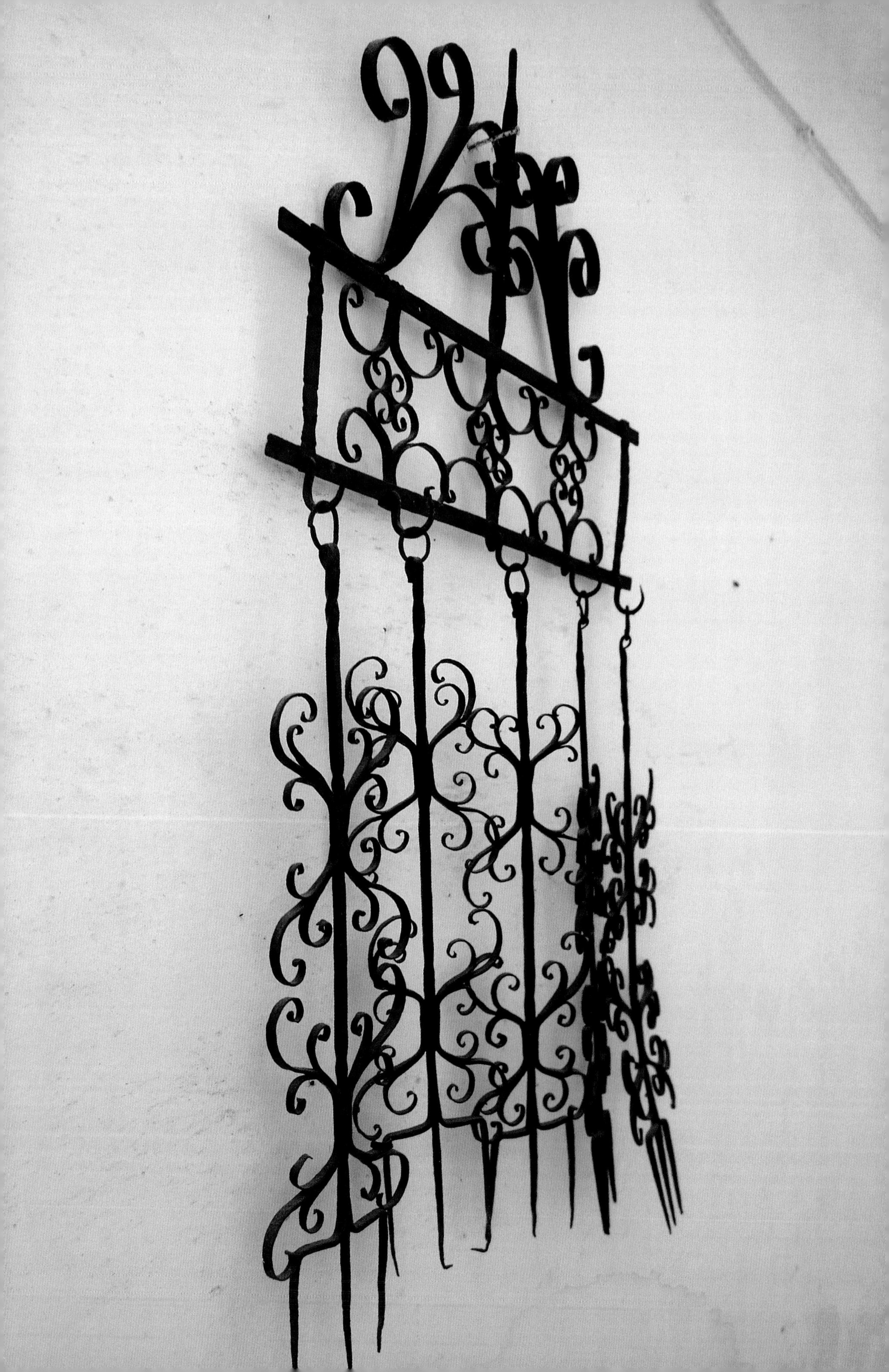

AVE
MARIA

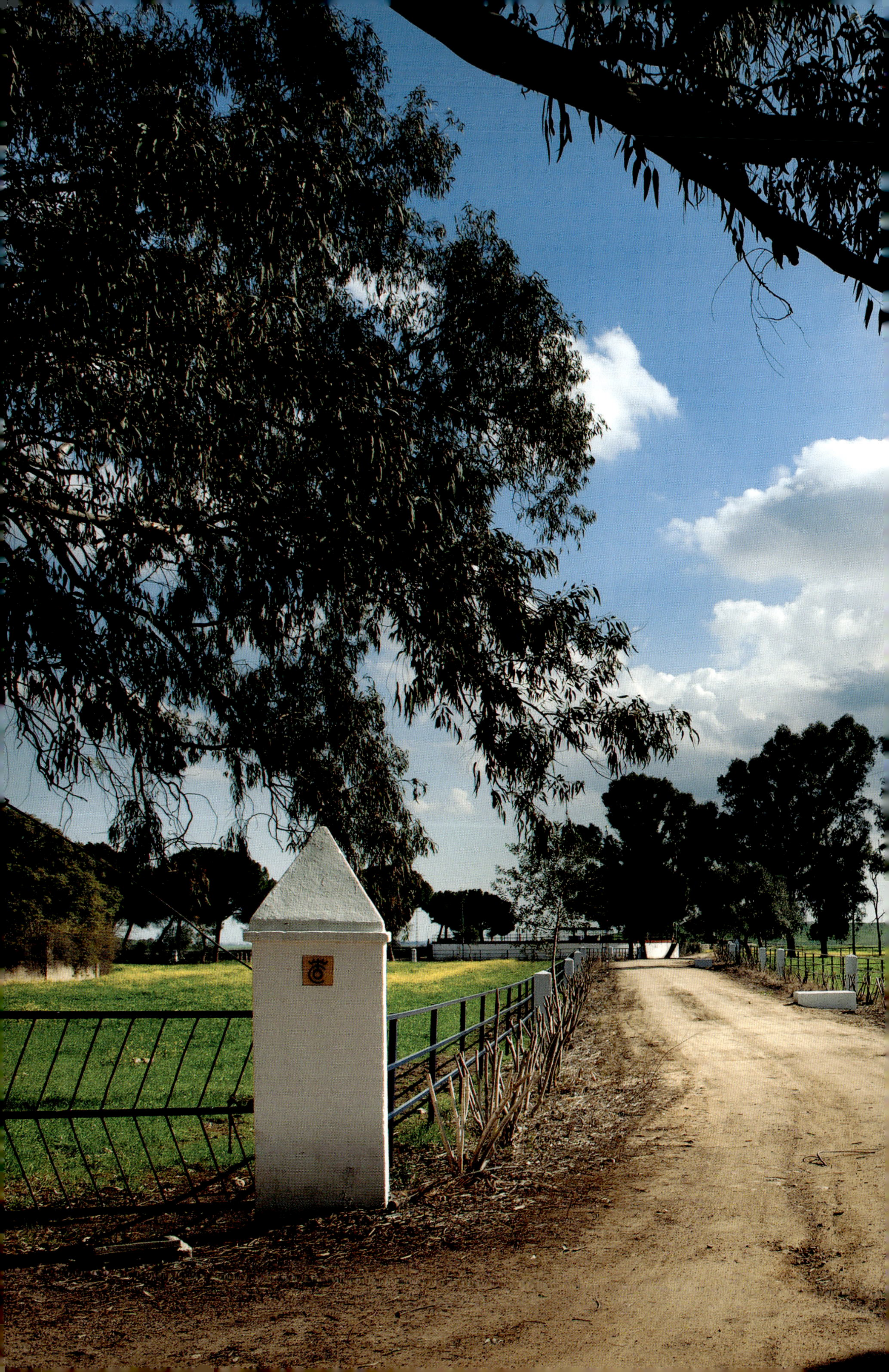

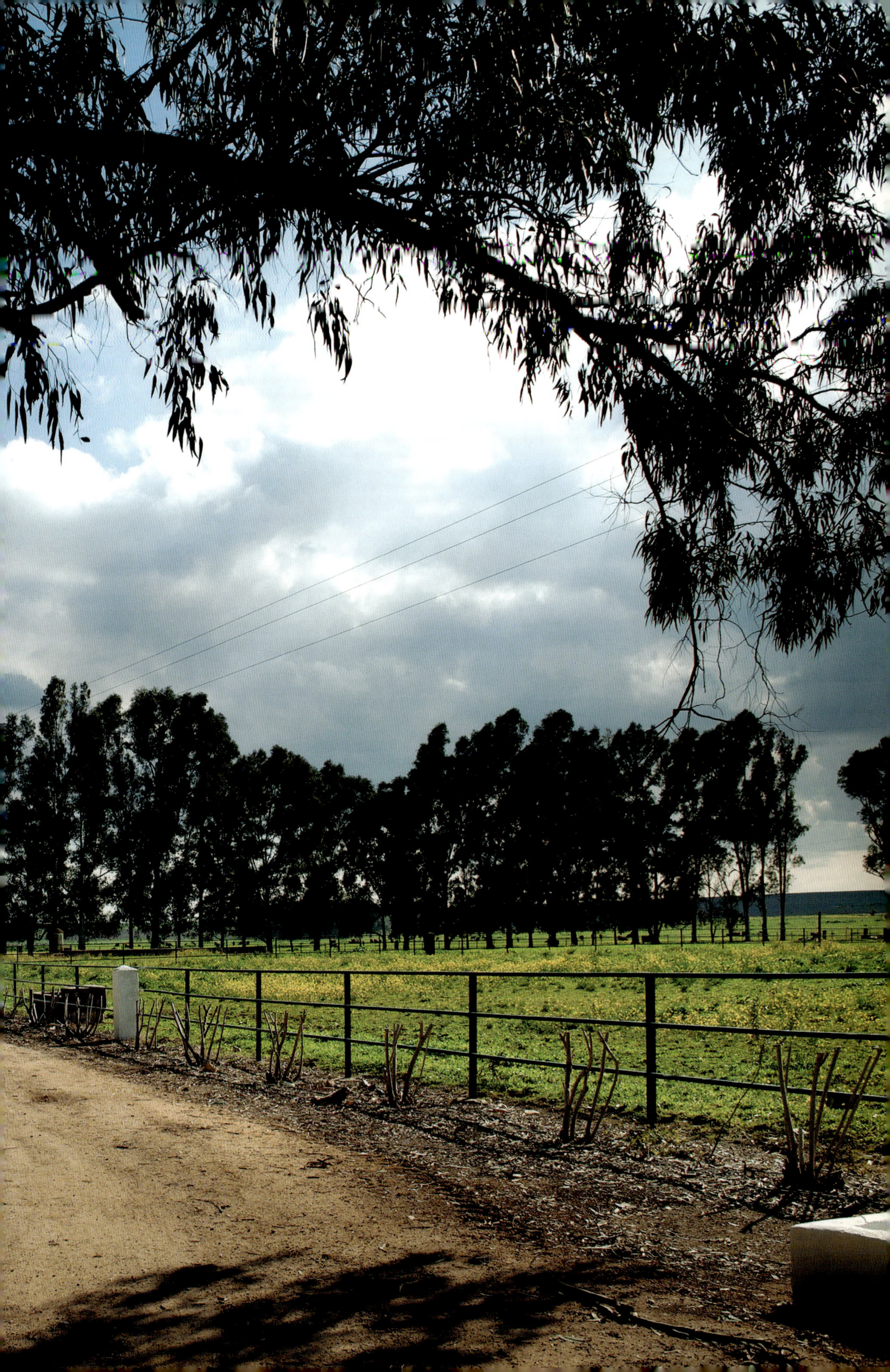

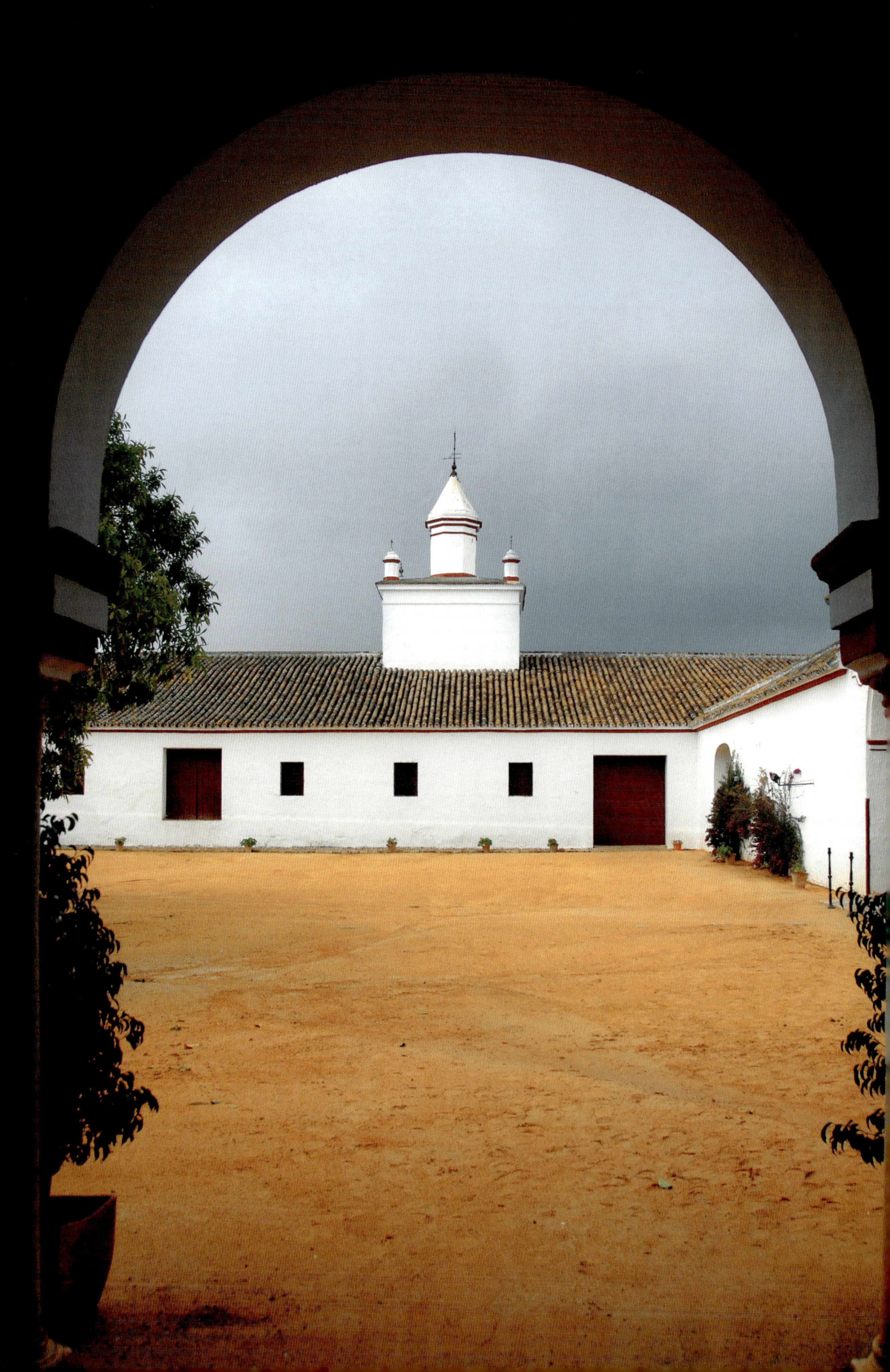

Clockwise from opposite: Courtyard of a Sevillian country estate; a horse near the stables of a Sevillian country estate; a herd of pigs at a pig farm near Seville; a traditional tiled roof; a loggia looking out onto a courtyard; horses grazing in a meadow on the grounds of El Esparragal; Torre de la Reina, a luxury hotel in the countryside outside Seville; rustic simplicity at El Esparragal.

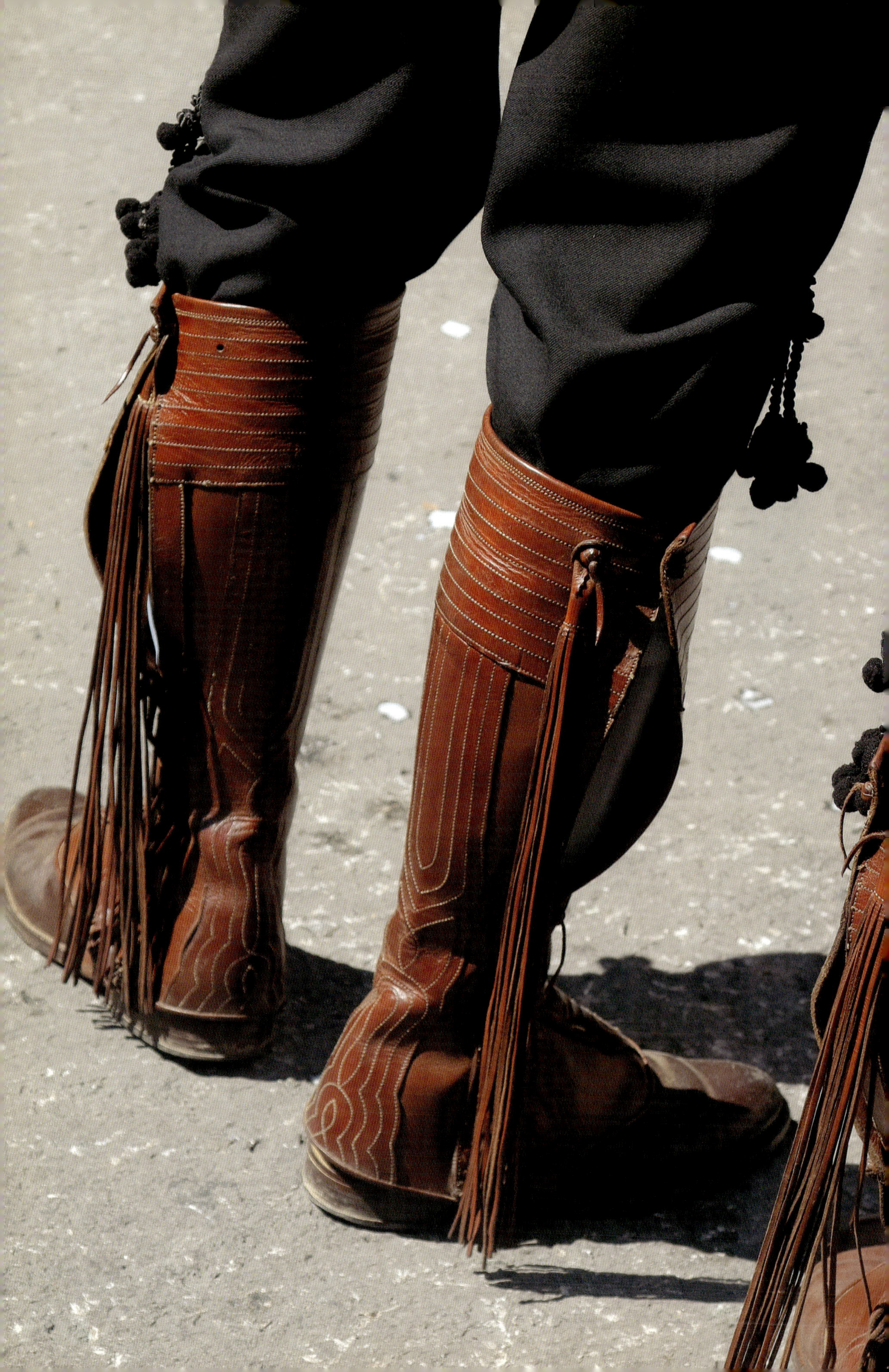

BARS, SHOPPING, & HOTELS: ADDRESSES

Seville is so much more than a beautiful city. Brimming with hot spots for tourists and locals alike—romantic hotels, glamorous and luxurious stores, and a vibrant bar scene—it's a dynamic, exciting place to eat, drink, shop, and get the most out of life.

It is necessary to speak of tapas bars when talking about Seville. While the city has a number of legendary fine-dining restaurants, such as Becerrita, Robles, or the famous Oriza, a sit-down meal is not always the first choice here. Instead, it's more common to go out for tapas. A tapa is a small portion of food, the size of an appetizer, to accompany a beer or a glass of dry or oloroso sherry. Every neighborhood or district of Seville has fantastic spots to *tapear* (the verb commonly used to express the act of going out for tapas with friends). In the area of the Plaza de la Maestranza, there are many places to choose from; most specialize in beef dishes. Mesón Serranito, La Bulla, and El Camerino are among the best in the neighborhood. Near the cathedral and in the neighborhood of Santa Cruz are Las Teresas, founded in 1870, and Taberna Poncio. Also known for their delicious tapas are the Álvaro Peregil and Las Columnas taverns, which can both be found on Mateos Gago Street. Las Golondrinas, in Triana, has the best sirloin cooked in whiskey.

Seville also has some of the world's most beautiful hotels—from the spectacular Alfonso XIII to the Europa and the Adriano, charming hotels each with only a few rooms, with shaded patios and tranquil rooftops with views of the Giralda. For a truly special experience, stay at the magnificent Casas de la Judería, a labyrinthine property in the former Jewish quarter, fused from twenty-seven separate homes joined together by patios and secret underground passageways that resemble Roman hot baths. Of course, there are also the marvelous palaces, such as the Fontecruz, the Casas del Rey de Baeza, and the Palacio de Villapanés. Last but not least, the Hotel Amadeus, decorated with old orchestral scores and original baroque instruments, is perfect for music lovers.

Seville's shops are unique and range from classic to modern. Francos Street, in the very center of Seville, near city hall, is where one can find ribbons, lace, and shawls for flamenco dresses, and all sorts of fabrics and religious objects for Holy Week. Other notable streets for shopping are Chicarreros, Tetuán, and Sierpes.

Traditional Sevillian boots.
Pages 154–155: El Esparragal, a luxury retreat in the countryside near Seville.

SHOPPING

Ana Abascal
(antiques)
Fernandez y Gonzalez, 15
954 224 540

Antik
(carpets, jewelry, fabrics, gifts)
Calle Alfalfa, 15
954 222 014
antiksevilla.com

Belle De Jour
(women's apparel)
Calle Asunción, 4
955 239 508
belledejoursevilla.com

Calzados Mayo
(boots)
Plaza de la Alfalfa nº2
954 225 555
calzadosmayo.com

Cuqui Castellanos
(shoes)
Calle Rosario, 8
954 560 996

Diza-Dizal-Zadi - Abanicos de Sevilla
(fans)
Calle Tetuán, 5
41004 Sevilla
954 214 154
abanicosdesevilla.net

Koma
(women's apparel)
Pasaje Ateneo, 5H
954 563 710
facebook.com/koma.sevilla

Sombreros Maquedano
(hats)
Calle Sierpes, 40
954 564 771
maquedano.com

Mordisco de Mujer
(online fashions, vintage, and contemporary)
954 225 809
mordiscodemujer.mitiendy.com

Patricia Buffuna
(hats)
Calle Don Alonso el Sabio, 8
954 537 824
patriciabuffuna.com

Pitusa Gasul
(Sevillianas dresses)
Calle Chapineros 1, local 4
954 234 149
pitusagasul.wordpress.com

Populart
(ceramics)
Pasaje de Vila 4
954 229 444
populartsevilla.com

Reyes Hellin
(hats)
Calle Alfonso XII, 48
954 380 430
reyeshellin.es

Roberto Diz
(bridal gowns)
Calle Chicarreros, 2
656 569 050
robertodiz.es
facebook.com/pages/-
robertodiz-/133132306741340

Rocio Porres Domecq
(jewelry)
Archeros 19, junto a Sta. Mª
954 217 309

Shaw Joyero
(jewelry)
Plaza Nueva, 13
954 217 249
shawjoyero.com

Left: Women with traditional Sevillian fans below: front window of a jewelry store.

Below: A plate of jamón, a favorite at Sevillian tapas bars.

Above: Plaza de San Francisco; below: the Albariza restaurant; following pages: window of the Maquedano hat store.

La Albariza

40

Maquedano

RESTAURANTS

Abantal
Calle Alcalde José de la
Bandera, 7–9
954 540 000
abantalrestaurante.es

Antigua Abacería de San Lorenzo
Calle Teodosio, 53
954 380 067
antiguaabaceriadesanlorenzo.com

Gastromium
Avenida Ramón Carande, 12
954 625 555

Gastrosol
Espacio Metropol Parasol,
Plaza de la Encarnación
952 217 225
gastrosol.es

La Albariza
Calle Betis, 6
954 338 960
laalbariza.es

La Raza Seises
Don Remondo, 2
954 232 024
grupolaraza.es/seises

Puerto Delicia
Muelle de las Delicias
955 115 656
puertodelicia.es

Puerta Grande
Calle Antonia Díaz, 33
954 216 896
facebook.com/pages/Puerta-Grande-Sevilla/122037801197993

HOTELS

Casas de Santa Cruz
Calle Pimienta, 4
954 293 698
casasdesantacruz.com

Fontecruz Sevilla
Calle Abades, 41–43
902 444 099
fontecruzhoteles.com

Hospes Las Casas del Rey de Baeza
Plaza Jesús de la Redención, 2
954 561 496
hospes.com

Hotel Adriano
Calle Adriano, 12
954 293 800
adrianohotel.com

Hotel Alfonso XIII
Calle San Fernando, 2
954 917 000
hotel-alfonsoxiii-sevilla.com

Hotel Amadeus
Calle Farnesio, 6
at Calle San José, 10
954 501 443
hotelamadeussevilla.com

Hotel Bécquer
Calle Reyes Católicos, 4
954 228 900
hotelbecquer.com

Hotel Casa 1800
Calle Rodrigo Caro, 6
954 561 800
hotelcasa1800sevilla.com

Hotel Convento La Gloria
Calle Argote de Molina, 26–28
954 293 670
hotelconventolagloria.es

Hotel Elvira Plaza
Plaza de Doña Elvira, 5
954 293 698
hotelelviraplaza.com

Hotel Europa
Calle Jimios, 5
954 500 443
hoteleuropasevilla.com

Hotel Husa Los Seises
Calle Segovias, 6
954 229 495
hotelhusalosseises.com

Hotel Inglaterra
Plaza Nueva, 7
954 224 970
hotelinglaterra.es

Hotel Las Casas de la Judería
Calle Santa María la Blanca, 5
954 415 150
casasypalacios.com

NH Central Convenciones
Avenida Diego Martínez Barrio, 8
954 548 500
nh-hoteles.es

Palacio de Villapanés
Calle Santiago, 31
954 502 063
almasevilla.com

——————— **BARS** ———————

Álvaro Peregil
Calle Mateos Gago, 20
954 218 966
tabernasperegil.com

Bodeguita Polavieja
Calle General Polavieja, 22
954 225 493
bodeguitapolavieja.blogspot.com.es

Bodeguita Romero
Calle Harinas, 10
954 229 556
bodeguita-romero.com

Casa Morales
Calle García de Vinuesa, 11
954 221 242

Casa Moreno
Calle Gamazo, 7
954 228 315

Casa Ricardo
Calle Hernán Cortés, 2
954 389 751
casaricardosevilla.com

El Camerino
Calle Dos de Mayo, 34
954 500 022

El Loco Sibarita
Calle Jesús del Gran Poder, 83
673 111 269
facebook.com/pages/El-Loco-Sibarita-Tapas/267887876677291

El Rinconcillo
Calle Gerona, 40 at Calle Alhondiga, 2
954 223 183
elrinconcillo.es

La Bulla
Calle Dos de Mayo, 26
954 219 262
barlabulla.com/contacto

La Azotea
Calle Jesús del Gran Poder, 31
955 116 748
laazoteasevilla.es

La Flor de Toranzo
Calle Jimios, 1–3 at Calle Joaquín Guichot, 9
954 229 315
andalunet.com/trifon

Las Golondrinas
Calle Antillano Campos, 26
954 331 626
barlasgolondrinas.com

Las Teresas
Calle Santa Teresa, 2
954 213 069

Ovejas Negras
Calle Hernando Colón, 8
666 674 338
ovejasnegrastapas.com

Taberna Poncio
Calle Ximénez de Enciso, 33
954 460 717
facebook.com/TabernaPoncio

Zelai
Calle Albareda, 22
954 229 992
restaurantezelai.com

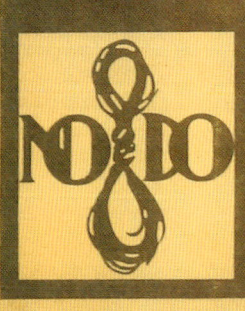

SEVILLA
FERIA DE ABRIL
FIESTAS PRIMAVERALES 193

ANDALUCIA POR SI PARA ESPAÑA Y LA HUMANIDAD

Acknowledgments

First, I would like to extend my utmost appreciation for my editor Martine Assouline. I was introduced to Martine in Seville, in front of the gates of the Alcázar, and from there we began a beautiful friendship, one that I am sure I have gotten more from than she has.

I would also like to thank Prosper Assouline, of course. Prosper loves creating beautiful books, and he knows how to search for and find beauty through his great perseverance.

Thank you, too, to the staff at Assouline, especially Shoshana Thaler, for her patience and for the love she has put into this book; photo editor Rebecca Stepler, who understands the music that lives in the images; Cecilia Maurin who designed this beautiful book; and Valerie Tougard, editor of the French edition of the book.

I would like to mention fondly here Ramón Ybarra Valdenebro, who was the mutual friend who introduced me to Martine. In addition, the Duchess of Alba, for the generosity she showed me, and Father Ignacio Jiménez Sánchez-Dalp of Seville, whose help with making Cayetana and the House of Dueñas accessible was invaluable.

Finally, I wish to thank the many friends who, when called upon, didn't hesitate to assist in editing this work. There are so many that I can't name you all, but you know who you are, and to each of you I offer my heartfelt appreciation.

—Antonio del Junco

Prosper and Martine Assouline would like to thank all those who helped them to discover and love Seville, especially, Cédric Reversade, Paul-Maxime Koskas, Father Ignacio Jiménez Sánchez, Ramón Ybarra, and his wonderful family including its reigning matriarch, the great Mayda, and of course, Antonio del Junco for his work and passion.

A very special thanks to the Duchess of Alba for writing such a beautiful foreword.

Poster from the 1934 Seville April Fair.

Page 4, clockwise from top left: The Harness Exhibition, one of the popular events during the Seville April Fair; Mayda dancing; the Giralda seen from the rooftop of the Seville Cathedral; matador Morante de la Puebla; the Harness Exhibition at the Maestranza; Rita Hayworth at a bullfight during the April Fair, 1950; a canopy of *velas*, or awnings, over an alleyway; matador Víctor Puerto and his wife, Noelia Margotón; a flamenco guitarist; actress Norma Duval with designers Victorio y Lucchino at the Harness Exhibition; Mayda with her father; Tom Cruise during a break while filming *Knight and Day* in Seville.

Page 5, clockwise from top left: The Maestranza and the Giralda, seen from Triana; on the set of a flamenco-themed film in the María Luisa Park; poster for the 2013 bullfighting season; Orson Welles at a bullfight; Cameron Diaz during a break while filming *Knight and Day* in Seville; Sevillian actress Paz Vega (*left*) at the Seville Fair; bullfighters' capes; Sofía, then-Princess of Asturias, at the Seville Fair; nuns playing basketball in the cloister at the convent of San Leandro; matador Paquirri, who was tragically killed in 1984 during a bullfight, and his wife, Carmen Ordóñez; orange trees in the gardens of the Alcázar; façade of the Church of San Ildefonso; Nati Abascal at the wedding of her son Rafael; reflection of the Giralda in a puddle in the Plaza Virgen de los Reyes; painter Reyes de la Lastra.

Photo Credits

Photography by Antonio del Junco, except the following:

Page 4, clockwise, from top left: © Antonio del Junco; © Assouline; © Assouline; © Carlos Nuñez; © Antonio del Junco; © *Diario ABC*; © Antonio del Junco; © Aníbal González; © Antonio del Junco; © Aníbal González; © *Diario de Sevilla* - Sevilla Film Office; © Assouline; page 5, clockwise, from top left: © Antonio del Junco; © Hemeroteca Municipal - Sevilla Film Office; © Assouline; © *Diario ABC*; © *Diario de Sevilla* - Sevilla Film Office; © Aníbal González; © Antonio del Junco; © *Diario ABC*; © Antonio del Junco; © Antonio del Junco; © *Diario ABC*; © Antonio del Junco; © Antonio del Junco; © *Diario de Sevilla*; © Antonio del Junco; pages 22, 24: © *Diario ABC*; pages 25, 26: © Assouline; page 27, clockwise, from left to right: © Antonio del Junco; © *Diario de Sevilla*; © Assouline; © Antonio del Junco; © Antonio del Junco; © Antonio del Junco; © *Diario de Sevilla*; pages 30–31: © Raul Caro; pages 32–33: © Europa Press via Getty Images; page 44: © Private Collection/Ken Welsh/The Bridgeman Art Library; page 47: © Shutterstock; page 51: © Assouline (tapas bar and gambas); page 57: © Colección Carmen Thyssen-Bornemisza; page 58: © Muzeum Narodowe, Poznan, Poland / The Bridgeman Art Library (painting); page 62: © Eric Cuvillier for the Hotel Alfonso XIII; page 69: © Assouline (bar, stained-glass, tile); pages 70, 73: © Catherine Ashmore; page 74: © Hamburger Kunsthalle, Hamburg, Germany/The Bridgeman Art Library; page 75: © Musée d'Orsay, Paris, France/Giraudon/The Bridgeman Art Library; page 77: © New Line Cinema/Photofest; page 80, clockwise, from top left: © All rights reserved; © Explorer/J.L. Charmet/ coll. Bibliotheque de du Musée de la Comédie-Francaise, Paris; © Giraudon/Coll. Musée des Beaux Arts, Dunkerque; © All rights reserved; page 81: © All rights reserved; pages 82–83: © Artephot/Oronoz/Coll. Galeria Sammer, Madrid; page 88: © *Diario ABC*; page 89: © Assouline; page 91: Private collection, © All rights reserved; page 98: © *Diario ABC* (Jacqueline Kennedy Onassis); © Assouline (pocket detail, saddle detail, girls in traditional dress); page 90: © Assouline (harness exhibition); page 101: © Gamma-Rapho via Getty Images; page 109: © Assouline (rooftop, chapel, Giraldillo, crucifixion, San Miguel Portal); page 124, clockwise, from top left: © Diario ABC; © Antonio del Junco; © Diario ABC; © Raúl Caro; © Raúl Caro; © Antonio del Junco; © Aníbal González; © *Diario ABC*; page 125: © Raúl Caro; page 128: © Assouline (top); page 129: © *Diario ABC* (Ava Gardner, Ernest Hemingway); page 133: Courtesy of Ramón Ybarra, photograph by Ignacio Gil; pages 148, 149, top right, 151–153, 157, middle right, 158, 161, 162–163: © Assouline; page 166: Private collection, © All rights reserved.

SEVIL

1. Arraual dela puerta de Carmona	5. Castilleia de Guzman	9. Caños de Carmonas	13. Iglesia maior	17. Plaza de Don Pedro Ponce
2. Arraual dela puerta de Macarena	6. Castilleia dela Cuesta	10. El Mattadero	14. Monasterio de S. Pablo	18. Plaza del Duq de Arcos
3. Casas del Duq de Alcala	7. Camas	11. El quemadero	15. Plaza de S. Francisco	19. Plaza de Palazio
4. Casas de Colon	8. Calle delas armas	12. El Algaba	16. Plaza del Duq de Medina	20. Plazio del Rey